NINETEENTH-CENTURY DESIGN

CENTURY | DESIGN

FROM PUGIN TO MACKINTOSH

CHARLOTTE GERE
AND
MICHAEL WHITEWAY

WEIDENFELD
AND
NICOLSON
LONDON

First published in Great Britain in 1993 by
George Weidenfeld and Nicolson Ltd
Orion House, 5 Upper St Martin's Lane
London WC2H 9EA

British Library Cataloguing in Publication Data
A catalogue record for this book is available from the British Library.

ISBN 0 297 83068 6

Design: Harry Green
House Editor: Alice Millington-Drake

Phototypeset by Keyspools Ltd, Golborne, Lancs
Colour separations by Newsele Litho Ltd
Printed and bound in Italy

ENDPAPERS Owen Jones: detail from the competition design for the
1857 Manchester Exhibition building; see PL. 70.

FRONTISPIECE Christopher Dresser: 'Crow's Foot' decanter, silver
and glass; made by Hukin & Heath, design registered 9 October
1878.

PAGE 6 A. W. N. Pugin: tile, to a design from the title page of
Floriated Ornament, 1849 (PL. 46); for Minton & Co.

PAGE 9 A. W. N. Pugin: majolica-ware stove tile; made by Minton,
*c.*1850; detail from PL. 60.

PAGE 30 L. N. Cottingham: medieval-style tile, for Minton;
see PL. 23.

PAGE 110 Christopher Dresser: tile; made by Minton,
designed *c.* 1870.

PAGE 196 C. F. A. Voysey: bird design.

CONTENTS

FOREWORD

The purpose of this book is to document experimental design in the nineteenth century by relating surviving furniture, interiors and decorative art to drawings, published and patented or registered designs, exhibition catalogues, jury reports and criticism, and recorded commissions; and to examine the avant-garde against the social and cultural background of Victorian life. The momentum of experiment and invention was maintained by a succession of remarkable men – artists, architects, planners, engineers, critics, educationalists and philanthropists – whose legacy is the design industry in the twentieth century.

The eighteenth-century Palladian country house complete with its art collections amassed in the course of the educational Grand Tour on the Continent, the essential culmination of a gentleman's preparation for life, is still widely regarded as the summit of British aesthetic achievement, a belief that the recent *Treasure Houses of Britain* exhibition (Washington, 1986), did much to promote. In spite of the great advances in nineteenth-century scholarship the decorative art of the Victorian period is still in a cultural twilight. The old aphorism 'Good taste ended in 1820' has continuing currency. Victorian taste is not 'good' in the accepted sense, but robust. Ignored and largely forgotten during the first half of the present century, the massive task of recovering the identities and works of the leading nineteenth-century designers was begun in the 1930s by Nikolaus Pevsner with his *Pioneers of the Modern Movement from William Morris to Walter Gropius* (1936). The criteria for the chronological study of stylistic trends were set by Peter Floud in 1952, when he was working on the pioneering exhibition of *Victorian and Edwardian Decorative Arts* held at the Victoria and Albert Museum in that year.

Floud defined his aims as to include only objects that could be authoritatively attributed to the leading Victorian and Edwardian designers, and objects that were exactly datable and attributable to specific firms even though it was not possible to assign them to a particular designer owing to the emphasis on anonymity by Victorian manufacturers. 'It was intended,' he explained, 'that the exhibition should include the best examples of the work of all Victorian and Edwardian designers whose work showed originality, competence and sincerity, and had some influence on their own or subsequent generations.' Under these criteria local and traditional material was omitted, and also examples of everyday commercial production – for example, transfer-printed pottery – or decorative objects of purely technical significance such as Tunbridge ware, papier-mâché and 'Berlin' woolwork. With the added dimension of influence from foreign contemporaries and a consideration of some economic and industrial factors, these guidelines have provided the framework for the present study.

The Oxford English Dictionary definition of 'Designer' (a word first recorded in 1662) relegates the practitioner to the role of a mere functionary making patterns for the benefit of manufacturers; however, Simon Jervis includes in his *Dictionary of Design and Designers* (1984) artists from as early as the mid-fifteenth century. It was accepted that the architects of Greece and Rome controlled the style and arrangement of the contents of a building as well as the structure itself. No doubt this tradition remained unbroken, but little documentary evidence exists from any period before the Middle Ages. The early designers were responsible for individual objects or engraved pattern books of ornament.

In the eighteenth century it was increasingly architects rather than painters or sculptors who designed the interior details, the furniture and the decorative equipment of the house. By publication

PL. 1 George Walton: painted hoarding for the Kodak Company, *c*. 1900.

of their models they began to influence the style of manufactured articles. The nineteenth century saw the birth of the design profession, the role of the designer being defined with the establishment in 1836 of the Government Schools of Design. The purpose of these schools was to train artists for industrial design, with the aim of improving manufactures. The practical element seems to have been insufficiently stressed: in 1894 Charles Campbell of the decorating firm Campbell, Smith & Co. remarked:

> 'I consider a proper architectural training, as well as an educated eye for colour and form, essentially necessary to the art of a decorator, and I think, our art schools would show more practical results were this a part of the education. As it is, a student from South Kensington is of little use to us until he has spent two or three years in learning what he might well have acquired there.' (*The Topical Times*, 17 November 1894.)

The architectural profession expanded greatly in the nineteenth century, particularly in Britain, encompassing many men of independent means who might in the past have practised only as amateurs. Many of the domestic and ornamental objects designed by architects that were taken up by manufacturers were furniture and ornaments which were essential to their integral schemes but could not be obtained in the shops. There are examples of this progression from patronage to commercial exploitation in the cases of Thomas Hope, A. W. N. Pugin, William Morris, E. W. Godwin and most of the Arts and Crafts architects. These were often the result of an architect being in a position to build, furnish and decorate his own house or that of a particularly indulgent patron.

Even a century and a half ago the opportunities to design a house and its furnishings down to the last detail were few. Some examples are documented: Hope's Deepdene (his London mansion in Duchess Street was not built for him); Thomas Hopper's Penrhyn Castle for the Earl of Carnarvon; Pugin's own houses at Salisbury and Ramsgate in Kent (PL. 71); Morris's Red House at Bexleyheath (PL. 73), designed and furnished in collaboration with Philip Webb; Godwin's Dromore Castle in Ireland for Lord Limerick (PL. 160–2); William Burges's commissions for the Marquess of Bute (PL. 116–18) and his own Tower House in Kensington; Charles Rennie Mackintosh's Scottish commissions, Hill House, Hous'hill and Windyhill, and his own flat in Glasgow; and houses for their own occupation by Arts and Crafts architects such as C. F. A. Voysey (PL. 302), Ernest Gimson and Sidney Barnsley, as well as Barnsley's Rodmarton Manor for the Biddulph family. This list is by no means comprehensive, but its great span of time gives some indication of the rarity of this particular privilege.

The usual process was to hand the completed structure over to a professional decorating firm, the course followed by Prince Albert at Osborne. This Italianate 'marine residence' of the royal family, on the Isle of Wight, was the epitome of prosperous bourgeois aspirations. Carefully designed with obsessive attention to detail by the conscientious and cost-conscious Prince and soundly contructed by the master builder Thomas Cubitt, it contained sumptuous interior schemes worked out by Ludwig Grüner in the palatial Renaissance manner that spelled luxury for well-to-do householders. In spite of his involvement with design reform Prince Albert maintained the traditional division of responsibility between builder and furnisher. Cubitt was to supply all the fixtures and fittings in the house. The list of these was comprehensive, including the baths, hot-water systems, warm-air apparatus, sinks, kitchen fixtures, stoves, grates, brass picture rails, boxes for candles and lavatory paper, copper coal scuttles, fire irons, fenders and doormats. For the furniture and upholstery the Prince turned to the Regency classicist Henry Whitaker, who had recently furnished the new Conservative Club. The silk-covered and gilded pieces were made by Dowbiggin. Whitaker, who had earlier issued *Designs of Cabinet and Upholstery Furniture in the Most Modern Style*, in 1825, produced a new pattern book in 1847, the *Cabinet Maker and Upholsterer's Treasury of Designs*, in which versions of the Osborne furniture are included.

Also typical is the history of Earl Manvers's Thoresby Hall, Nottinghamshire (1864–75), the last great house to be designed by Anthony Salvin (1799–1881), the most successful country house builder in Victorian England. The architect's involvement with the interior ceased in 1871 on completion of doors, windows and ceilings. The chimneypieces, often part of the architectural brief, were here supplied by Fisher & Dyson; Gillow's were responsible for the bedroom suites and other furniture; otherwise the rooms were a mixture of treasures salvaged from a previous house and pieces acquired on his travels by the Earl, with a large quantity of French furniture inherited by his wife, daughter of the Duc de Coigny. Most other large ensembles were achieved in a similar way.

'Originality, competence and sincerity', to quote Peter Floud, emanated overwhelmingly from architects, but their designs influenced taste only when they were sufficiently admired to be exploited commercially. In this context the career of Dr Christopher Dresser is significant. Unusually, his name appears on a wide range of manufactured articles, and was clearly a valuable marketing device (PL. 245–8). As more information emerges about the production of his designs on a commercial scale it is apparent that they had wide currency among the public. He has been described as the first professional designer; he is also credited with the architectural design of two houses, but he was not an architect. It is possible that his activities mark the beginning of the division between the architect as a universal man – the description applied to Karl Friedrich Schinkel – and the specialized and trained professional who must chose between one or other aspect of the subject.

In 1891 Philip Webb, Richard Norman Shaw and Walter Crane, among others, voiced their objections to the parliamentary bill to limit the practice of architecture to those who had passed qualifying examinations, setting out their views in *Architecture, A Profession or an Art* (1892). To them, such a move seemed to demote the 'mother of the arts'. In practice the long-term result has been to create exclusive professional compartments, rather than to maintain the fruitful dual function of the nineteenth-century architect-designer.

INTRODUCTION

For cultural and economic reasons Britain was destined to play the lead in the development of design throughout most of the nineteenth century. An immensely strong financial position was supported by the most advanced industrial economy in the world and a vast empire. While the rest of Europe was impoverished and devastated by war, and continually disrupted by political upheaval and revolution, the narrow channel separating Britain from the Continental mainland enabled it to remain impregnable. At the turn of the century Hermann Muthesius, an architect commissioned in 1896 by the German government to write a history of recent British domestic architecture, was to open his discussion of *The English House* (*Das englische Haus*, 1904) with this observation:

> 'A deeper insight into English life confirms what one has heard, that in all its ideas and feelings, in its *mores*, its philosophies and in its whole outlook on life, England stands apart from the countries of the continent of Europe, that it is a world of its own displaying an individuality of a quite special character in every aspect of culture.'

Long years of peace in Britain had allowed art and trade to flourish, and also to achieve an unprecedented prominence in Europe and the United States. In the 'workshop of Europe' economic stability encouraged industrial investment in transport and mechanization, as well as pioneering initiatives such as the Great Exhibition in 1851, which realized Prince Albert's cherished concept of 'art in industry'.

With the Great Exhibition the British made a public bid for preeminence in trade and manufactures. That this crucial lead fell to London was the result of historical accident. But for the revolution of 1848 the French would certainly have won the contest to stage the first international trade exhibition. Throughout the nineteenth century France was to suffer repeatedly from the bitter economic consequences of war and revolution.

Together the 1851 official catalogue and the *Art Journal Illustrated Catalogue* constituted a huge and unprecedented visual compendium of consumer products. Prince Albert, who had been largely responsible for this winning coup and for official encouragement of the cultural development of his adopted country, used the *Art Journal* as a means of publicizing his collection and patronage of art. The architectural and decorative activities of Queen Victoria and the Prince provide a perfect reflection of the middle-class aspirations of their time.

Two further exhibitions followed in 1853, in New York and Dublin, but these have faded into insignificance. The French were quick to regain the initiative with their own exhibition in 1855. Jackson & Graham, a leading London cabinet-making firm, were prominent exhibitors. A view of their stand shows an ormolu- and porcelain-mounted cabinet designed by the fashionable French decorator Eugène Prignot. A damaging legacy of 1851 was the widespread perception of the French as superior to the British in taste and craftsmanship. Emulation seemed to be the answer, and Jackson & Graham had the satisfaction of securing a Grand Prix with this ambitious cabinet in the French baroque style. The German architect and designer Gottfried Semper tried to devise a style that would combine the French grand manner with an English character. The cabinet designed by him and made by Holland & Sons, also shown at the 1855 Paris Exhibition, is set with porcelain plaques in reference to the French taste for Sèvres-mounted furniture, but the subject of the centrepiece is taken from a painting by William Mulready. Both cabinets were acquired for the South Kensington Museum. According to the 1862 *Art Journal Illustrated Catalogue*, a lesson learnt in 1851 was that 'it taught our designers

that the French taste which they had been following was in the main false', the 1855 episode being conveniently overlooked.

The impact of the 1851 exhibition on industrially ambitious nations was enormous; in Germany, for example, the term *Kunstgewerbe*, applied art, came into currency in the 1860s. Exhibitions represented a commercial and scientific 'coming-of-age', an important affirmation of progress all over the industrialized world.

Avant-garde designs emanated overwhelmingly from the architectural profession, in Britain an already large and growing force in the cultural development of the country, supported by a prosperous middle-class consumer movement. Architecture was traditionally a gentlemanly occupation and many nineteenth-century practitioners had adequate private means to protect them from the rigours of commercial competition. The most radical design ideas emerged from small, very distinctive offices where the personality of the architect was unchecked by the requirements of larger public commissions; notable examples were William Burges, Philip Webb and C. F. A. Voysey.

Fierce competition took its toll of those in the front line. Too many died in what should have been their prime: Augustus Welby Pugin at forty years of age, Prince Albert at forty-two, Henry Hobson Richardson at forty-three, I. K. Brunel, William Burges and E. W. Godwin at fifty-three, G. E. Street and Eugène Viollet-le-Duc at fifty-seven, Karl Friedrich Schinkel at sixty, and Joseph Paxton at sixty-two, all worn out with the strain of working under great pressure. Dante Gabriel Rossetti and William Eden Nesfield also died young, aged respectively fifty-four and fifty-three, but this was caused by pressures of a different kind. Thomas Jeckyll died insane in Norwich Asylum at fifty-four; Bruce Talbert died of drink aged forty-four, also the result of overwork.

The nineteenth century was a period of great social upheaval. The Industrial Revolution had altered the face of Britain and transformed the fortunes of many of the inhabitants. A vast increase in population and the resulting class mobility had an effect on moral, intellectual and cultural values. Great and rapid change is disquieting: half fascinated and half repelled, many Victorians took

PL. 3 The Indian Court; for the same publication. From the standpoint of a satellite-communications culture it is difficult to imagine the impact of these exotic artefacts on people whose visit to the exhibition was their first excursion outside their native village.

refuge in a romantic vision of the past, clothing the benefits of industrial progress in the decorative forms of medieval and Elizabethan architecture, disguising factory chimneys as Italian campaniles and warehouses as Egyptian palaces. A great technological triumph, the tubular railway bridge by Robert Stephenson at Conway on the Chester to Holyhead railway, which opened in 1848, had castellated pylons so that it should harmonize with Conway Castle rising above it.

This dichotomy was neatly expressed by Schinkel on his return from the travels in England that had revealed to him the exciting potential of industrial building methods:

'The new age does everything lightly; it no longer believes in an established state ... On the other hand, the complete contempt for everything established, which they desire to replace as quickly as possible by putting another in its place, this tendency and preference for change, which ultimately allows no time for anything to be recognized and enjoyed, is a sure sign of the vanity of the age and those who stand at its head.' (Alfred, Freiherr von Wolzogen, *Aus*

Schinkels Nachlass, Reisetagebücher, Briefe und Aphorismen, vol. III, 1863, p. 371.)

New transport systems reduced the known world to the compass of the intrepid traveller. The most significant was the vast railway network that developed throughout Europe. J. M. W. Turner's *Rain, Steam and Speed, The Great Western Railway* (PL. 25) was exhibited at the Royal Academy in 1844 and at the Manchester Jubilee Exhibition in 1887. Turner had painted the most compelling vision of the exhilaration, if not the precision, of new technology. He was observed as the inspiration for the painting struck him.

Lady Simon, who had been travelling on an Exeter to London train, gave this account to the Royal Academician and diarist George Richmond:

'In the coach seated opposite her was an elderly gentleman, short and stout, with a red face, and a curious prominent nose. The weather was very wild, and by-and-by a violent storm swept over the country, blotting out the sunshine and the blue sky and hanging like a pall over the landscape. The old gentleman seemed strangely excited at this, jumping up to open the window, craning his head out, and finally calling to her to come and observe a curious effect of light. A train was coming in the other direction, through the blackness, over one of Brunel's bridges, and the effect of the locomotive, lit by the crimson flame and seen through driving rain and whirling tempest, gave a peculiar impression of power, speed and stress.'

Overhearing a critical visitor to the Royal Academy exhibition remark, 'Just like Turner, ain't it? Whoever saw such a ridiculous conglomeration?' Lady Simon replied, 'I did.'

In the 1840s the railways were dramatically extending the potential of the canal network that had served the industrial revolution in the eighteenth century. The possibility of transporting heavy materials with relative ease and economy allowed provincial manufacturers to expand into a countrywide market.

Queen Victoria travelled by train for the first time in 1842, giving an enormously valuable boost to railway development in Britain. Pugin's diaries are full of references to the train journeys that allowed him to cram still greater prodigies of work into his intensely active career. The entries for June 1851 gave an idea of his peripatetic existence: in the space of five days he went from Birmingham to Holyhead; from Holyhead to Dublin and on to Maynooth; from Dublin to Birmingham and from Birmingham to London, then down to Ramsgate where he stayed for a short while. The miracle of modern communications quickly became common-place. Pugin wrote to his wife in November 1850 detailing endless frustrations: 'Travelling miserable', he complained. (See Alexandra Wedgwood, *A. W. N. Pugin and the Pugin Family*, 1985, pp. 71, 118.) Ultimately the railway network was to transform the pattern of urban spread as suburban living became a practical possibility.

Well into the present century, in contrast to the raw mechanism of the engine, the design of railway coaches was still related to earlier carriage-work. At the 1851 Exhibition casings in Gothic Revival style were a prevalent feature of mechanical exhibits, including electric telegraph instruments by William Reid (Class 10, item 427) which look like wall monuments in a church. The concept of 'form and function' only truly arrived in the present century, lagging far behind the basic tenet of Reformed Gothic, 'truth to materials' in building and furniture design.

For those lacking the opportunity to travel, the world was brought within their scope in 1851, when a vast array of scientific and natural marvels and manufactures of every description was displayed in Hyde Park. Inducements were offered to enable a wide spectrum of the population to enjoy the exhibition, from cheap entry charges to day excursions (the provision of such excursions for temperance groups led to the growth of Thomas Cook's great travel empire). Queen Victoria noted in her *Journal* (14 June 1851):

'Quite forgot to mention that on the morning of the 12th we saw 3 whole parishes Crowhurst, Linchfield and Langford, from Kent and Surrey (800 in number) walking in procession 2 and 2, the men in smock frocks, with their wives looking so nice. It seems that they subscribed to come to London, by the advice of the clergymen, to see the Exhibition, it only costing them 2s and 6d.' (Quoted in C. H. Gibbs-Smith, *The Great Exhibition of 1851*, London, 1981, p. 19.)

The shows enjoyed a phenomenal level of publicity; the catalogues themselves opened up a consumer paradise, offering a range of choice hitherto unknown.

Imaginary voyages through time and space were provided on a more permanent basis at the Crystal Palace – the 1851 exhibition building re-erected at Sydenham in 1854 – and in the newly established museums. *Travels in South Kensington* (1882) was a tour of the national decorative art museum conducted by the American journalist Moncure Conway. For the privileged the works of artist-travellers and the expensive new colour-illustrated publications offered an inspiring view of antique and exotic art and architecture. The importance of printing, and of colour illustration in particular, in developing and stimulating the consumer culture can hardly be overstated. The intellectualism of nineteenth-century architectural polychromy was inspired by the astonishing diversity of antique and historical references.

The coloration of the monuments of ancient Greece formed a special study, notably among French Beaux-Arts trainees; similarly, once attention had focused in the 1820s on the Alhambra in Spain the colour theories of the Moors preoccupied architects and decorators, especially Owen Jones. The neoclassical architects of the previous generation had presented a view of antiquity that was colourless, in spite of the evidence offered by returning travellers of polychrome decoration on ancient monuments. Jones and his collaborator Jules Goury made painstaking analyses of the surviving colour in the Alhambra in order to reconstruct its original appearance. Goury had become interested in the coloration of ancient monuments when travelling with Gottfried Semper in Greece. Semper had been in contact with Jacques Hittorff in Paris, and thus with French Beaux-Arts studies of antique polychromy. The influence of this work extended beyond architecture, inspiring intricately ornamented interiors and painted and inlaid furniture.

The influence of Cairene tomb buildings, evident in the bold striping that forms a distinctive element in, for example, the polychrome ornament used by William Butterfield, came probably from the published works of artist-travellers; while the patterns of

PL. 4 The New Palace of Westminster, from the Thames; photograph *c.*1900. The building of the new Houses of Parliament in the Gothic style marked a crucial change of direction for official architecture. The brilliantly inventive use of Gothic ornament made this the most important secular commission of the Gothic Revival. An iron model of the building was shown in Paris at the 1855 Exhibition.

Continental Gothic were noted at first hand on the extensive visits to monuments in Northern France, Flanders and Spain undertaken by Burges and Street. Nineteenth-century designers assumed a culturally sophisticated and well-informed audience familiar with their publications, and expected subtle references to earlier civilizations to be understood and appreciated.

Excitement and pride at the visible and tangible advantages of industrial and scientific development and the enormous increase in domestic and other forms of daily convenience was balanced by ethical reservations. Religious faith faced fearful challenges. In a frenzy of building the Victorians erected a rampart of new churches against the terrifying onslaught of religous doubt. For most architects – and certainly the Gothic Revivalists – the main business of their practice was church architecture or restoration. The Tractarian Movement and the spread of Ritualism brought commissions for all the accessories of church ritual; embroidered vestments and cloths, metalwork vessels and pastoral staffs, stained glass windows and painted decoration filled churches both old and new. However, a study mainly devoted to domestic design is not the place to attempt an adequate overview of the overwhelming importance in the nineteenth century of ecclesiastical architecture and its related decoration and furnishing.

Pugin, primarily an architect of churches and ecclesiastical dependencies – vicarages and church schools – and one of the Gothic Revival's most impassioned religious proselytizers, achieved unprecedented access to public attention through his involvement in the greatest secular commission of the century, the rebuilding in the Gothic style of the Houses of Parliament which had been destroyed by fire in 1834. For this enormous project techniques were evolved, for example, in tile manufacture and the use of mechanically executed ornament, that affected future production for the domestic market.

In his *History of the Gothic Revival in England* (1872, p. 153 [new edn 1970]) Charles Eastlake remarked:

'The carver, the cabinet-maker, the silversmith who sought his assistance, or whose work he was called upon to superintend, might reckon with safety on the rich fertility of his inventive power, and in truth Pugin's influence on the progress of art manufacture may be described as more remarkable than his skill as an architect. For the revival of mediaeval taste in stained glass and metal work we are indebted to his association with Mr Hardman. The attention which he bestowed on ecclesiastical furniture has been the means of reviving the arts of wood-carving and embroidery – of improving the public taste in the choice of carpets and paper-hangings.'

Brilliantly innovative Gothic Revival architects such as Butterfield and Street were destined to play a lesser part in design reform and the development of manufactures because their careers were focused so relentlessly on the design of church building. Although this involved some domestic and institutional architecture in the provision of rectories, schools and cottages, the opportunities to design furniture and ornamental pieces were relatively few. When Street did design domestic furniture it was strikingly original, almost abstract in conception, and it was his experiments with ecclesiastical embroidery in the 1850s that inspired Morris in his important 'art needlework' venture.

The Art Movement developed in the early 1860s when a vast house-building programme redressed the balance between ecclesiastical and domestic architectural commissions and, through the design work of Webb, Norman Shaw, Nesfield and Godwin, confirmed the importance of the architect-designer to the furniture and decorating trade, already hinted at in Pugin's career. With the increasing dominance of the manufacturer in the applied arts the carefully evolved design principles of the Art Movement gave way to a purely decorative, 'Art for art's sake' philosophy. This phase of decorative design has been known since the 1890s, appropriately, as the Aesthetic Movement. The Aesthetic Movement grew out of the Art Movement; many designers are common to both, and in both there is an area of confusion as to where the balance of responsibility lies between the designer and manufacturer. The word 'art' was much used in relation to decoration and furnishing in the nineteenth century, and here we have tried to follow the terminology of the designers themselves.

Max Beerbohm found the Aesthetic Movement sufficiently remarkable to attempt a summary of its origins:

'In fact, Beauty had existed long before 1880. It was Mr Oscar Wilde who managed her *début*. To study the period is to admit that to him was due no small part of the social vogue that Beauty began to enjoy. Fired by his fervid words, men and women hurled their mahogany into the streets and ransacked the curio-shops for furniture of Annish days. Dados arose upon every wall, sunflowers and the feathers of peacocks curved in every corner, tea grew quite cold while the guests were praising the Willow Pattern of its cup. A few fashionable women even dressed themselves in sinuous draperies and unheard-of greens.' ('1880', *Works and More*, 1930, p. 38.)

Beerbohm was in fact chronicling the decline of a movement and the trivializing effects of its popular success. The early days were different.

In the sharp but rarely cruel ridicule of George Du Maurier's *Punch* cartoons we can find the visual annals of the Aesthetic Movement. In his life of Whistler, James Laver remarked of the magazine:

'During this period *Punch*, than which there is no more accurate reflection of the opinions and prejudices of the more philistine of the British upper middle classes, devoted a considerable portion of its space every week to ridicule of the Aesthetes. The master of the revels was Du Maurier.' (James Laver, *Whistler*, revised edn 1951, pp. 138–9.)

Frank Burnand sought Du Maurier's advice about the set for his play, *The Colonel*, an Aesthetic satire:

'Try & have a room papered with Morris' green daisy, with a dado six feet high of green-blue serge in folds – and a matting with rugs for floor (Indian red matting if possible) – spider-legged black tables & side board – black rush bottom chairs & armchairs: blue china plates on the wall with plenty of space between – here & there a blue china vase with an enormous hawthorn or almond blossom sprig . . . also on mantlepiece pots with lilies & peacock feather – plain dull yellow curtains lined with dull blue for windows if wanted. Japanese sixpenny fans now & then on the walls in this picturesque unexpectedness.' (From a letter of 28 July 1880, in Yale University Library, quoted in Leonée Ormond, *George Du Maurier*, 1969, pp. 279–80.)

Du Maurier's advice consists of a round-up of artistic clichés that had become deliciously absurd by 1880, but in the 1870s many artistic houses were decorated in precisely this manner, while artists and architects had been living like this for upwards of two decades. The artful simplicity of rush-bottomed chairs and 'Daisy' wallpaper was the hallmark of Morrisian Aestheticism; another strand of artistic taste inclined towards Godwin's spidery Japanese-inspired tables; the Japanese pots and fans, with Oscar Wilde's lilies and peacock feathers, were the staple accessories of Japonisme, to be displayed against plain walls and combined with textiles in subtle unassertive colours.

Interior Decoration in the Regency

'We have before observed, and it cannot be too deeply impressed on the mind of the reader, that the first glance at the exterior of a house, like hearing the sound of the first bar of a piece of music, ought to give a correct idea of the style of all which is to follow. Whoever has a cultivated taste for architectural beauty must feel the force of this truth.' (Loudon, *Encyclopaedia*, 1833, p. 1088.)

The role of the architect-designer was not invented in the nineteenth century, but it was then that his sphere of influence was greatly enlarged. In the eighteenth century the Adam brothers, Robert

(1728–94) and James (1732–94), fulfilled this role, creating of every last detail of the complete ensemble, not only the ornate plasterwork walls and ceiling but the furniture, the curtains and even the doorknobs.

Their elegant neoclassicism swept through English architecture and furniture in the 1760s and 1770s, and spread rapidly on the Continent and in America. Patterns for architectural ornament, furniture and silver or plated wares were diffused through the *Works of Robert and James Adam* (from 1771). As Sir John Soane remarked, 'To Mr Adam's taste in the ornament of his buildings and furniture we stand indebted, inasmuch as manufacturers of every kind felt, as it were, the electric power of this revolution in art.' Thomas Sheraton's designs, published in *The Cabinet-Maker and Upholsterer's Drawing Book* (1793–4), were copied in Germany, where a translation of the book appeared as early as 1794.

The influence of Napoleon's architects Percier and Fontaine, and the Prussian court architect Karl Friedrich Schinkel, followed a similar pattern: architectural commissions fully realized down to the smallest details of lighting and furnishing were subsequently published in pattern-book form. Percier and Fontaine's *Receuil de décorations intérieures*, which included imperial commissions, commenced in 1801 and was quickly plundered for ideas; Rudolph Ackermann's *The Repository of Arts* has many plates based on the designs of 'Mr Persee'. Publication of Schinkel's architectural plans and details started in 1835, and his furniture and decorative objects appeared between 1835 and 1837. His designs had already been appearing in the *Vorbilder für Fabrikanten und Handwerker* since 1821, and the complete set was many times reissued.

Examples of manufactures were circulated and copied as well. From the late eighteenth century Josiah Wedgwood's distinctive 'Etruscan' and 'Jasper' ceramic wares were imitated in Paris and Berlin; he developed a creamware, called 'Queen's Ware' in honour of Queen Charlotte, which was so widely exported and subsequently copied that it threatened the survival of the Continental trade. Wedgwood's inventions were still spoken of with awe throughout the nineteenth century, his Jasperware in particular being admired for its originality. These strands of influence through architectural pattern books and manufacturing initiatives, so important to the diffusion of ideas in the nineteenth century, were already firmly established by the end of the eighteenth century.

In contrast to the luxurious French furniture and *objets d'art*, the British designs were suitable for production at a price within the reach of a large public. The roots of the Biedermeier style lie in this turn-of-the-century Anglomania. Although the characteristic pale woods and discreet ormolu mounts used for the furniture derive

PL. 5 Karl Friedrich Schinkel: armchair in painted cast iron; the first example cast *c*.1825. A novel and exotic material for furniture Schinkel's chair was matched with other decorative objects in cast iron: candelabra, urns and tripods. The pieces were finished matt black, as here, or to imitate bronze and patinated bronze. Although the technology used by Schinkel to shape the individual elements is sophisticated, great advances in furnace technology were later to improve immeasurably the quality of casting, as in the products of British foundries such as Coalbrookdale.

from French *bois clair* pieces of the Directoire and Empire periods, many of the forms recall Adam's or Thomas Sheraton's designs, stripped of their neoclassical swags and arabesques.

One of the earliest of the Viennese Michael Thonet's chair models of about 1836, exploiting his bent laminate method of manufacture (PL. 6), was a fashionable Biedermeier sidechair based on a typical English Regency 'Grecian' chair, a type that was ubiquitous in the

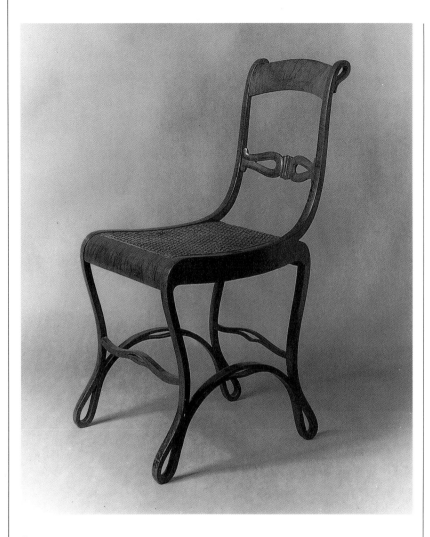

first quarter of the nineteenth century. Later, in the 1850s, Thonet developed his own forms which were no longer dependant on currently fashionable styles, and this successful formula has survived to the present day. With the use of outstanding designs from architects such as Josef Hoffmann (PL. 334), Otto Wagner and Adolf Loos, both Thonet and his principal rival J. & J. Kohn gained a place in the mainstream of design development at the turn of the century. The sound economic basis and adventurous design policy of both Wedgwood's and Thonet's enterprises enabled them to withstand the cultural and commercial pressures that had destroyed the manufacturers of luxury goods and fashionable novelties.

It is no coincidence that the term 'interior decoration' should have been coined at the very beginning of the nineteenth century. An indication of the way this new preoccupation would develop can be inferred from the decorating activities of Thomas Hope, whose schemes for his own Duchess Street mansion were published in 1807

in his *Household Furniture and Interior Decoration* – a prophetic title indeed.

The Duchess Street interiors (PL. 7), strongly influenced by Hope's friend Charles Percier, were relentlessly classical in inspiration and too didactic to attract many imitators. Hope stated his decorating precepts in strong terms: Sidney Smith wrote of *Household Furniture* in the *Edinburgh Review*;

> 'Everything is to be adorned according to Mr Hope, with emblems and symbols connected to the uses to which it is applied, and all these emblems are to be derived from classical mythology. He has made a perfect hieroglyphic or enigma of most of his appartments by this means, and produced something so childishly complicated and fantastic as to be impenetrable without a paraphrase and ridiculous when it is interpreted.'

None the less, distinctive forms such as the Klismos chair (PL. 8) were easily assimilated into fashionable schemes.

Below PL. 8 George Bullock: Klismos-style chair from Great Tew Park; before 1810, made for Matthew Robinson Boulton at Soho House.

However impenetrable the effect of Hope's schemes may have seemed, the fact is that he was setting a much publicised precedent for British architect-designers who followed in his footsteps. The diarist Joseph Farington recorded the opinion of George Dance the Younger:

'Dance told me He thought it better than He expected, & that by the singularity of it good might be done as it might contribute to emancipate the public taste from that rigid adherence to a certain style of architecture & of finishing & unshackle the Artists.' (Quoted in David Watkin, *Thomas Hope and the Neo-Classical Ideal*, 1968, p. 213.)

Hope died in 1831, so we cannot know what he would have made of the new developments in architecture and design. In the biographical introduction to the posthumous publication of Hope's *History of Architecture*, his youngest son wrote: 'He died just before the great Gothic revival, but not until he had done enough to show that he never would have been among its fierce antagonists.'

The scale of Hope's decorating activities was far surpassed by the Prince of Wales (later King George IV), who built, altered and embellished his residences at Carlton House; at his exotic Chinoiserie Pavilion in Brighton; at Royal Lodge, his picturesque cottage orné; and, after he had succeeded his father in 1820, at Buckingham Palace and Windsor Castle. The work of the royal architects and decorators at Carlton House and the Brighton Pavilion was known in detail through highly influential colour-illustrated volumes, further promoting the concept of an independent art of 'interior decoration'. Prominent among them were Henry Holland, James Wyatt, Thomas Hopper, John Nash, William Porden, Humphry Repton and Sir Jeffry Wyatville. Holland's team of French *émigré* decorative painters and cabinet-makers, as well as a great number of London craftsmen and tradesmen, among them Marsh & Tatham and Morel & Hughes, were busy decorating and furnishing at Carlton House during the forty years of the Prince's ownership. The

Above PL. 9 Windsor Castle from the Great Park. The extensive reconstruction of the castle in picturesque Gothic instigated by George IV was carried out in the 1820s by Wyatville.

Right PL. 10 A. W. N. Pugin: side chairs, painted and gilded; an example of the design supplied for the Gothic-style renovations at Windsor Castle, 1827.

Crace family were responsible for the Pavilion interiors. The youthful A. W. N. Pugin was employed at Windsor as early as 1827, designing furniture for manufacture by Morel & Seddon (PL. 10).

These interiors were fitted out regardless of expense. They were lit by magnificent chandeliers; the examples in the Rose Satin room at Carlton House were judged the finest in Europe. Ornamental porcelain vases and urns decked suites of fixed consoles. There were the most mechanically advanced clocks – George IV was an enthusiastic patron of Breguet – and vast table services of silver gilt with sculptural table centres and garnitures, as well as carpets and curtains of unbelievable opulence. Much of the material was French: the gilt bronzes from Thomire, the porcelain from the Sèvres factory, and the furniture by Weisweiler and Roentgen.

British manufacturers represented turned to artists such as the sculptor John Flaxman, who made designs for Wedgwood and the royal goldsmiths Rundell & Bridge.

The architect Charles Heathcote Tatham was well versed in the repertoire of classical ornament and was capable of supplying the design needs of his brother Thomas, of the furnishing firm Marsh & Tatham. He had been dispatched to Rome as a young man when working in Henry Holland's office. From Tatham's drawings, sent back in letters, Holland devised a number of classically inspired pieces for the Prince. At the Pavilion Crace used ideas for Chinese ornament and furniture proposed by Sir William Chambers in the 1750s, but the Chinoiserie chairs of simulated bamboo made by Marsh & Tatham were based on Chinese export furniture. Another contributor to these schemes was George Smith, author of several books of designs for furniture and decoration, who styled himself in 1826 'Upholsterer and Drawing Master to His Majesty'.

These artists and craftsmen who enjoyed the King's patronage were not directly influencing the design of manufactures, but such large-scale activity had an effect on the development of an independently British decorative art industry. However, as Prince and King, George IV retained his taste for sumptuous decoration in the French style, and this was to remain the touchstone of rich men's houses throughout the nineteenth century. Typical of this preference for lavish gilding and carving is the suite of white and gold furniture for the Court Drawing Room at Goldsmiths' Hall, designed by the architect Philip Hardwick the Elder in the 1830s and made by the firm W. & C. Wilkinson.

The death of the King in 1830 marked the end of an era: he had provided, in the style of the eighteenth-century aristocracy, an unparalleled example of adventurous, sometimes outrageous, but cultivated patronage. He was the last British monarch to make a significant contribution to the appearance of the capital when, with Nash, he initiated the development in the classical style of Regent Street and Regent's Park. Nash lacked the grandiose opportunities enjoyed by Schinkel in Berlin or Leo von Klenze in Munich, but his work established the classical character of domestic and commercial architecture in London for half a century. The King was extravagant, unpopular, ridiculed for his matronly mistresses and despised for his treatment of his wife, but as a connoisseur of painting and a knowledgeable patron of architecture and design he provided a model that was eagerly emulated.

At the time of his death he was engaged on a project of considerable contemporary relevance, the extensive remodelling in the picturesque Gothic style of Windsor Castle (PL. 9). But he was succeeded by his brother, the seafaring Duke of Clarence, an unashamed philistine, who finished the work at Windsor and Nash's uncompleted alterations to Buckingham Palace as cheaply as possible. Royal patronage was never again to be so visible: Queen Victoria's building, decorating and furnishing activities were concentrated on her private family residences in Scotland and at Osborne on the Isle of Wight, a domestic example most congenial to the majority of her subjects.

Thomas Hope's approach was in great contrast to the widely spread patronage of the King. He was not in need of an architect. Wary of the increasing use of machine production by fashionable firms such as Gillow's and Crace, he sought out obscure but highly qualified craftsmen of particular merit in their own area of specialization to carry out his designs for furniture and decoration.

PL. 11 L. N. Cottingham: Gothic-style chair, 1844; made by Samuel Pratt of Bond Street, patentee in 1845 of a wood-carving machine. Pratt's interest in simplifying the production of ornamental designs by using machinery may have influenced Cottingham's continuing attachment to highly decorated Gothic, a contrast to the structural emphasis in Pugin's work in the 1840s. Cottingham's chair resembles designs by Pugin dating from 1830. Cottingham was ahead of his time in knowledge and appreciation of Gothic, his pattern books of metalwork designs and his *Working Drawings of Gothic Ornaments etc., with a design for a Gothic Mansion* (1824) dating from the period when he was working on drawings of Henry VII's chapel at Westminster Abbey for publication. A collection of fragments and casts in his London house formed the basis for the Architectural Museum, established at Westminster in 1852.

PL. 12 A. W. N. Pugin: chair modelled on the 'Glastonbury' chair; for one of his early commissions, the college at Oscott, Birmingham. Henry Shaw and Sir Samuel Rush Meyrick, *Specimens of Ancient Furniture*, 1838, shows the original chair, which had belonged to Horace Walpole. It was already being copied in the eighteenth century. Pugin chose this chair, one of the very few surviving pieces of English medieval furniture, as being the most suitable to a pure structural style of Gothic. He pursued the ideal of cheap furniture through simplification of form rather than technology.

His patronage has been compared by David Watkin (1968, p. 53) to that of William Morris in the 1850s, who was also engaged in building and furnishing his own house. An analogy with Pugin might seem appropriate as well.

Morris's experiment was to have much more far-reaching results, not least of which was the creation of Morris & Co., but Hope was a pioneer in many of the initiatives that were later to transform the status of design in Britain. Hope's inspiration was fundamentally French-oriented, and his influence was too fragmentary and diffused to affect the subsequent development of industry and domestic manufactures, the route through which Victorian designers were to make their fullest impact. However, he had tried to raise the standard of art instruction for the artisan by proposing the idea of a school of design, and he promoted public patronage to fill the gap created by the increasingly private character of royal commissions.

Cut off by the blockade during the Napoleonic Wars from the classical monuments of the Mediterranean, with the Grand Tour ended, or at least suspended, Britain developed a new architectural language from the native heritage and indigenous materials. Furniture models associated with British victories, such as the 'Trafalgar' chair and the Egyptian pieces commemorating the Battle of the Nile, inevitably had an insular appeal. The overwhelm-ing preference for mahogany furniture had perforce to be set aside in favour of beech, yew, walnut, rosewood and oak. In January 1824 the following comment appeared in Ackermann's *Repository*: 'The manufacture of British woods such as pollarded oak and elm cut transversely near the roots is now so well understood and so beautiful when thus applied that they need no other recommend-ation to the admirers of superior furniture.' The 'Regency' style – the term now widely accepted to describe the decorative arts of the period from 1790 to 1830 – combined Greek Revival with an elegant Gothick, some exotic influences from China and India, and the newly discovered Tudor.

The Regency cabinet-maker George Bullock was noted for his employment of native woods and Mona marble from his own quarry, and for the use of decorative motifs taken from native plants rather than from the repertoire of popular classical ornament. With his partner Richard Bridgens he experimented in 'Elizabethan' furniture using oak. A Bullock-like design for a pier table, published in the *Repository* in 1818 (the year of Bullock's death) recommends the use of rosewood and 'oak transversely cut and highly polished, which in splendour rivals foreign woods'. The use of native woods lent individuality to French and Austrian furniture as well, pale birch and fruitwoods giving distinction to the Continental Bieder-meier style.

Opposite, left PL. 13 A. W. N. Pugin: oak pedestal table stamped 'A. Pugin' and made by Pugin's Covent Garden firm; *c.*1830. Pugin has extracted the essence of form from Tudor designs and arrived at a severe undecorated type that foreshadows his abstract, structural furniture of the 1840s.

Opposite, right PL. 14 George Bullock and Richard Bridgens: library table in oak inlaid with ebony with Gothic details; supplied *c.*1817 for Battle Abbey. The base mouldings are derived from medieval stonework.

Right PL. 15 A. W. N. Pugin: circular centre table in rosewood; *c.*1835. The mouldings, similar to those used by Bullock, terminate in masks based on medieval sculptural stonework. Pugin published the 'octagon' table in *Gothic Furniture* (1835).

In the eighteenth century 'Gothick' designs had generally been made up in mahogany, but in the 1820s British oak was seen to be more in keeping with an archaeological approach to historical revival styles. The use of oak was to remain a distinguishing feature of reformed historical revival furniture until this was superseded in the 1870s by mahogany, seen as more appropriate to the revived 'Queen Anne' style.

Bullock was involved in the decoration and furnishing of Walter Scott's Abbotsford, an important milestone in the development of nineteenth-century antiquarianism. Scott's novels were immensely popular, and widely read in translation. His romantic view of the past played a crucial part in popularizing historicism in architecture and decoration. Abbotsford itself was a model antiquarian confection.

At the beginning of the nineteenth century mainstream European neoclassicism was almost in its final stages. The long years of war had succeeded in fragmenting a style already eclectic and increasingly unfocused; the massive *Néo-grec* of the Second Empire classical revival was undeveloped and the Italianate manner used by Barry and Cubitt still two decades in the future. In Britain the resulting vacuum might almost have been created to allow the romantic and antiquarian strand of Gothic that had emerged in the eighteenth century to rise to a place of dominance. As Kenneth Clark wrote in *The Gothic Revival* (1928, new edn 1964, p. 197), 'It changed the face of England ... filling our towns with Gothic banks and grocers, Gothic lodging-houses and insurance companies, Gothic everything, from a town-hall down to a slum public-house ... There cannot be a main street in England quite untouched by the Revival.'

Culture and Consumer

In the century between 1750 and 1850 profound social changes had taken place in Britain. The population at the time of the first census in 1801 was 10.8 million; by the middle of the century it had more than doubled. In that period the whole balance of the population

PL. 16 Palaces on the Riva degli Schiavoni in Venice; mid-nineteenth century photograph by G. Naya. Photographic collections, widely available from the 1850s, were an important medium of communication. Photographs were on show at the Great Exhibition, and the Photographic Society of London was founded in 1853. Prince Albert was an early enthusiast, and was persuaded with the Queen to become patron of the Society. As Ruskin perceived photography, combining science and art, reflected the spirit of the age. He saw the potential for accurate recording and used daguerreotypes in preference to watercolours.

shifted from an agricultural to a manufacturing economy; from a predominantly rural community to the reverse, with 80 per cent living in towns and dependent on industry for employment. The population of London increased from 1,117,000 in 1801 to 2,685,000 in 1850. By the end of the century the numbers had again doubled.

Apart from the need for employment which brought people to the economic centre of the country, the attractions of the capital were obvious; theatres, clubs, pleasure gardens and fashionable shops provided endless opportunities for amusement for the newly prosperous urban population. Fashionable society was relentlessly focused on London during the Season, dispersing thereafter to great landed estates in the country, centred on houses filled with historic collections of paintings and works of art and masterpieces of eighteenth-century cabinet-making. The private palaces of London were conspicuous for their magnificence – Queen Victoria thought her own quarters were quite outclassed by the Sutherlands' Stafford House (now Lancaster House) – rather than for innovative design.

The design reform movement in the nineteenth century was fuelled as much by industrial new money and middle-class prosperity as by aristocratic patronage, thus diminishing the cultural gulf that had previously existed between the capital and provinces. Northern industrial towns such as Manchester and Liverpool grew up in the nineteenth century and soon reached their zenith of architectural grandeur and cultural autonomy, only to face a demoralizing decline of prosperity in the present century.

Town halls, museums and libraries ordained by civic pride exploited the full grandeur of Victorian historicism. 'Manchester is a more interesting city to walk over than London. One can scarcely walk about Manchester without coming across frequent examples of the *grand* in architecture. There has been nothing to equal it since the building of Venice.' This eulogy appeared in *The Builder* in 1861. The recently completed Assize Courts (1859), designed by Alfred

Waterhouse, might perhaps have prompted the comparison with Venice, being in the Venetian Gothic style recommended by John Ruskin. Ruskin's *The Stones of Venice* had an immediate impact on the development of an appropriate secular vocabulary. Usually he loathed the style which his enthusiasm had inspired, but he admired the Assize Courts, remarking that the building as a whole was 'much beyond everything yet done in England on my principles'.

By the 1850s the Perpendicular style of the Palace of Westminster was already outmoded. Studies of earlier structures and increased knowledge of the Continental Gothic heritage had broadened the basis of Victorian Gothic. G. E. Street and William Burges headed the group of 'thirteenth-century men'. Manchester already boasted two fine classical public buildings by Sir Charles Barry, the Royal Manchester Institution (1824) and the Athenaeum (1837); in 1868 Waterhouse's thirteenth-century Town Hall was to complete a notable grouping.

Local architects were provided with opportunities on a large scale. For example, in Leeds the imposing complex of Town Hall, Corn Exchange, Mechanics' Institute and Oriental Baths was carried out in the 1850s and 1860s by Cuthbert Brodrick of Hull. The intricate, leafy Ruskinian Gothic designs of J. H. Chamberlain (PL. 175) are undeservedly little known because his career was based in Birmingham. Local industrial manufacturers developed lines in ornamental wares, often to the original designs of innovative architects, notably Skidmore of Coventry (Bruce Talbert [PL. 136]) and the Coalbrookdale iron foundry (Christopher Dresser [PL. 137]). Furniture manufacturers based in, for example, Leeds (Marsh, Jones & Cribb), Manchester (Lamb) and Lancaster (Gillow's) having been contractors in important architectural commissions, found themselves in a position to employ architect-designers such as Talbert, Charles Bevan and W. R. Lethaby, and thus to evolve a distinctive style.

The increasing scale and splendour of successive waves of mainly terraced urban housing is witness to the rise of the middle class in the mid-nineteenth century. In the wake of middle-class prosperity came the consumer culture that we know today. Domestic requirements that had been met *ad hoc* at local level were now supplied by an extensive network of manufacturers increasingly reliant on mechanized production. The establishment of shops and, later, department stores presented an unprecedented degree of choice. Design reform was in conscious opposition to the danger, of which many were aware, that novelty for its own sake would dictate taste.

Large families attended by an army of servants lived in considerable opulence. Throughout the nineteenth century the second-largest employment for the population as a whole was domestic service; for women it was the largest. Hippolyte Taine, visiting England in the 1860s, was impressed by this aspect of London:

'They turn out houses as we turn out Paris fancy-goods. What a multitude of easy, comfortable, of wealthy households! The whole implies large profits from quick turnover, an opulent free-spending middle-class very different from our own, financially straightened and looking twice at every penny spent.' (*Notes sur l'Angleterre*, transl. Edward Hyams, 1957, p. 15.)

Muthesius regarded as a significant mark of individuality this preference for living in houses, as opposed to the apartments which had been the usual dwellings of townspeople on the Continent since the eighteenth century. 'We must be clear about one thing,' he wrote: 'for all our efforts on behalf of art, an artistic culture can only begin with the individual and the individual can only exercise his artistic sense by shaping his immediate surroundings, his living room and his house.'

Although 90 per cent of families lived in rented properties and were thus unable to influence the style of the exterior, the creative embellishment of the interior provided the domestic market with excellent commercial opportunities. The nineteenth century saw an increase for all classes except the very poorest in shopping for non-essentials, an activity described in 1899 by the American economist Thorstein Veblen as 'conspicuous consumption'. By the end of the century shopping in the new department stores was a major leisure and social activity. In the mid-nineteenth century the professional middle class in England was enviably prosperous; Hippolyte Taine compared the fees and salaries of the teaching, medical and legal professions in Britain and in Second-Empire France: 'There are ten such fortunes and such kind of lives in England for every one in France.' (p. 16.)

A new class of patron for art and design emerged in the wake of this prosperity. Whereas the houses of the aristocracy and the very rich all over the world continued to show a uniformity in taste of specifically French inspiration – furniture and decorative objects in the revived rococo style were overwhelmingly in the ascendant at the Great Exhibition of 1851 – now, through the influence of the 'Art' or Aesthetic Movement, middle-class architecture and decoration developed a distinctive character. Some unexpected recruits to the Aesthetic Movement came after the publication of Matthew Arnold's provocative *Culture and Anarchy* (1869), in which the landed and upper classes were stigmatized as philistines and 'Barbarians', their most undesirable characteristic being their resistance to new ideas. Eager to prove him mistaken, the aristocratic intelligentsia were quick to form artistic coteries, centring, for example, on Little Holland House where Mrs Prinsep cherished G. F. Watts; around the activities of Sir Coutts Lindsay's Grosvenor Gallery in Bond Street; and in the adventurous patronage of the 'Souls', an exclusive group who had made friends among artists – notably Edward Burne-Jones – as well as writers and poets. Ultimately this trend resulted in the creation of such philanthropic ventures as the Royal School of Art Needlework, and various charitable craft guilds (the Duchess of Sutherland, who ran a successful Cripples' Guild, was an 'occasional Soul'). At Naworth Castle in 1874 Rosalind Howard (wife of George Howard, later Earl of Carlisle) had looked forward with a certain apprehension to her first meeting with William Morris, fearing that he might share Arnold's prejudice: 'he was rather shy – and so was I – I felt he was taking an experimental plunge among the barbarians … Not that I think he will like me – but he puts up with me.'

When he arrived in London Muthesius established himself in Hammersmith, where he numbered among his circle of friends Walter Crane, Charles and Margaret Mackintosh and Herbert McNair. His book reflects an intimate understanding of the artistic milieu from which the best of late nineteenth-century British domestic design derived.

Rural Architecture

Muthesius also noted the English preference for living in the country, which had resulted from what he described as the 'desolate monotony' of the English city. The new class of house owner needed a size and type of dwelling that was neither a mansion nor a farmhouse. In the eighteenth century this gap was filled by the picturesque 'cottage orné', of which John Nash's designs for Blaise Hamlet (1810) are among the best examples. These were built as almshouses, but many of the contemporary essays in this style were substantial country houses, and George IV's Royal Lodge in Windsor Great Park, a cottage orné also designed by Nash, was palatial.

Initially the architectural gap was filled through the publication of pattern books of 'villa' types in all the modish styles. The success of, for example, P. F. Robinson's *Designs for Ornamental Villas* (1827) is apparent from the many houses built to his suggestions clustered on the outskirts of country towns and villages. In 1835 the millionaire farmer Joseph Neeld selected James Thomson to build the Egypto-Italian Tower House and farm buildings on his estate on the outskirts of Bath on the basis of Thomson's *Retreats, a Series of Designs Consisting of Plans and Elevations for Cottages, Villas and Ornamental Buildings*. The result was a distinctive group, a number of the farms having ornate towers based on Italian belvederes, in style

akin to H. E. Goodridge's Beckford Tower at nearby Lansdowne. Less self-consciously picturesque than Robinson, Thomson shows in his designs the influence of the massive monuments of ancient Egypt and is a true precursor of the compact, organic Gothic used by the reforming architects of the 1850s.

John Claudius Loudon's *Encyclopaedia of Cottage, Farm, and Villa Architecture and Furniture* (1833) was intended as a manual of self-help; 'Every gentleman ought to have some knowledge at least of architectural drawing,' he wrote, 'so as to be able to design the buildings to be erected upon his estate, which are now often built from the coarse plans of ignorant workmen.' (p. 799.) Loudon's book was many times reprinted and was immensely influential (PL. 17), notably on the American architect Andrew Jackson Downing, whose own book, *The Architecture of Country Houses* (1850), acknowledges this debt. However, cultivated patrons were not to be fobbed off with the type of ornamental villa that was designed to be a dependency on an ancestral estate.

Muthesius pinpointed the problem:

'As a result of the growth of a class of educated architects on the one hand and the swift rise of the middle classes on the other, the architect was more and more often called in for these small commissions. He was at first too highly educated for them. He brought with him an archetectonic ambition that made him attempt monumental architecture on these ordinary little commissions – this was the architect's fundametal failure in the last century.'

Muthesius identified the solution as the recovery of the vernacular tradition, which he credits to the English architects and dates to the 1860s.

Although the self-consciously rural theme of the cottage style became a side issue with the rise of Reformed Gothic in the 1840s, it had established an anti-classical individuality for country dwellings,

PL. 17 The Palm House at Bicton House, Bicton, Devonshire; constructed in the 1820s for Lord Rolle, a noted horticulturalist. This is the type of structure proposed by John Claudius Loudon for experimental 'forcing houses' in Bayswater (1815–18), and described by him as 'non-architectural'. The palm house is built of iron and glass, using a masonry back wall to retain heat. Freestanding structures at Bretton Hall (1827) and the Palm House at Kew (1844–8), both by Decimus Burton, are the predecessors of Paxton's Great Stove at Chatsworth, itself the precursor of the Crystal Palace of 1851, also by Paxton.

INTRODUCTION
Rural Architecture

using a variety of building materials, an asymmetrical plan and an irregular roofscape. Twenty years later the thread re-emerged in the vernacular architecture of W. E. Nesfield and Norman Shaw, and in the Arts and Crafts houses of Voysey and Ernest Gimson at the turn of the century. Architecturally the 'model village' of the 1800s was the precursor of the garden suburb of the 1880s.

Pugin, Butterfield, Street, G. F. Bodley and Webb were all pioneers of the middle-class Gothic Revival house. Loudon had realized (*Encyclopaedia*, p. 1088) that to go beyond the simple pattern-book solution, even in furnishing a house, required an architect:

'What passes for Gothic furniture among cabinet-makers and upholsterers is, generally, a very different thing from the correct Gothic designs supplied by Architects who have imbued their minds with this style of art. Wherever, therefore, a house is to be furnished in the Gothic style, we repeat our recommendation to put the whole under the direction of a competent Architect.'

In 1830 Pugin was not yet twenty years old, but he had already established his own cabinet-making firm at 12 Hart Street, Covent Garden (1829–31) to produce furniture and metalwork in the Gothic, Elizabethan and Jacobean styles (PL. 13). With an increasing understanding of medieval architecture he realized that he should no longer improvise and invent, and by 1834 he had worked out a set of guiding principles that mark the beginning of the Reformed Gothic style. In architecture and furniture design Pugin was to initiate revolutionary changes, not least in his ability to address a new audience. Largely through the activities of Pugin and his successors, the patronage of architects and decorators, once the nearly exclusive prerogative of the landed aristocracy, was to become a practical possibility for the middle classes.

Pugin had aristocratic patrons, the Duke of Devonshire and the Earl of Shrewsbury for example, but his most effective contribution towards architectural reform was on a modest domestic scale, stemming from his design for his own house near Salisbury. The compact, brick-built and carefully detailed family house paved the way for the enduringly popular vernacular or 'Old English' style house which has never been entirely dropped from the English country building repertoire.

For the first two-thirds of the nineteenth century country house builders were still substantially of the upper class, relying on their land for the means to sustain an enormously expensive way of life. In subsequent decades a fall in the value of agricultural land prompted sales from the great estates to financiers and industrial millionaires and gave the Rothschilds, for example, a way into the landowning class. Baron Ferdinand's Waddesdon Manor was built on land acquired from the Duke of Marlborough. The landless great house achieved and sustained by industrial money, such as Cragside, built in 1870 for Sir William Armstrong by Norman Shaw, was a comparatively late development.

Although Cragside was landless in the economic sense, Armstrong eventually owned 1,729 acres of gardens, pleasure grounds and woodland, acquired piece by piece as rocky moorland. He created a romantic showcase of formal gardens, glasshouses, parkland and contrived wildness in a rocky gorge, where an elaborate system of dams and lakes – a pleasing feature in itself – provided hydroelectricity for lighting and central heating. Cragside was the first private house to boast such a system. Telephones were installed so far in advance of the development of a telecommunications network that Armstrong was reduced to calling his guests in their rooms and singing to them.

Recession in the 1880s

Dependence on acreage as a source of revenue was to have disastrous consequences in the 1880s, when many estates were ruined by the agricultural depression. The drop in the value of land, which hit particularly at the country estates of the aristocracy, had a wider effect on the economy as a whole. After Pugin's death a significant realignment had occured in the pattern of patronage for decorative art, shifting from the individual to the manufacturer or entrepreneur. This paved the way for his successors to become career designers, like Bruce Talbert and Charles Bevan, and many architects maintained a sideline in commercial ranges of metalwork, wallpapers and textiles, with a significant improvement in their earnings. The quality of manufactures was raised, and many examples of furnishing and decoration attained the status of works of art.

Spending by the middle classes had risen particularly steeply in the 1850s and 1860s, and prosperous professional men with families had become accustomed to making a show of culture and style as part of a comfortable and expensive way of life. While they were anxious to cut down expenditure in ways that would not diminish an appearance of affluence, essential economies in the eighties left a trail of impoverished or bankrupt firms, including Gillow's, Jackson & Graham, Minton, and Holland & Sons, all formerly profitable purveyors of the opulent interior.

A steady decline in public interest had also hit the once popular exhibitions which had proliferated all over the world after 1851. These had promoted a particular genre of technical display in every category of decorative domestic object. Without exhibitions to

26

stimulate demand for these, many of the manufacturers found themselves in difficulties. 1874 saw the last of the annual South Kensington trade shows, a significant pointer to industrial recession. Another factor was that increased professionalism and the trade orientation of the majority of the exhibitors had squeezed out the freaks and curiosities, such as cathedrals modelled from millions of matches and baskets of flowers woven in human hair, which had been an enormous attraction for the general public.

The 1878 Paris Exhibition had a purpose, to demonstrate France's recovery from the Franco-Prussian War, but G. A. Sala's comment sums up a general dissatisfaction:

> 'I will, in the outset, candidly own that, although I have the proud privilege to be a free-born Briton of the Victorian era, I went about the Exhibition in the spirit of an ancient Athenian, perpetually demanding some new thing; and quite as frankly must I admit that, so far as my first visit to the Exhibition went, I was disappointed.'
> (*Paris Herself Again*, 1882, p. 60.)

The exhibits featured in the Inventions and Health Exhibitions in London in 1883 and 1884 – in 1884, for example, the fitted wardrobe was introduced, hygienic but not visually exciting – were of a very different type from the extravagantly praised masterpieces of technique. The exhibition carousel continued successfully on the Continent, the 1889 International Exhibition in Paris being the first to make a profit since 1851.

It might almost seem as if the design reform movement, with its patrons in the intellectual and artistic middle class and its logical destination the classless art and architecture of the Arts and Crafts Movement, had developed to withstand the recession. The Aesthetic Movement actually benefited from it. One mark of social arrival was to become a patron of art, and this involved substantial sums to purchase paintings and sculpture. The Aesthetes, with their preference for a restrained and cultivated style of decoration, rather looked down on the plutocratic taste for walls covered in a mosaic of gilt-framed paintings. The saving of outlay on works of art justified a lavish, but still much smaller, expenditure on embroidered hangings or tapestries, painted tiles, stained glass and ebonized furniture.

Yet 'art for art's sake' carried the seeds of its own destruction. The public felt increasingly uneasy at its absence of moral purpose, and the scandalous downfall in 1895 of Oscar Wilde, the Aesthetic Movement's most prominent publicist, promoted the simple ideological certainties of Arts and Crafts philosophy.

The direction taken by the Arts and Crafts Movement marks the decline in Britain's long maintained position as the leading innovator in architecture and design. Although the establishment of the Art Worker's Guild and Arts and Crafts Exhibition Society gave the movement a collective impact, particularly in theoretical propositions about the role of design in society, there is less evidence of the influence of individual designers. There are notable exceptions in Mackintosh and his Glasgow group, who operated outside the narrowly based Arts and Crafts aesthetic, and C. R. Ashbee, who assiduously cultivated contacts in America including Frank Lloyd Wright and the brothers Charles Sumner and Henry Mather Greene.

Recognizing the importance of British designers in forming the basis for a recognized profession, the Kunstindustriemuseet – the decorative arts museum – at Trondheim in Norway made purchases from Siegfried Bing's Art Nouveau exhibitions of pieces by W. A. S. Benson, Morris and Liberty & Co. The collection was made with an educational purpose, to learn from, and the choice of items shows what was regarded as significant in design terms nearly a century ago. The contrast with the present-day idea of the most important design developments of the period is startling. The choices carefully avoid extremes in form or handling. The work of Godwin and Dresser is conspicuously absent.

In the 1820s Schinkel had been searching for a domestic style for the royal palaces in Berlin that would alter the intimidating scale of earlier royal patronage. He found it in England on his travels in 1826. From Decimus Burton's Athenaeum Club and Robert Adam's Lansdowne House he took chair designs in simple unornamented shapes. These were to become widely popular in Germany in the 1830s, and were during the same period the standard equipment of modest English houses, recommended by Loudon in his influential *Encyclopaedia* as ideal villa furniture. The theme of design reform was to be this search for beauty in appropriateness, in the functional, in truth to materials and in the possibility of art for all.

At Trondheim great emphasis was placed on simple country forms for furniture, and pure undecorated shapes in glass and ceramics. Eastlake had written: 'Lost in the contemplation of palaces we have forgotten to look about us for a chair.' By the end of the century simple functional chairs had become a major preoccupation with many of the designers associated with the Arts and Crafts Movement. One of the examples at Trondheim, a green-stained beech country chair made for Liberty's, would now pass unnoticed in any second-hand furniture shop, whereas in 1902 it was recognized as a significant acquisition. When these purchases are compared with our own public acquisitions from international exhibitions in the second half of the century, it is obvious that appreciation of the vernacular – which was to emerge as a thread of nationalistic culture in many European countries as well as in the United States – represented an enormous and important revolution in taste.

PL. 18 C. Harrison Townsend: the Horniman Museum, Forest Hill, London. The purpose-built museum was commissioned by Frederick Horniman, Member of Parliament and chairman of the family tea firm, to house his anthropological collections. It was started in 1897, in an idiosyncratic style more reminiscent of the Vienna of the Secessionists than *fin-de-siècle* London. The façade, with its eye-catching tower clock, is decorated with a mosaic by Robert Anning Bell.

PL. 19 J. M. Olbrich: the Secession Building in Vienna. The building was begun in 1897 with the founding of the Vienna Secession, and completed in the following year. Like the movement itself, the details were inspired by English Arts and Crafts ideas.

REFORMED GOTHIC
AND ENGINEERING

The revival of the Gothic style in the eighteenth century can be traced to the architectural publications of Batty Langley and the brothers William and John Halfpenny. Such pattern books were to remain an important, if erratic, route for the dissemination of ideas well into the nineteenth century. For example, it was by chance that Robert Lugar's *Architectural Sketches for Cottages, Rural Dwellings and Villas in the Grecian, Gothic and Fancy Styles* (1815) came into the hands of the Prussian Princess Augusta. Thus a derivative work by a little known architect provided the first inspiration for the 'English' Gothic Babelsberg, designed by Karl Friedrich Schinkel in 1833.

The eclectic fantasy of Strawberry Hill, Horace Walpole's house at Twickenham, caught public imagination in the 1750s, and thereafter development of a Gothic architectural style ran parallel to the classical idiom. Even if Walpole was not the first to investigate the possibilities of Gothic, his well publicized building activities at Strawberry Hill provided a focus for the growing interest in the style. Walpole had been grounded in the classical tradition and his early enthusiasms were formed by the Grand Tour which he took in 1739; he therefore understood more clearly than many of his fellow Gothic enthusiasts the implications of departing from the classical 'Rule of Taste'. 'One must have taste to be sensible of the beauties of Greek architecture; one only wants passion to feel Gothic', he wrote in *Anecdotes of Painting* (1762).

Strawberry Hill was the principal model for the so-called 'Gothick' decoration of the late eighteenth century. But Walpole initiated many more serious antiquarian preoccupations that were to persist in architecture and design well into the nineteenth century. For example, he was an early enthusiast for medieval heraldic tiles, and the first to install a collection as part of a Neo-Gothic interior. He owned a number of pieces of furniture, including the 'Glastonbury' chair and a set of ebony bobbin-turned Indo-Portuguese chairs thought to be medieval, that served as models for nineteenth-century designers. Walpole was a pioneer collector of old stained and painted glass, and Strawberry Hill was decorated with this as well as contemporary work. As Clive Wainwright has pointed out (*The Romantic Interior*, 1989, p. 84), Walpole was one of the people responsible for creating a market for ancient glass. The interest developed into a full-scale revival of painted and stained glass in the nineteenth century.

In its early stages the vocabulary of the Gothic Revival was based on some implausible notions; for example, that a canopy from a medieval shrine can be adapted to a fireplace, or a cathedral provide the model for a country house; the purpose of reform in the nineteenth century was to replace these fantasies with an archeologically correct Gothic style for modern architectural development.

The publication in 1817 of Thomas Rickman's *An Attempt to Discriminate the Styles of English Architecture, from the Conquest to the Reformation* provided a framework for the development of an authentic Gothic vocabulary with a system of classification by periods ('Norman' from around 1066; 'Early English' from 1189; 'Decorated English style' from 1307 and 'Perpendicular' from 1377 to about 1640). This served well as long as Gothic performed the function of a national style, but difficulties arose when the wider appreciation of Continental Gothic architecture meant that further, and rather clumsy terms had to be devised. Scholarly manuals were published at much the same time for the classification of the French, Italian and German Gothic types. An element of nationalism determined many of the supposed differences between, for example, French 'romantic' Gothic and the German style of the same period.

In the early nineteenth century the architectural 'battle of the styles' had resolved into an almost straight confrontation between the rival claims of classical and Gothic. The battle lines had a certain attractive symmetry, with classicism identified as pagan and Gothic as Christian, adding a moral dimension to purely aesthetic considerations. The Gothic, or medieval, style of building and decorating was identified with a stable and uncorrupted society, having values untainted by the turmoil of the Industrial Revolution. Later, schisms within the Gothic Revival were to complicate the issue. C. L. Eastlake, writing in *The Gothic Revival in England* (1872), understood the dangers of Pugin's Roman Catholic proselytizing to the development of an architectural style.

By 1850 George Gilbert Scott could claim that the Gothic Revival was 'the great architectural fact of the age. . . . a style which will be pre-eminently that of our own age . . . meet all its requirements and embrace all its arts, improvements and inventions'. (*Remarks on Secular and Domestic Architecture*, 1857, preface, p. xi.) However, he was outfaced by Palmerston who insisted on the choice of the Renaissance style for the new government offices (now the Foreign Office), and Scott was regarded by his colleagues as a betrayer of the cause.

With the spread of Gothic as a domestic style came the need for furniture and ornamental details for the interior. The Gothic-style furniture designed by Sir John Soane for the Library at Stowe is plain to a fault, a contrast with the fussy crockets and pinnacles generally employed to suggest the romance of the past. Unlike the already relatively severe forms proposed by Rudoph Ackermann in 1810 (*Repository of Arts*, vol. III, pl. 36, 'Gothic sopha, table, chair & footstool, for a library') Soane had not made the error of simply tacking Gothic ornament on to Regency shapes. William Porden achieved a sort of halfway house in this respect for Eaton Hall; while the general concept remained irredeemably conventional, the detailing was successfully Gothicized.

In 1815 Sir Jeffry Wyatville had designed an octagonal table using a medieval font as the inspiration for the pedestal, and supporting the top with brackets like those on a hammerbeam roof. A. C. Pugin, father of A. W. N. Pugin, also succumbed to this tendency. The title page of *Pugin's Gothic Furniture*, published by Ackermann in 1827, uses Gothic decorative details on what are still coventional Regency forms. However, his manipulation of the source was superior to the slab-like efforts of E. B. Lamb, who, as late as 1835, was still translating ecclesiastical stonework into panels of wood to create a clumsy Neo-Gothic furniture style. In the 1830s, dissatisfied with the purely ornamental Regency Gothic style, the younger Pugin was looking for architectural elements with which to forge a new structural vocabulary for furniture. His massive oak table (PL. 15), illustrated in *Gothic Furniture in the Style of the 15th Century* (1835), uses sculptural and architectural details from Gothic churches in much the same way as Wyatville, without sufficiently redefining them. His subsequent transformations of pointed arches and buttresses into the understructure of tables and chairs were to leave Wyatville's clumsy font far behind.

Meanwhile, in the 1840s at Snelston Hall in Derbyshire, designed by Lewis Nockalls Cottingham (1787–1847) in 1828, the architect was attempting radical solutions to the problem of furnishing in the Gothic style. Cottingham by no means entirely resolved the problems of remaking furniture design to a Gothic concept (PL. 11), but he did devise forms that were based on historical precedent rather than merely Gothic in detail and ornament. He had his friend Henry Shaw's magisterial survey of *Specimens of Ancient Furniture* (1836) for inspiration as well as Pugin's *Gothic Furniture*. Simon Jervis ('Gothic rampant: designs by L. N. Cottingham for Snelston Hall', *V & A Yearbook*, vol. 3, 1984, pp. 323–31) has traced an interesting source for the pedestal of the octagonal drawing-room table, which is in a form of the base of a boxwood reliquary 'formerly in the possession of Mr Bullock, Egyptian Hall, Piccadilly', included by Shaw in *Specimens*.

For thirty-five years before the Great Exhibition in 1851, which marked the public début of Gothic manufactures, architects and designers had been playing with varieties of 'Old English', looking for alternatives to the neo-rococo that dominated nineteenth-century middle-class taste. In contrast to the architectural inspiration of the Gothic, the source of the Tudor and Jacobean revival was furniture and woodcarving. The painfully evolved structural element characteristic of Reformed Gothic was lost in the resulting 'Tudorbethan', a style marked by an obsession with carved ornament.

For Mamhead in Devon in the 1840s Anthony Salvin devised a form of Tudor that preserved a clean linear character, eschewing the masks and grotesques of Walter Scott-influenced antiquarianism. Salvin was not always so restrained, as may be seen in the riotous excesses of ornament perpetrated by him at Harlaxton. A rare exercise in Neo-Norman, Thomas Hopper's Penrhyn Castle of the 1830s is decorated in a bold, almost rough-hewn manner, which has parallels in the strong lines of Reformed Gothic. The specially designed furniture is thought to have been made by carpenters on the estate, introducing the element of honest craftsmanship favoured by Pugin, and anticipating ideologies usually associated with Ruskin and Morris and the Arts and Crafts Movement. By the mid-century the scene was set for the consolidation of Reformed

Gothic and its commerical exploitation by Seddon, Bruce Talbert and Charles Bevan.

The cult of natural ornament, an important feature of Reformed Gothic, can be traced in many illustrated publications of the period. Pugin's *Floriated Ornament* appeared in 1849 (PL. 47). In *The Seven Lamps of Architecture* (1849), Ruskin puts forward the proposition that beauty may be achieved by imitation of, or inspiration from nature. The theme is pursued in *The Stones of Venice* (1851–3), and in his lectures on 'Natural ornament' of 1855, continuing throughout his subsequent publications. It is a thread that can be followed throughout the century. Christopher Dresser's doctorate was awarded for botanical studies; he published 'Botany as adapted to the arts and art manufactures' in the *Art Journal* (1857–8), and his first book *The Art of Decorative Design* (1860) expanded the theme. Morris & Co. is still identified with the floral papers and textiles that were the hallmark of the firm's style. The adaptation of plant forms to flat pattern was pursued through Japonisme in the 1880s and culminated in the flowering – literally – of Art Nouveau.

A. C. Pugin and his Son

By his own account, Augustus (or Auguste) Charles Pugin was a nobleman of Swiss descent who had supported the French king in 1789. He arrived in England, a penniless *émigré* with nothing to offer but an immature talent for drawing, in 1791. The story of his origins and his adventures before arriving in London given in detail by Benjamin Ferrey (*The Life of Pugin the Architect*, 1861, pp. 1–4) has not been substantiated, but the fact that his son believed it was to be important to him in his architectural career, particularly in his dealings with his patrons. In response to an advertisement A. C. Pugin entered the office of John Nash, then one of the busiest in the country – with Robert Smirke and Sir John Soane, Nash was employed as Architect to the Board of Works, whose most important patron was the Prince of Wales, later George IV.

The elder Pugin's skill as a watercolourist made him indispensable to Nash, who handed over to him the responsibility for the buildings in the newly popular Gothic style, for which Nash himself had little taste. Pugin was a pioneer in the investigation of ancient examples of Gothic architecture, and the drawing of these for Nash, as patterns and for reproduction, was the main part of his work in Nash's office. One of the most significant of the Ackermann publications on which Pugin collaborated was *Westminster Abbey* (1812; see PL. 20). Between 1825 and 1827 he was responsible for twenty-seven Gothic-style illustrative plates for Ackermann's *Repository of Arts*, possibly in collaboration with his precocious son, who was working with his father at that date. Although described as an architect, A. C. Pugin never achieved his own architectural practice, his functions remaining those of teacher, illustrator and architectural draughtsman.

His work as an architectural draughtsman added significantly to the basis on which the nineteenth-century Gothic Revival evolved. As Ferrey remarked, 'The superior knowledge of Gothic architecture which the elder Pugin was known to possess, led many architects whose aquaintance with medieval art was superficial, to apply to him for aid. ... Many buildings might in strictness claim him as their author instead of the architect to whom they are publicly ascribed'. (pp. 50–51.) However, his greatest importance to

PL. 20 Frederick Mackenzie:
Westminster Abbey; watercolour
made for Ackermann's two-
volume work on the history of
the Abbey, 1812, illustrated with
100 hand-coloured plates by
Mackenzie, A. C. Pugin, Thomas
Uwins and G. Shepherd.
Investigation of the native
heritage of Gothic architecture
was given an enormous impetus in
the early nineteenth century with
the publication of a series of
studies of Westminster Abbey, of
which this is one of the first and
the most lavishly produced.
Ackermann's publication was
followed in 1818 by an important
antiquarian study by Edward
Brayley, and in 1822 by L. N.
Cottingham's *Plans, Elevations,
Sections and Details of Henry VII's
Chapel*, a dazzling display of
draughtsmanship that discernibly
influenced the drawing styles of
Barry and Pugin.

PL. 21 View of the flying buttresses of Henry VII's chapel at Westminster Abbey, with the entrance front of the New Palace of Westminster beyond; from a photograph taken by Lockett of Bloomsbury Street in the nineteenth century. The view is deliberately angled to show the close relationship between the architecture of the chapel and Barry's revivalist architecture.

the development of design in the nineteenth century rests on his having fathered and educated Augustus Welby Northmore Pugin, his only child.

In 1802 A. C. Pugin married Miss Catherine Welby, daughter of a barrister-at-law who was the third cousin of Sir William Welby of Denton Hall in Lincolnshire; ten years later in 1812 their son was born. From an early age Pugin went on architectural tours of the Continent with his father and fellow pupils, and he embarked on an independent career, designing plate for the royal goldsmiths Rundell & Bridge, at the age of fifteen. This led to work for Sir Jeffry Wyatville, designing furniture for the recently completed Gothic-style apartments at Windsor Castle, to be made by Messrs Morel & Seddon (PL. 10).

The Windsor furniture is typically Regency in style. Ferrey praised it cautiously:

> 'Without asserting that this work, when completed, was wholly successful, it may fairly be said, that the furniture was remarkable for great variety of form and detail, producing a fitness not to be found in any other modern attempts; and it may be reasonably doubted whether any person but Pugin could have designed such a multitude of objects with equally happy results.' (p. 53.)

Precocious though Pugin was, it is hardly surprising that he worked in a style consistent with the recommendations of Ackermann. Pugin himself was not pleased when he looked back on these youthful efforts; writing in 1841 of the spiky and over-ornamented designs used for Gothic furniture, he remarked: 'I have perpetrated many of these enormities in the furniture I designed some years ago for Windsor Castle.' (*The True Principles of Pointed or Christian Architecture*, 1841, p. 35.) Performing a remarkable imaginative leap, he shook off the constraints of decorative 'Gothick' which he had used for Ackermann and the Windsor designs. Thereafter his aims were to be simplicity and fitness for purpose.

While still in his teens Pugin established his own business at 12 Hart Street in Covent Garden, to provide 'all the ornamental portions of buildings which could by possibility be executed apart from the structure and be fixed afterwards'. An oak table (PL. 13) of about this date stamped 'A. Pugin' is in the 'Jacobean' style currently being explored by Bullock's partner Richard Bridgens and the architect Anthony Salvin. Pugin had made drawings at Hatfield in 1829 as inspiration for the firm's products and for one of his early independent commissions, the furnishing of Perry Hall at Handsworth in Birmingham for Mrs Gough.

The firm had a brief existence, then Pugin's fancy was caught by sailing and the sea. After his carefree travels in 1831 Pugin employed his seamanship in going to and fro across the North Sea to Holland and Belgium, importing fragments of church carving and pieces of antique furniture for his business owned jointly with the dealer Edward Hull. The wreck of his first boat, coupled with severe financial problems, brought him back to the architectural fold and, as if he had some presentiment of his early death, he began the feverish pursuit of a career which was to leave him totally worn out and mad by the age of forty.

PL. 22 Thomas Hopper: detail from the base of a Gothic-style candlestand in Coade stone; for the conservatory at Carlton House, inscribed 'Coade & Sealy, 1810'. The conservatory, dating from 1807, was modelled on Henry VII's chapel in Westminster Abbey, with the interstices of the fan-vaulted roof inset with glass panes. The design of the stands was also inspired by Westminster Abbey, which was then being restored by James Wyatt. The stands supported six-branched candelabra, also in the Gothic style. The conservatory was demolished with the house in c.1826. The candelabra were reused in 1827 by Sir Jeffry Wyatville in his Gothic scheme for a coffee room in the King's Apartments at Windsor Castle, and were to influence Pugin when he came to design candelabra for the dining room and the gallery.

Left PL. 23 L. N. Cottingham: encaustic tiles in the medieval style; for Minton's, the images taken from the pavement of the Westminster Abbey Chapter House. The Chapter House, completed in 1253, was used until 1865 for the Public Record Office and the medieval floor was covered by wooden boards. The tiles were rediscovered and the technique and designs put into production by Minton's initially for the newly-restored Temple Church (Edward Blore, 1841, at that time architect to Westminster Abbey; he was succeeded by George Gilbert Scott). The art and artefacts of the Abbey continued to influence design throughout the nineteenth century – the sermon at Gilbert Scott's funeral made reference to the Abbey as having inspired the Gothic Revival – and Burges used the design of the star-shaped panels of the great painted retable that had been rediscovered and reinstated by Blore for a corner cupboard in his Buckingham Street chambers.

Above PL. 24 Table, the top inlaid with mosaic in a pattern imitating the thirteenth-century Cosmati-work of the 'Great Pavement' at Westminster Abbey, by H. Stevens of Pimlico, exhibitor at the 1851 Exhibition.

Engineering and the Structure of Gothic

*I*n the eighteenth century the 'Gothick' style was used as an ornamental alternative to the severity of classicism without any understanding of its constructional purpose. It is no coincidence that use of Gothic forms should have developed at a period of unprecedented advance in the history of engineering. The creations of Thomas Telford and Isambard Kingdom Brunel had as great an effect on the landscape of Britain as the finest masterpieces of ecclesiastical and domestic building. Engineering not only permitted a vastly increased roof span through the use of iron supports; it fed architecture with new materials and techniques, encouraging development away from a slavish historicism. It was not the exquisite neoclassical houses of Thomas Hope and Sir John Soane that impressed Karl Friedrich Schinkel on his tour of Britain in 1826, but the monumental factory and warehouse architecture of the northern industrial cities.

We know from contemporary paintings that T. F. Pritchard's iron bridge at Coalbrookdale (completed 1779) was a popular tourist attraction. The site is known as 'the birthplace of the Industrial Revolution' from the pioneering use of this new constructional material. Brunel's Clifton suspension bridge at Bristol, designed in 1831 but not completed until 1864, was another wonder of the industrial age (PL. 26); with its huge battered-pylon supports, it stands as an impressive experiment in the Egyptian Revival style, even though Brunel's intended Egyptian decorative details were,

PL. 25 J. M. W. Turner: *Rain, Steam and Speed: The Great Western Railway*; exhibited at the Royal Academy, 1844, and Manchester Jubilee Exhibition, 1887.

perhaps happily, never executed. Sphinxes and winged globes would surely have diminished the austere power of the unadorned piers.

Significantly, Brunel's name features among those in competition for the building to house the Great Exhibition of 1851. In the event he had to console himself with the great triple-arcaded concourse at Paddington station, on which he was then working, assisted by Matthew Digby Wyatt. When it came to the building of the Crystal Palace opposition to Joseph Paxton's remarkable design (PL. 58) might have prevailed but for the existence of such important and successful industrial precedents. Once the decision to build in iron and glass was taken the choice of Paxton's design was inevitable, since he was responsible for the Great Conservatory at Chatsworth, the largest structure of the type then achieved.

An analytical appreciation of the mechanics and engineering of Gothic architecture marked the emergence of Gothic as a force for architectural reform. One important step was the building in 1820 to 1824 of St Luke's Church in Chelsea, designed by James Savage, the first Gothic Revival church constructed with a structurally functional stone vault. The most complete synthesis of Gothic and engineering is to be found in the publications of Eugène Viollet-le-Duc (PL. 27), immensely influential in the mid-nineteenth century. English Gothic Revival architects acknowledged their debt to Viollet-le-Duc and his massive *Dictionnaire raisonné de l'Architecture* (from 1858) – as Burges confessed, 'we all cribbed from Viollet'. Reservations among his contemporaries about the radical restoration of the buildings of France's medieval heritage did not extend to his publications, which were mined for inspiration in structural and decorative details. His romantic reconstruction and decoration of medieval castles at Pierrefonds and Roquetaillarde was mirrored in Burges's fantasies for the Marquess of Bute at Cardiff Castle and Castell Coch. In spite of the strong emotional appeal of the medieval past, a purely decorative style would not have provided a viable alternative to classicism.

Opposite PL. 26 I. K. Brunel: suspension bridge at Clifton, Bristol; designed 1831, completed 1864. E. W. Godwin, who was born in 1833 and brought up in Bristol, must have seen all the stages of its erection: his father was a friend of Brunel, as was Pugin. The obvious relationship between engineering and the Gothic and Egyptian phases of nineteenth-century reformed design is no coincidence.

Above PL. 27 Eugène Viollet-le-Duc: plate from the *Dictionnaire raisonné de l'architecture*, 1854–86. In spite of their profound reservations about the doctrinaire character of Viollet's reconstruction of ancient structures, Victorian architects owed – and acknowledged – a great debt to his writings.

Above PL. 28 Hector Guimard: Ecole du Sacré-Coeur, avenue de la Frillière, Paris, 1895. The building was originally open at ground level to provide a play area for the pupils. It has since been converted into apartments. Guimard's model is the drawing for a market hall published by Viollet in *Entretiens*, XII, vol. 2, pl. 21, and the relationship with the struts supporting the domed roof in the previous illustration is also obvious. Earlier influence from Viollet was rarely so direct, with Burges and his contemporaries interpreting his examples in a historicist spirit. This is another route by which his influence developed after the Gothic Revival. Although the architectural basis is still essentially Gothic, the façade with its dormers and small-paned windows reflects Guimard's interest in English vernacular revival ideas which he had admired on a visit in 1894, only a year before the date of this building.

Left PL. 29 View of the east end of the cathedral of Notre Dame in Paris. Pugin had made studies of details at Notre Dame when travelling with his father in the 1820s. From 1842 Eugène Viollet-le-Duc was engaged on a major restoration programme of the cathedral – not universally admired. The polychromatic decoration of the interior was published by Oradou in 1870.

Above PL. 30 Hector Guimard: cast iron support for an illuminated Métro sign, Paris. The majority of Guimard's metro stations were designed and built 1899–1900 for the Métropolitain line from Porte de Vincennes to Porte Maillot. The design drawings in the Musée des Arts Décoratifs in Paris are among the most inspiring documents of French Art Nouveau.

Augustus Welby Northmore Pugin, Architect

Commissions had not been lacking for the furnishing firm in Covent Garden, but Pugin was no businessman and failure was inevitable. Within the three years following 1832, the year in which his first wife and both his parents died, Pugin came to the notice of one of his most important patrons, the Earl of Shrewsbury; he designed furniture for the antique dealer Edward Hull; he made a tour of English and French cathedrals; he was converted to Catholicism and embarked on his trailblazing architectural career with a modest commission for a church in Salisbury. The character of his work was to be coloured from the moment of his conversion by his vision of life in pre-Reformation England. In 1835 he bought half an acre of land three miles from Salisbury, and built himself a house, St Marie's Grange, in what he conceived to be the style of the fifteenth century. Benjamin Ferrey, Pugin's first biographer, described the house:

'Here he set boldly to work, and designed and built a house for himself exhibiting all the peculiar arrangements common to domestic dwellings of the 15th century. The structure was principally of brick. It was quaint and odd, and much noticed by people of the neighbourhood who took an interest in such matters. It can scarcely be said that he was successful in this work; there was nothing very inviting in the exterior design, and a great absence of modern comfort in the interior arrangement. The building tended rather to show the eccentricity of its owner than his superior skill in design; still it was not without merit, and undoubtedly formed a striking contrast to the class of modern suburban houses generally erected.' (*The Life of Pugin the Architect*, 1861, pp. 72–3.)

Pugin's house cost £2,000 to build. The workmen were unaccustomed to the methods insisted upon by the architect, the very thick walls causing particular trouble. He had great difficulty in selling it – as Ferrey remarked, '[he] never thought, when erecting it according to his own fancy, that the house would be unsuited to other people's requirements in the event of his wishing to sell it' – and he finally had to let it go for £500 to Mr Staples, from whom he had bought the land for the same sum.

Pugin's first publications appeared in 1835 and 1836, one of furniture designs 'in the style of the fifteenth century', two on Gothic architecture – one of which was the celebrated and controversial *Contrasts between the Architecture of the 15th and 19th Centuries* – and two of metalwork designs. *The Glossary of Ecclesiastical Ornament and Costume*, of 1844, illustrated with the finest chromolithographed plates, was a new departure after these slim polemics. With his *True Principles* (1841), and *Floriated Ornament* (1849; see PL. 47), they formed the visual reference material for the Gothic Revival style in England. In 1836 the decision was taken to rebuild the new Palace of Westminster in the medieval style (PL. 4); this made Pugin's involvement a foregone conclusion, although the fact that he was a Catholic meant that he could only occupy a position subordinate to Charles Barry, author of the winning design. Barry himself was a 'pre-archaeological' Goth accustomed to working in the invented style that Pugin had already rejected.

In summoning Pugin as his 'ghost' Barry had conjured up a genie, but he had no apprehension of the power that he was unleashing. The exuberance of Gothic detailing produced a building of unparalleled impact, 'the initial letter in the chapter of our architectural history which the age has been composing', as one critic was to write in 1869 in the newly founded *Architect* magazine. He was describing a structure that soon became a landmark recognized the world over.

By the 1840s the perception of Gothic as it should be applied to contemporary architecture and design had very much changed. Even the use of the Perpendicular style for the Palace of Westminster was to be condemned as outdated in 1850, long before it was finished. Study of appropriate models on the Continent had convinced Pugin that he should place a strong emphasis on structure above ornament in his furniture, and he preferred carved pieces to those ornamented with inlay, which he stigmatized as false in effect. Forms were further simplified, and the contribution of the craftsman valued above mechanically executed ornament. When it suited him however, Pugin willingly sought out technological solutions, even using a carving machine.

Of his furniture for the Convent of Mercy at Handsworth, Birmingham (PL. 36), Pugin wrote: 'The whole are extremely simple in design but yet of strictly ecclesiastical character; and from the unity of style which pervades the whole of this edifice, and which extends to the furniture and other fittings, it produces a striking illustration of the old religious houses.' The plainness of the furniture had an ideological as well as an aesthetic purpose. Pugin wished to serve a relatively impecunious market as well as to indulge a wealthy patron. He wrote a letter to Crace in about 1850, outlining his ideas for cheapening his structures still further:

'I am anxious about this plain furniture and I send you at once a lot of designs, rely on it the great sale will be in articles that are within the range of the middling class, clergymen furnishing parsonage houses etc. . . . you ought to produce a dozen of each to make them pay and keep them all ready seasoned for putting together at a day's notice keeping one sort always on show . . . I am anxious to introduce a sensible style of furniture of good oak and *constructively* put together that will compete with the vile trash made and sold.'

Pugin's work on the rich and intricate interiors and furnishings at Westminster was demanding, ill-remunerated and, owing to the somewhat equivocal position with Barry, uncrecognized; but Pugin was happy to promote the cause of Gothic architecture through his work on what was early accepted as the most important secular commission of the century. Meanwhile he was engaged on a number of projects, including the remodelling of Alton Towers for Lord Shrewsbury, and of Scarisbrick Hall in Lancashire; on furniture for Barry's Birmingham Grammar School, for Oscott College, for the Convent of Mercy at Handsworth, and for the Duke of Devonshire's Lismore Castle; as well as wallpapers, textiles, carpets, ceramics, metalwork and jewellery for various manufacturers. In the 1840s he was again building a house for himself, this time at Ramsgate in Kent (PL. 71). The culmination of his extraordinary output was the Medieval Court at the Great Exhibition in 1851 (PL. 59), achieved just before overwork drove him to madness and his untimely death in 1852.

Pugin's most original design work was not to be found in his publicly visible achievements such as the Palace of Westminster and the Medieval Court. Nor do his publications do justice to the most uncompromising of his ideas. The most abstract and structural of his furniture designs were hidden in schools and convents, or were designed for his own use. In his *History of the Gothic Revival in England*, C. L. Eastlake remarked of the house at Ramsgate: 'Here may be seen some of the quaint furniture which Pugin so cleverly and readily designed. . . . It must be confessed that in his house and the church at Ramsgate one recognises more thorough and genuine examples of Pugin's genius and strongly marked predilections for Medieval architecture than elsewhere.' (1872, p. 164.)

As Eastlake surmised, Pugin put his heart into his own houses. Ramsgate was a triumph of hope over experience, of a belief that the difficulties encountered at St Marie's Grange were not fundamental to domestic Gothic Revival architecture. Ramsgate survives with traces of Pugin's occupancy, providing an intimate and revealing glimpse of a romantic medievalist.

In 1888, looking back on Pugin's remarkable achievements, the

architect J. D. Sedding remarked: 'We should have had no Morris, no Street, no Burges, no Shaw, no Webb, no Bodley, no Rossetti, no Burne-Jones, no Crane, but for Pugin.'

Ironically, the Medieval Court, Pugin's last stand against the 'complete burlesque of pointed design' (*True Principles*, p. 35), was buried in the midst of the Great Exhibition, a shrine to that 'confused jumble of styles and symbols borrowed from all nations and periods' that he had stigmatized in *An Apology for the Revival of Christian Architecture* (1843, p. 4). All the technical ingenuity of which the age was capable, and it was considerable, was expended on a profusion of ornament. The 'Rococo Revival' was the style prevalant among the commercial manufacturers from all parts of the world. Few of the exhibits outside the Medieval Court are admired now for their design, though the importance in contemporary estimation of this French-led taste is recognized. The achievement of the building and its decoration is, however, seen as of enduring magnitude.

Opposite PL. 31 A. W. N. Pugin: drawing for the kitchen at Scarisbrick; part of the remodelling of the sixteenth-century half-timbered mansion, comissioned in 1837, based on the monks' kitchen at Glastonbury Abbey. The bold roof timbers are mirrored in the understructure of the large centre table. His structural principles were derived from medieval timber architecture, as confirmed by the following comment from *True Principles* (1841): 'In ancient timber houses we do not find a single feature introduced beyond the decoration of what was necessary for their substantial construction.'

Above PL. 32 A. W. N. Pugin: oak table; probably designed *c.*1840. The severely simplified structure follows on from the still decorated carved supports of a table designed *c.*1834 and illustrated in *Gothic Furniture in the Style of the 15th and 16th Centuries* (1835).

Left PL. 33 A. W. N. Pugin: line engraving from *Gothic Furniture* showing a view of a carved oak table with parallel stretchers.

End

Above PL. 34 A. W. N. Pugin: line engraving from *Gothic Furniture*; see PL. 33.

Right PL. 35 A. W. N. Pugin: oak table, end view; see PL. 32.

PL. 36 A. W. N. Pugin: oak side table with drawer; from the Convent of Mercy, Handsworth, Birmingham, *c*.1841. The cast iron handles pre-date Pugin's association with Hardman. Pugin's experiments with structural principles are illustrated by the different solutions he applies to fitting drawers into this type of table. The frame has immense strength, its X-braced sides being united by a stretcher with a central support also buttressed from the base. The drawer is hung on runners from the top and extends only half the width of the top, as far as the central member. For other examples he made the drawer unit a self-contained box fitting under the top within a similarly buttressed frame. These represent radically architectural resolutions to the problem of simplifying furniture design.

PL. 37 A. W. N. Pugin: oak side table for the Houses of Parliament. Pugin's taste for severe structure is modified by the requirements of this public commission, the discreet carved ornament in the Gothic taste probably representing a consensus of what was appropriate to the dignity of government. More than a hundred types of table were designed for the Palace of Westminster, among the grandest being the octagonal tables for the Princes' Chamber, which have a more ornately carved version of this curving stretcher.

PL. 38 A. W. N. Pugin: oak side table of 'knock-down' construction; *c.*1850. An example of the type of table urged by Pugin on Crace for 'poor vicars', to be kept always in stock ready for assembly.

PL. 39 A. W. N. Pugin: his own cabinet; made by George Myers in carved oak with painted heraldic devices on shields, *c*.1845. A number of drawings for a comparable commission survive in the Myers family. Pugin provided only the most sketchy indications of carved ornament, believing that the craftsman's interpretation added to the validity of the design.

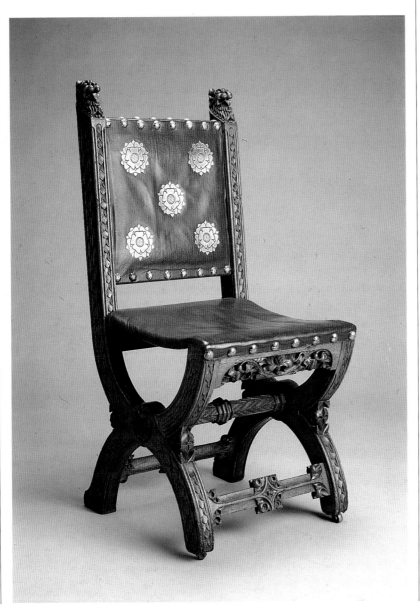

Left PL. 40 A. W. N. Pugin: Robing Room Chair, carved oak upholstered in gold-stamped leather. The chair is based on a design by Crispin de Passe from the *Officina arcularia*, published in Amsterdam in 1642.

Above PL. 41 A. W. N. Pugin: design for a fireplace; one of his proposals for the remodelling of Eastnor Castle for Earl Somers, *c.*1850. Eastnor was built between 1812 and 1814 by Robert Smirke as a romantic Neo-Norman castellated fortress. The shortage of wood occasioned by war on the Continent caused Smirke to devise, with considerable ingenuity, roof-trusses of metal, a foretaste of important Victorian building developments. The decoration of the castle went through various phases, summed up by David Watkin as Regency Baronial, Catholic Gothic and Aesthetic Italian.

Left PL. 42 A. W. N. Pugin: candlestick, silver-plated and gilded with enamelled shields bearing an initial 'B' and arms on the reverse; made for Henry R. Bagshawe and recorded in the Hardman Daybooks in 1842. Possibly made using electroplating techniques learned during Hardman's association with Elkington.

Above PL. 43 A. W. N. Pugin: one of a pair of brass and steel andirons, *c.*1846; from the Large Drawing Room at Adare Manor, with armorial shields bearing engraved Wyndham and Quin coats of arms. Similar to those designed by Pugin for the entrance hall at Adare, for which the drawing survives in the possession of the Dunraven family.

Right PL. 46 A. W. N. Pugin: clock; designed in 1851 and made by Hardman. In a letter to Hardman Pugin complained that the details of the design for the clock had caused him as much trouble as 'a small church'.

Left PL. 45 A. W. N. Pugin: silver milk jug; made by Hardman, 1851. From Treverbyn Vean, the Cornish house of Colonel Somers Cocks.

PL. 44 A. W. N. Pugin: silver jug; made by Hardman, 1849. A jug of similar lobed form formed part of Pugin and Hardman's display, 'a large variety of these quaint and beautiful works', at the 1851 Exhibition. This jug dates from the year of the Birmingham Exposition of Arts and Manufactures, when ill health had not yet seriously diminished Pugin's vigour and enthusiasm. By 1851 much of the structural quality of the ornament had been abandoned in favour of a smoothly conventional Gothic shape, lacking the stylish and structural flat strap and rivets which, with the foliate termination, form the decoration of the piece.

Left PL. 47 A. W. N. Pugin: title page to *Floriated Ornament*, 1849.

Above PL. 48 A. W. N. Pugin: jardinière and stand; designed for Minton's with an all-over Gothic pattern printed on to the ceramic body by Collins and Reynolds patent lithographic process, date marked 1850.

PL. 50 A. W. N. Pugin: ceramic garden seat with Gothic-style decoration; designed for Minton's, *c*.1850.

PL. 49 A. W. N. Pugin: ceramic bread plate; made by Minton's in the encaustic process, this version in six colours. The first example, in four colours, was exhibited at the Birmingham Exposition of Manufactures in 1849. Many examples survive, suggesting that this was a popular model. The ethical message is simple and clear, appropriate to a time when the problems of the 'hungry forties' were a frequent topic.

The New Palace of Westminster

The fire that devastated the old Houses of Parliament in 1834 forced into prominence the bitter debate as to the suitability of the classical or Gothic style for this great public building. The decision in favour of Gothic was seen as a victory for the thrusting middle class against the official guardians of taste among the aristocracy. It was an irony that Barry, principal author of the Italianate Renaissance revival, should have found himself building the greatest secular Gothic commission of the age. With the Manchester Institution and the Travellers' Club he had established an impressive architectural language for spacious, well-finished premises with stately pretensions. This broad canvas had to be abandoned in favour of intricate, minutely detailed ornament and extreme richness of colouring to give an appropriately medieval atmosphere to the Palace of Westminster. Here Pugin's passion for colour and ornament, his attachment to heraldic devices and his knowledge of the decorative arts of the Middle Ages were an invaluable support, and to him must go the credit for most of the interior decoration.

While there were accessible precedents for stained glass windows, floor tiles, great oak tables, pew-like benches, open fireplaces and massive firedogs, it was no mean feat to make a convincingly consistent 'medieval' interior that must be lit by gas, carpeted, hung with wallpaper, and supplied with kneehole desks, upholstered armchairs, clocks and inkstands.

J. G. Crace's verdict, voiced in 1858, gives a hint of the team effort that this great task involved:

> 'That great benefit had been derived by the application in the Houses of Parliament of the true principles of decoration in metalwork, especially in gas fittings in the general lighting of the building, in ornamental ironwork, carpets, paper-hangings, furniture and every branch of medieval ornament. The theories on which this system of decoration were based came into definite practice when the great building was in progress and it was there shown that the principles were sound and capable of being carried out more ornamentally and beautifully than the false principles previously in vogue.' (E. M. Barry, *An Account of the New Palace of Westminster*, quoted in M. H. Port, ed., *The Houses of Parliament*, 1976, p. 297.)

The team was composed of both old-established firms subcontracted by the Commissioners and newcomers, coached and bullied by Pugin into realizing his medieval vision. Of the former, Gillow, the most respected decorating firm of the period was awarded the furniture contract. Holland & Sons, one of the largest and most prominent nineteenth-century cabinet-making firms, already under contract for a number of government offices, were brought in when one of Gillow's estimates was rejected. Much of the internal woodwork was supplied by them as well as furniture. Pugin's friend John Hardman (1811–67) of Birmingham was one of the newer group. He was eventually to find himself responsible for the metalwork – appropriately, as his main business was ecclesiastical metalwork – and the stained glass. Crace, retained for the ornamental painting, and Herbert Minton, who won the contract for the encaustic tiling, had both been recommended by the Fine Art Commission, but they too were protégés of Pugin.

Pugin had been responsible for persuading Hardman to expand in 1838 from button-making into a new venture supplying church metalwork in the Gothic style to Pugin's designs. There was an element of self-interest in his promotion of Hardman for the work at Westminster; when Pugin worked through Hardman he drew an extra fee as the firm's designer.

Pugin needed men who understood his methods. He drew with great rapidity and his sketches, though showing a nervous intensity, contain little in the way of precise detail. They had to be interpreted with imagination, thus putting a considerable burden of responsibility on the manufacturer. Pugin believed that this need to participate so actively in what became, in effect, a collaboration conferred dignity on the workman's task.

It has been remarked that Crace's ten-year involvement with Pugin was unique in his career (see Alexandra Wedgwood in 'J. G. Crace and A. W. N. Pugin', *The Craces*, Megan Aldrich, ed., 1990, p. 137). Crace's dependence on Pugin's inspiration lasted for much longer. Apart from finishing Pugin's incomplete projects in an appropriate style, Crace continued to use Pugin's designs unaltered or slightly adapted throughout his working life. But his Puginesque cabinet for the 1862 London International Exhibition (PL. 104) does not rival the great Gothic cabinet of 1851.

Hardman also continued to use Pugin's designs long after his death. He had more claim on them, since his nephew and successor John Hardman Powell married Pugin's daughter Anne in 1850.

Some indication of Pugin's preferences among the Palace of Westminster team may be inferred from his choice of collaborators on the Medieval Court in 1851; here he worked with Crace, Hardman, Herbert Minton and his builder Myers. These were the men whom he had so greatly benefited, from whom he had demanded new methods and solutions as the problems of achieving the great project in Westminster were imaginatively overcome. He had found these men when they were mere artisans and apprentices; bullying and persuading, but never doubting that they would achieve what he asked, he made them into craftsmen.

The Act of Emancipation in 1829 did not entirely protect Pugin from the temporal disadvantages of his conversion to Catholicism. In the new climate of religious tolerance his employment on the decoration of the Houses of Parliament was condoned, particulary as the extent of his contribution was not immediately apparent, but it could not protect him from bigotry. John Ruskin, having been accused of plagiarizing Pugin with his use of contrasted examples in architecture, and inspired by a Nonconformist hatred of Pugin's religion, wrote a devastating indictment of his career: 'It is often said that I borrow from Pugin. I glanced at Pugin's *Contrasts* once, in the Oxford architectural reading room, during an idle forenoon. ... I never read a word of any other of his works, not feeling from the style of his architecture, the smallest interest in his opinions.' He continued, 'It is very necessary that all should know at once that he is not a great architect, but one of the smallest possible or conceivable of architects.' (*Modern Painters*, vol. III.) Pugin replied, 'Let the fellow build something himself'.

More than simply devastating was Ruskin's decision not to mention Pugin in his books; his influence was enormous and the result was a century of oblivion.

PL. 51 C. Barry and A. W. N. Pugin: the top of the clock tower at the Palace of Westminster with 'Big Ben'.

Above PL. 52 The Lobby of the House of Lords, showing the carved Gothic panelling and the patterned floor tiles.

Right PL. 53 A. W. N. Pugin: encaustic floor tiles with heraldic devices in the Lobby; made by Minton's.

William Butterfield

*P*ugin's Catholicism barred him from involvement with the Cambridge Camden Society, founded in 1839 – and known from 1846 as the Ecclesiological Society – to 'promote the study of Ecclesiastical Architecture and the restoration of mutilated architectural remains'. The Society published an influential journal, the *Ecclesiologist* (1841–68), in which the works of a number of the leading Gothic architects were shown. It was William Butterfield, a firm Tractarian two years Pugin's junior, who edited and made most of the drawings for the Society's design guide to church metalwork and furniture 'of the ancient form', *Instrumenta Ecclesiastica* (1844–7, with a second series 1850–6). Butterfield's church plate designs were made up by John Keith & Son (PL. 56), who won a medal for their display at the 1851 Exhibition. They were exhibitors again in 1862 showing, with pieces by Butterfield, the Bishop of Brechin's chalice designed by G. E. Street.

Butterfield set up his architectural practice in 1840 and one of his important early commissions, dating from 1845, was St Augustine's College at Canterbury, 'remarkable' as Eastlake observed, 'for its extreme simplicity' (*A History of the Gothic Revival in England*, 1872, p. 226). Butterfield was an innovator and his work has parallels with Pugin's; but, aside from the Ecclesiological plate scheme, he was no proselytizer. His writings were few and he lived in a Georgian house in Bedford Square, not seeing the need to adapt his own home to conform with the style of his church buildings. An uncompromising architect, whose severely foursquare buildings were relieved only by a rather harsh polychromy of white Bath stone and black, yellow, blue and blood-red brick, he was first and foremost a church builder. Butterfield did not set out to repel or shock: as he remarked to Philip Webb, he regarded his use of colour for the façades of Keble College, Oxford, as 'gay'. The interiors of churches such as All Saints, Margaret Street, in London (1849) glitter with a brilliant mixture of mosaic and painted decoration. The geometric formality of his fonts (PL. 55) – his most outstandingly original contribution to Victorian church art – has few parallels until the present century.

One of Butterfield's rare country houses, Milton Ernest Hall in Bedfordshire, built for his brother-in-law (1854–8), is a development of Pugin's domestic Gothic: austere, ecclesiastical in feeling and without extraneous ornament, a fit setting for the deeply

Left PL. 54 William Butterfield: architectural inkstand, silver, cut glass and ebony; made by Keith & Co., *c.*1847. This inspired design, from Pugin's most original contemporary, anticipates the related ideas of William Burges by more than a decade.

Below PL. 55 William Butterfield: font in the Church of Ottery St Mary; one of the most intricately architectural of the eighty fonts and font covers designed by Butterfield in a singularly forward-looking geometric manner. The details bear an obvious relationship to those of the inkstand. Butterfield's domestic buildings were the acknowledged starting point for Philip Webb's vernacular Gothic style.

religious Starey family. The dependencies and village houses, also by Butterfield, are of simple brick and tiled construction with no antiquarian ornament, a model for future rural development. Unlike Pugin, who had written: 'I seek *antiquity* and not *novelty*. I strive *to revive, not invent*', Butterfield used modern materials for his utilitarian buildings, for example red brick, and anachronistic sash windows of eighteenth-century design which he found pleasing because they were more practical than casements. The Milton Ernest furniture is straightforward and in the Regency tradition; as Eastlake said, Butterfield always 'steered a middle course between reverence for the past and the necessities of the present age' (p. 277).

Seen in the context of the Ecclesiological Society's 1862 Exhibition Medieval Court (PL. 80, 81), Butterfield's bold architectural polychromy and showy use of painted and applied decoration for church interiors, furniture and metalwork, was pioneering and influential. His successors as superintendents of the Society's church plate scheme were, appropriately, G. E. Street and William Burges, the leading medievalists of the next generation. As to his effect on domestic architecture, Philip Webb admired him above all his contemporaries. Red House, built for William Morris, is Webb's most visible homage to Butterfield, and although his subsequent work developed away from the Gothic style, echoes remain of Butterfield's influence throughout his career.

PL. 56 William Butterfield: silver flagon; made by Keith & Co., 1844. In the sectarian divisions that marked the Gothic Revival in the forties and fifties Hardman and Keith emerged as the two principal rivals for ecclesiastical metalwork commissions.

John Ruskin

It is difficult to describe Ruskin's activities in such terms as to give an idea of the scope and power of his influence. He was born in 1819 and died in 1900, falling short by one year of being an exact contemporary of Queen Victoria. He was an author, critic and teacher. His spheres were, broadly speaking, art, architecture, natural sciences and political theory. He was the most popular writer on art history and theory and the most influential critic, certainly in his own time, possibly of any age. The inevitable reaction against him was total and for years his work was completely ignored. Diffuse and wordy, unable to resolve an argument logically, the thread of his discourse is hard for the modern reader to follow, but his effect on his contemporaries was overwhelming. He was only thirty when the *Seven Lamps of Architecture* appeared in 1849; *The Stones of Venice* followed two years later, and there was hardly a single Gothic Revival architect thereafter who did not acknowledge the inspiration of this magisterial work. The famous chapter 'On the Nature of Gothic', with its thesis on the dignity of hand craftsmanship, acted as a catalyst for ideologies from Morris to the Arts and Crafts Movement.

Although he was a passionate collector of paintings and medieval manuscripts, and despite his work *The Two Paths, Being Lectures on Art and Its Application to Decoration and Manufactures* (1859), Ruskin was not notable as a patron of architecture and design. The modest houses he lived in were undistinguished and had furnishings of the most conventional taste, purchased from a firm of decorators named Snell, who provided everything down to the carpets, curtains and china. As Arthur Severn remarked in his memoir of Ruskin: 'The Professor never cared for the high art movement in furniture and china. He had no taste for such matters.' (James Dearden, ed., *The Professor*, 1967, p. 132.) With impassioned and often inconsistent criticism of current ideas, in *The Two Paths* Ruskin added moral and ethical questions to the already weighty aesthetic problems of interior decoration. However, it is true that a 'Ruskinian' style can be identified in architecture and furniture. Morris is an example of a committed Ruskin disciple, whereas Owen Jones and Dresser, with their scientific and mathematical 'propositions', represent the amoral opposition.

In the *Seven Lamps* Ruskin had itemized the appropriate styles from the past that could be adapted to the architecture of the Victorian age: they were Pisan Romanesque, Venetian Gothic and the earliest English Decorated from the late thirteenth and the early fourteenth century – he is said to have fainted with emotion when first seeing St Wulfram's church (*c.* 1280) in Grantham. George Gilbert Scott, Pugin and Butterfield had already experimented with early English Decorated, but the Continental styles were relatively new territory to architects in Britain. After his profound study of Venetian architecture for *The Stones of Venice*, Ruskin became so infatuated with this style that he suggested that its use for secular buildings should be enforced by the government. 'Ruskinian' Gothic is distinguished by its basis in inspiration from nature – the definition of 'Beauty' in the *Seven Lamps*. Ruskin's own exquisite drawings of Venetian buildings and architectural details for the illustrations to *The Stones of Venice* (PL. 57) were recognizably the source for much 'Ruskinian' ornament and decoration.

Ruskin's other sphere of influence was political. Though his socialism and many of his initiatives, such as a road-building scheme and another to sell tea, now look at best naive they were an important prelude to the utopian ideals of the Arts and Crafts Movement. Ruskin's Guild of St George, founded in 1878, was the precursor of the handicraft guilds that proliferated at the turn of the century. It was based on proto-communist financial rules, exacting contributions from the members according to strict percentage calculations of capital and income, although in reality the only large sums came from Ruskin himself. However, he managed to fund some interesting projects, including a museum, before the scheme was overwhelmed by mismanagement and insolvency.

PL. 57 John Ruskin: plate from *The Stones of Venice*.

THE DUCAL PALACE.

Prince Albert and the Great Exhibition

Prince Albert of Saxe-Coburg-Gotha married Queen Victoria in 1840, but he was not officially created Prince Consort until 1857, three years before his early death at the age of forty-two. Frustrated from the start by his subordinate position which prevented him from wielding direct political influence, he turned to the spheres of art and culture. The Prince had a scholarly turn of mind and the historical bent of Victorian architecture and design was congenial to him. He also appreciated the importance of art and design to the British economy. He gathered an impressive team, known as 'the Prince's men', first among these being the Secretary of the Science and Arts Department Henry Cole. Richard Redgrave was Cole's able lieutenant, and Matthew Digby Wyatt was his companion on the mission to investigate the Paris 1849 Exhibition which was the immediate inspiration for the Great Exhibition in 1851. In 1845 the Prince appointed the German Professor Ludwig Grüner (1801–82) to be his artistic adviser; Gruner's hand is present in many of his undertakings, but most notably in the building up of his picture collection.

The Prince, with Grüner's assistance, supervised the continuing work on the royal palaces. However, the design of Osborne House, in the Italianate style popularized by Sir Charles Barry, was largely his own, with the assistance and technical advice of Thomas Cubitt. The Prince's involvement with the mural decorations for the new Houses of Parliament gave him much pleasure, but his greatest impact on the artistic fortunes of his adoptive country lay in his schemes for the Great Exhibition in 1851 and the subsequent creation of 'Albertopolis', a 'culture centre' on the German model, the complex of institutions that eventually included the South Kensington Museums, the Royal Schools of Music, the Albert Hall and the Imperial Institute. These institutions were showcases of newly developed construction materials and methods, combining art and science in the structure as much as in the purpose or contents.

The Prince was a thoughtful and informed patron of new manufactures. To give a particular instance, he was interested in the important and rapidly expanding tile industry, and many of his projects included schemes to demonstrate their uses. At Osborne the Marble Corridor designed to house a collection of sculpture and the open colonnades, intricately decorated under the supervision of Grüner, are paved with armorial and geometric-patterned encaustic tiles designed by the Prince and made by Minton, Hollins & Co. The Royal Dairy, one of the buildings on his model farm at Windsor, was designed between 1857 and 1859 by the architect and sculptor John Thomas to provide a showcase for a large range of brilliantly coloured tiles and sculptural elements of 'majolica' in the form of bas-reliefs and fountains, also by Minton's, which had recently developed the 'majolica' technique. The dairy was completed in 1861.

The complex of farm buildings including the dairy was the last and in many ways the most personal of Prince Albert's building projects. The idea of a tiled dairy was not new but the brilliant colouring of the interior was certainly an innovation, reflecting the mid-century taste for polychrome decoration, and it became the forerunner of many restaurants, public houses and food shops for which tiled surfaces seemed practical and appropriate. The Prince had already overseen two previous tiled schemes: not only the Marble Corridor at Osborne, but also the Frescoed Pavilion in the grounds of Buckingham Palace (which no longer survives) had a tiled floor. In the dairy printed border tiles edge friezes and surround plaques executed in low relief in imitation of della Robbia work. In the frieze below the pitched roof are portrait roundels of the royal children; the floor tiles have impressed patterns and the sculptural fountains are of majolica ware.

John Thomas had worked for Barry on a number of commissions including the Houses of Parliament. Ornaments for various railway buildings for Brunel followed, and for the Prince at Buckingham Palace, where he carved two large reliefs of *Peace* and *War* in 1848. His last Royal commission was for a chimneypiece for Windsor Castle. He designed and made the great St George fountain which was the centrepiece of Minton's display at the 1862 International Exhibition. It was completed only just before he died.

Prince Albert deserves much of the credit for reviving the influence of the Society of Arts – founded for the 'Encouragement of Arts, Manufactures and Commerce' – and for uniting the efforts of artist and manufacturer to the great benefit of British design. Cole attributes to him the coining of the term 'art applied to industry', clearly an echo of the conclusion arrived at in 1835 by the Select Committee on Arts and Manufactures: 'To us, a peculiarly manufacturing nation, the connection between art and manufactures is most important.' The Annual Exhibitions of 1847 to 1849, instituted by Henry Cole and held at the Society of Arts, were the forerunners of the 1851 Exhibition.

For several years there had been a feeling that action was needed to reform design. In 1846 the painter Richard Redgrave, sensible of the deplorable artistic choas that passed for taste in Britain at that time, wrote to the Prime Minister, Lord John Russell: 'It is in the application of *design* that manufacturing industry is most deficient as compared with the advance in other directions.' It was intended that the Great Exhibition should improve matters, although what it actually achieved was to throw into unwelcome prominence all those deficiencies remarked by Redgrave.

Meanwhile, Cole initiated a brave attempt to influence taste with a pioneering venture, Summerly's Art Manufactures. In 1846, using the pseudonym Felix Summerley, he had entered and won the Society of Arts competition to promote good design with a tea service manufactured by Minton's. This confirmed his belief that it would 'promote public taste' if well-known painters and sculptors could be persuaded to design everyday articles, on the medieval model: 'In fact,' he wrote, 'there was scarcely a great medieval artist, when art was really catholic, who did not essay to decorate the objects of everyday life. Beauty of form and colour and poetic invention were associated with everything. So it ought still to be, and we will say, shall be again.'

Summerley's Art Manufactures was set up in 1847, with an impressive team of artists, among them Redgrave, Daniel Maclise, William Mulready, and the sculptor John Bell. The first advertisement, in October 1847, offered twelve items for sale, by December there were thirty-six. Several of the models bore the name of the designer with the 'FS' monogram, and the advertisements emphasized the individual artists. Cole's prize-winning designs bore the impressed mark 'Society of Arts Prize Pattern, 1846' as well as the name of the manufacturer. The designs show a preoccupation with form and function, as in Cole's 'Prize' beer jug wreathed with hops, Redgrave's water carafe decorated with waterlilies, and the wine coaster with bacchantes and bunches of grapes. A number of retailers undertook to stock the Summerley range; but the venture was unsound financially, and only broke even through the success of John Bell's figure sculpture *Dorothea*, reproduced in Parian statuary porcelain by Minton's. Cole, increasingly preoccupied with plans for the Great Exhibition, withdrew in 1848, and in 1851 the firm ceased trading. However, a number of enterprising manufacturers continued to use the designs, which marked a significant point in the campaign to improve design in industry. Most importantly, the concept of 'art manufactures' now existed.

The Great Exhibition opened in London on 1 May 1851, in the Crystal Palace (PL. 58) designed by Joseph Paxton and raised in hardly more than five months in a minutely planned engineering operation. The structure itself was an example of the most advanced technology that the age could offer. A remarkable feat was to use the rising construction itself, with no more elaborate support than wooden poles, in place of a separately erected scaffold. The ingenious gutters devised by Paxton, and the sash bars, were mechanically prepared and painted ready for use in lengths of 1 mile (1.6 km). The supply of panes of glass, 293,655 in all, accounted for one-third of the country's total annual production. The main building was 1,848 feet (563 m) long, three times the length of St Paul's Cathedral.

The sight of this astonishing structure provoked a predictable comment from Ruskin:

> 'The quantity of bodily industry which that Crystal Palace expresses is very great. So far it is good. The quantity of thought it expresses is, I suppose, a single and very admirable thought of Sir Joseph Paxton's, probably not a bit brighter than thousands of thoughts which pass through his active and intelligent brain every hour, – that it might be possible to build a greenhouse larger than had ever been built before. This thought, and some very ordinary algebra, are as much as all that glass can represent of human intellect.'

However, he well knew that it was a pointer to the future, paving the way for a succession of other large buildings constructed of iron and glass. It was not so very perceptive of Ruskin to see that the 'greenhouse' formed the essential transition between a bridge span and a vast arcaded exhibition hall. Indeed the same idea also occurred to Pugin.

Owen Jones was put in charge of the decoration of the interior (PL. 2, 3), for which he proposed revolutionary colour schemes based on the principles used by the Moors in decorating the Alhambra, on which Jones was a renowned expert. The proposal was for a startling combination of stripes of red, yellow and blue separated by narrow lines of white. It was accepted by Prince Albert and the Commissioners but provoked an outcry in the press – the critic in the *Art Journal* was particularly outspoken, employing such phrases as 'painful and unsightly' and 'the commonplace vulgarity of the conception' – and it was only in January 1851, when enough of the painting had been completed to judge the effect, that the violence of the debate began to abate.

Jones can hardly have expected the violent reaction to his scientific and historicist scheme, which was based on the pioneering colour theories of the French scientist Michel-Eugène Chevreul, demonstrated with colour plates in his *Principles of Harmony and Contrast of Colours* (1839) and Jones's own researches into the once

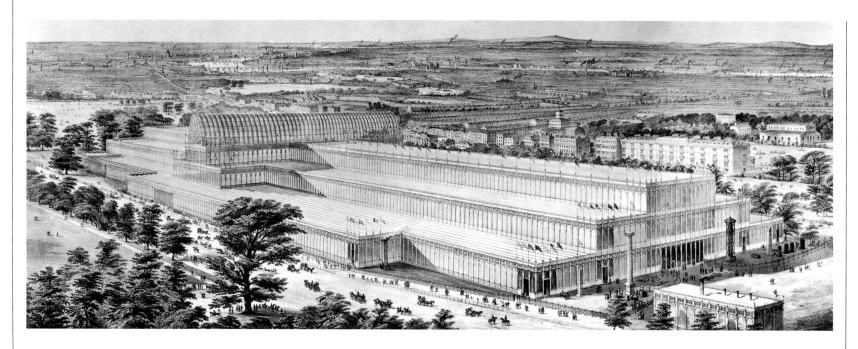

brightly coloured architecture of the ancient world. Counter-proposals included a plea for a uniform bronze-green colour for all the metalwork, and, even more understated and subtle, for a scheme of superimposed glazes designed to produce a grey similar to that in Titian's paintings. These showed both the taste of the time and a very imperfect grasp of the problems of decorating a vast space.

In the event the finished scheme was a great success and praise was lavished on Jones, *The Illustrated London News* commenting on the effect in eulogistic terms: 'To appreciate the genius of Owen Jones, the visitor must take his stance at the extremity of the building … looking up the nave, with its endless rows of pillars, the scheme vanishes from extreme brightness to the hazy indistinctness which Turner alone can paint.'

Although it was not the first display of manufactures aimed at promoting good design, the Great Exhibition realized Prince Albert's ambition in offering international coverage to the 'Industry of all Nations'. The advanced development in Britain of roads and railways enabled a vast public drawn from all classes of society to visit the show. It succeeded in opening up a prospect of hitherto undreamt-of consumer delights. The statistics are truly astonishing: in the 140 days during which the exhibition was open it was visited by more than 6 million people; 13,937 exhibitors contributed more than 100,000 exhibits the value of which was estimated at more than £2 million (excluding the Koh-i-noor diamond); the gate money and the sale of catalogues amounted to £300,000, of which £186,000 was profit. One baby was born in the building.

The Prince had contributed a pair of model houses which survive where they were re-erected, in Kennington. Grüner was responsible for the design of two table tops inlaid with coloured Derbyshire marbles in the Florentine manner, two fine Axminster carpets from Windsor Castle, a jewel casket made by Elkington's and an aesthetically indefensible garden seat made of coal.

Apart from the Medieval Court (PL. 59), which was entirely the work of Pugin, there was hardly a single memorable object in terms of design in the entire display, but even those who deplored the whole business thought it an important architectural experiment. One of the factors that ensured the project many imitators was the very large profit, that secured long lasting benefits to the nation in the form of 'Albertopolis', and the beginnings of a national collection of design. The implications for public taste were also far reaching, not least in the promotion of greatly enhanced expectations in the realm of choice and availability of goods.

A committee was set up to advise on the purchase of items from the Exhibition (PL. 62, 63), consisting of Cole, Pugin, Redgrave and Owen Jones. Redgrave had hoped for great things from the challenge of 1851, he was doomed to disappointment: in his *Supplementary Report on Design* appended to the official Jury Reports of the Exhibition he lamented 'that mixture of styles, and that incongruity of parts, which, perhaps, is itself "the style" of this characterless age'. He admired Pugin and praised his contribution, but he pinned his hopes on education, through Cole's *Journal of Design*, which he edited, and the network of Schools of Design.

Opposite PL. 58 Charles Burton: 'aeronautic view' of Paxton's iron and glass exhibition building; lithograph, 1851. This amazing structure stood for the highest technical achievement in nineteenth-century architecture, a celebration of industry harnessed to the service of art and education. The new railway system made the speedy completion of the building work possible, as the materials were transported from the factories and workshops of the Midlands.

Right PL. 59 The Medieval Court, arranged by A. W. N. Pugin; from *The Illustrated London News*. The names of Pugin's collaborators Hardman and Crace can be seen above the frieze of heraldic glass. Prominent in the foreground is Hardman's Great Stove with its Minton majolica tiles. The floor is laid with patterned encaustic tiles. Comments in the press were frequently unfavourable: 'On his entrance the visitor was struck with awe which is so often felt in a sanctuary: the place was, as it were, set apart from the rest of the Exhibition, looking dark and solemn for the display of the taste and art of dead men.'

Right PL. 60 A. W. N. Pugin: stove tiles, two of them pierced to release the heat, made in the newly revived 'majolica' process by Minton's and used for Hardman's Great Stove.

Far right PL. 61 A. W. N. Pugin: small silver-gilt and heavy crystal cruet jug; made by J. Hardman, *c.*1850. The jug was shown in 1851 in the group of 'ecclesiastical vessels, etc., ... designed by Mr Pugin and executed by Messrs J. Hardman & Co. of Birmingham'.

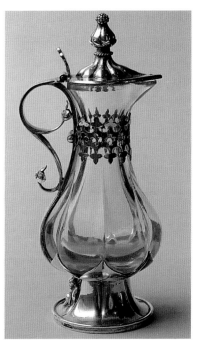

PL. 62 A. W. N. Pugin: Gothic cabinet in carved and painted oak with brass grilles and fittings; made by J. G. Crace, 1851. The cabinet was purchased from the exhibition for the newly established Museum of Manufactures and is now in the Victoria and Albert Museum.

PL. 63 Bernardo de Bernardis and Joseph Kranner: Gothic bookcase in carved oak; made by Carl Leistler & Son of Vienna. Shown in the Austrian section at the Great Exhibition in the 'Ladies' Library', one of a suite of rooms furnished by Leistler. This and Pugin's Gothic cabinet were considered to be the two most important pieces of Gothic Revival furniture in the exhibition. Emperor Franz Joseph presented the bookcase to Queen Victoria and it was removed after the exhibition to Buckingham Palace. It was later sent to Holyrood Palace in Edinburgh, and then to the Department of Forestry at the University there. In 1967 the University of Edinburgh gave it to the Victoria and Albert Museum.

Gottfried Semper

Above PL. 64 Ludwig Grüner: circular tile panel with Pompeian mask on pale purple ground; similar to those designed for the Marble Corridor at Osborne House, and made by Minton's, *c.*1845.

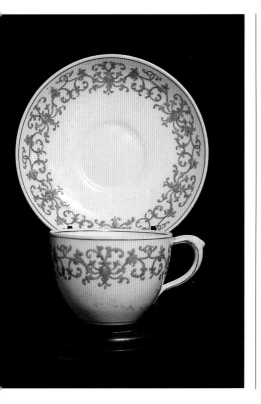

PL. 65 Henry Cole ('Felix Summerley'): prize-winning cup and saucer; made by Minton's. The Summerley holloware was also produced in a plain white, and the shapes were used by Pugin for his 'Gothic' pattern for the Houses of Parliament. The delicate, jewel-like enamelled decoration was to become a hallmark of Minton's finest tablewares.

Semper (1803–74) came to Prince Albert's notice in 1852, after he published *Wissenschaft, Industrie und Kunst*, a critical analysis of the effects of the Great Exhibition. He had trained as an architect in Munich before travelling to Paris, where he studied under the German-born architect Jacques-Ignace Hittorff (1792–1867). In Berlin in 1833 he met Karl Friedrich Schinkel; these contacts were the basis for his interests in antique polychromy and the architecture of the Italian Renaissance.

The studies of polychromy in ancient architecture pioneered by Hittorff and published in French in 1827 had made an important contribution towards the nineteenth-century taste for colour and contrast. Hittorff was a product of the Ecole des Beaux-Arts in Paris and had travelled in England in 1820, sketching buildings by Soane and Cockerell. He was in contact with Schinkel on a trip to Germany in 1821. These diverse influences produced the bold Italianate style deployed by Hittorff with impressive assurance, and which was to be used in various guises by architects all over Europe, providing the most conspicuous alternative to Gothic in the mid-nineteenth century.

Hittorff exemplifies the eclectic nature of an architect's development in the nineteenth century. Owen Jones, whose study of the architecture and decoration of the Alhambra made him a respected authority on colour in architecture, was one of many to be influenced by Hittorff's discoveries. Jules Goury, Owen Jones's collaborator on this book, had been Semper's travelling companion in Greece. So are the networks of example formed.

Semper's career as a designer in Germany was interrupted when he became involved with the revolutionaries in 1849 and had to flee to Paris. It was his employer in Paris who recommended him to Mr. Graham of the cabinet-making firm Jackson & Graham. In 1850 Semper moved to London and joined the team assembled by Henry Cole, designing the Egyptian, Swedish, Danish and Canadian sections at the Great Exhibition. He taught metalwork and furniture design at the School of Design at Marlborough House. In *Der Stil* (1861–3) he developed his ideas on the origins of style in art. The effects of this profoundly influential work are visible in the architecture and design of the twentieth century.

It has been suggested that the choice of the 'Early Renaissance

Lombardic' style for the brick and terracotta court of the South Kensington Museum was due to Semper's influence. The 'round-arch' style of brick architecture had been in use on the Continent since the 1820s.

Semper remained in England only until 1855, but the German example was important in stimulating interest in architectural polychromy and the Italian Renaissance. Grüner's *Specimens of Ornamental Art*, a study of Renaissance mural decoration and grotesques, appeared in 1850. The highly decorated Italianate style in architecture, complemented by furniture and decoration in the 'Neo-Renaissance' taste, formed a parallel strand to the progress of the Gothic Revival. Osborne was a prominent example of the genre and was immensely influential. Semper's association with Léon Arnoux at Minton's may explain his interest in 'Henri Deux' ceramic ware, a revival of the elaborate inlaid techniques practised in the sixteenth century at Saint-Porchaire. The greatest exponent of the Neo-Renaissance for decoration was Alfred Stevens, who made sculptural 'free Renaissance' fireplace models for the iron-working firm Hoole & Co. of Sheffield; but most of the art objects by lesser men are characterized by faithful historicism and intricate workmanship. The possibilities for development or evolution were few, and as a design trend the Neo-Renaissance was a dead end.

Owen Jones and Souvenirs of the Great Exhibition

Owen Jones was over forty years of age when he encountered the committee of the Great Exhibition. He was already known as the author of a magnificent illustrated account of the Alhambra in Spain (*Plans, Details, Elevations and Sections of the Alhambra*, 1842–5), the publication of which he had been forced to undertake himself, incidentally revolutionizing the printing of chromolithographic coloured illustrations. The production of the celebrated and hugely influential *Grammar of Ornament* (1856) was to an equally exacting standard. The range of the *Grammar* is vast, much wider than the title implies. The plates cover a universal spectrum of architectural details and pattern designs; China and India, Japan and Spain, botany and geometry are some of the subjects covered in the densely packed and richly coloured plates. Much imitated in subsequent publications, it was to provide a vocabulary of decorating ideas for his contemporaries and successors up to Frank Lloyd Wright. The book was continuously in print until 1910, and has been reissued.

Jones's writing and illustrating work was carried out in tandem with an architectural career that had begun in the office of the neoclassicist Lewis Vulliamy, but he designed few actual buildings. With the exception of the magnificently impressive, Crystal Palace-inspired, iron and glass showroom for the architectural and decorative glass manufacturers, Messrs F. & C. Osler, at 45 Oxford Street in London (who had supplied the fountain that provided the focal point in the great axial plan of the Crystal Palace), and similar schemes for exhibition buildings in Manchester (see PL. 70), and at St-Cloud on the outskirts of Paris, these architectural essays were of no great distinction. His conventional Italianate designs for the development at Kensington Palace Gardens in London suffered from the crucial defect of being five times as expensive as they should have been, a serious and financially embarrassing problem for the developer, John Marriott Blashfield. Large in scale and ambitiously ornamented, they set a precedent for the palatial character of the whole development.

Jones was to find his true artistic vocation in the field of decorative design. Although the work on the *Grammar* had provided him with a breathtaking width of reference, his decorative work was at its most striking and original when he remained faithful to the inspiration of Moorish Spain. Echoes of the *Alhambra* illustrations abound in the beautiful designs for textiles, including some silk weaving (PL. 146) in infinitely subtle colour combinations for the firm of Benjamin Warner of Braintree in Essex; and wallpapers (PL. 145) for John Trumble & Sons of Leeds and Jeffrey & Co. of Islington in London; and by logical extension in his interiors.

In his interior decorating work Jones's ideas were ambitious and expensive, so his clients tended to be public, as in his work on the reconstructed Crystal Palace at Sydenham (PL. 66) in South London and on the 1862 Exhibition; or commercial, as with Osler's showroom; or rich as the drapery multimillionaire Alfred Morrison. His most elaborate privately commissioned projects were carried out for Morrison, who owned a vast folly in Wiltshire and a London house at 16 Carlton House Terrace.

The tangible reminders of the Exhibition are the objects purchased after it closed, but it was commemorated in considerable detail in the *Official Catalogue* and the lengthy *Jury Reports*. The *Art Journal Illustrated Catalogue* was a pioneering initiative which offered what amounted to a pattern book of contemporary taste to a wide spectrum of manufacturers and their public. The line illustrations in the *Art Journal* and in other periodicals – notably *The Illustrated London News*, which gave extensive coverage throughout the months from May to November – might be said to provide the form but not the substance. The magnificent chromolithographic plates in Matthew Digby Wyatt's *Industrial Arts of the Nineteenth Century* (1851–3) show how sumptuous quality could deflect attention from defects in the principles of design.

It was Owen Jones who managed to wrest abstract principles from examples of international culture offered by the Great Exhibition and its successors. His *Grammar of Ornament* is a textbook of the world of pattern rather than an assembly of curiosities. Jones's credentials as a guide through the visual annals of exotic and ancient cultures were impeccable. His *Alhambra*, already a classic source of inspiration for the 'new style' deriving from Islamic precedents, was backed up by its three-dimensional counterpart, the Alhambra Court in the re-erected Crystal Palace at Sydenham which had opened to the public in 1854. Another product of Jones's extensive travels in the early 1830s was *Views on the Nile* (1843), a study of Egyptian buildings – an area in which his influence was to be crucial.

Writing of 'Egyptian ornament' in his *Principles of Decorative Design* (1873, p. 8), Dresser advised that 'further information may . . . be got from the South Kensington Museum library, where several interest-ing works on Egyptian ornament may be seen; – from the "Grammar of Ornament" by Mr Owen Jones, – the works of Egypt by Sir Gardiner Wilkinson [Sir John Gardner Wilkinson]; and, especially by a visit to the Egyptian Court of the Crystal Palace at Sydenham'. Gardner Wilkinson is no longer a household name; an explorer and Egyptologist, he had lived in Egypt for twelve years before publishing in 1837 his celebrated *Manners and Customs of the Ancient Egyptians*. Too late to have any effect on the neoclassical cult of ancient Egypt, its important message for designers was lost in a growing obsession with the Gothic Revival. The book was reissued in 1853 at a much more propitious moment. Pugin's experiments with a structural Gothic had reached a pitch of sophisticated simplicity, with forms free of anecdote or antiquarianism.

For his illustrations (PL. 67) Wilkinson had drawn on the examples of Egyptian domestic furniture uncovered at Thebes by the British Consul-General Henry Salt from 1815, which had been acquired for the British Museum between 1829 and 1835. In the 1860s and 1870s, these spare, abstracted pieces seemed to have a particular relevance, especially when seen in the context of the newly revealed art and architecture of Japan.

William Holman Hunt's chair (PL. 68), inspired by the Thebes furniture was made by J. G. Crace in about 1857, and Ford Madox Brown's plain variant was manufactured by Morris, Marshall, Faulkner & Co. in the 1860s. It is unlikely to have been a simple coincidence that resulted in so much of the Neo- or Anglo-Egyptian furniture being related to the plates in Gardner Wilkinson's book, though a note in Nesfield's 1862 sketchbook shows that he had seen the 'Thebes' stool in Semper's *Der Stil*. That books were often the source for ornamental motifs and forms even when the actual objects were readily accessible in the British Museum is confirmed by the inscription in one of Godwin's sketchbooks. Against ideas for chair legs he wrote: 'from the Parthenon Marbles', and underneath, the reminder: 'Ch. Daremberg & Edm. Saglio, Dictionnaire des Ants. Grecques, Paris 1873'. The chair leg features in his 'Greek' model (PL. 190) made from about 1885. Godwin's designs in the 1870s for 'Anglo-Egyptian' furniture follow Gardner Wilkinson closely.

Godwin's coffee table (*c*.1876), Dresser's stool for the Art Furnishers' Alliance (1881) and Liberty's 'Thebes' stool (PL. 277) all drew on this common source in the British Museum's Thebes material. Arthur Liberty was a shareholder in the Art Furnishers' Alliance. After the failure of the firm in 1883 he registered the Thebes stool with the Patent Office Design Registry (no. 16673, 1884). The three-legged Thebes stool, also from the Salt collection, was registered at the same time (no. 16674) though it had probably not formed part of Dresser's Art Furnishers' Alliance repertoire.

Left PL. 66 The 'Egyptian Court', showing full-size copies of the colossi of Abu Simbel in front of the north transept of the re-erected Crystal Palace at Sydenham; photographed in June 1854 by Delamotte. The towering Egyptian sculptures, rising almost to the roof, dwarf the wooden chairs, giving some idea of the awesome scale of this display. The effect of this and the material from extensive excavations at Thebes in the British Museum was to give an immediacy to Egyptian influence that no artist's view could match.

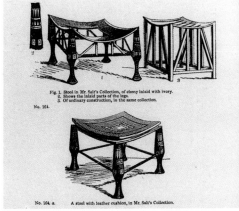

Above PL. 67 Sir J. Gardner Wilkinson: illustrations of the furniture from Thebes in the British Museum; from *Manners and Customs of the Ancient Egyptians*, first published 1837, reissued in a revised edition 1853. The discovery of the Thebes furniture provided models to counteract the picturesque fantasies of neoclassical Egyptian, such as the French-influenced room in Thomas Hope's mansion in Duchess Street (see PL. 7).

PL. 68 Chair of ebonized and turned wood; a variant of the model designed in 1857 by Holman Hunt and made by J. G. Crace.

PL. 69 Ford Madox Brown: chair of the 'Thebes' pattern; *c.*1860, and stocked by the Morris firm.

PL. 70 Owen Jones: competition design for the 1857 Manchester Exhibition building. In June 1856 *The Illustrated London News* mistakenly announced Jones as the competition winner. In fact the contract went to a local architect, Edward Solomans, later chief designer for the furniture manufacturers Lamb of Manchester. Although he was asked Jones declined to assist with the decoration of the interior, which was carried out by Crace.

George Edmund Street and his Pupils

Having served his articles with Owen Carter of Winchester, Street went into the London office of Sir George Gilbert Scott in 1844. Street's friendships, with Benjamin Webb, secretary of the Ecclesiological Society, and with Samuel Wilberforce, Bishop of Oxford, resulted among other appointments in his becoming diocesan architect of Oxford. His practice was therefore in Oxford at the moment when William Morris, having left Exeter College where he had been studying to be a clergyman, decided to study architecture. Morris made contact in Street's office with Philip Webb, a momentous meeting that was to determine the course of his life.

In the 1850s Street's office was the training ground for the élite of the next generation. It was the nursery not only of Morris & Co. but of the Queen Anne Revival and the Arts and Crafts Movement. Philip Webb had joined the practice in 1852 after an apprenticeship in Reading, just as Street secured his most important Oxford commission, Cuddesdon Theological Training College (1853–4) – according to Eastlake 'a simple but picturesque pile of buildings, chiefly depending for effect on artistic proportions' – for which he designed some remarkably inventive furniture. It was with the brutally simple circular table for Cuddesdon (PL. 75) that Street's debt to Pugin rather than to his former employer, Scott, was made apparent. In an equally austere X-frame trestle table, designed in 1865 for St Margaret's Convent at East Grinstead, he takes Pugin's functionalist ideas to their limit. Street's influence is obvious in the early furniture designs of the Morris firm, mainly by Webb.

After Webb's departure to set up his own practice he was succeeded in Street's office by Richard Norman Shaw who, with his friend W. E. Nesfield, is identified with the invention of the 'Queen Anne' style and the revival of the vernacular tradition. At the same time the brothers Edmund and J. D. Sedding arrived as pupils; Edmund died in 1868, but J. D. Sedding went on to become a founding member of the Art Workers' Guild, serving as Master in 1886 and 1887. T. E. Collcutt, an important Art Movement designer, was an assistant in the office with both Webb and Norman Shaw, before going on to work with Collinson & Lock. To complete a notable triumvirate of preceptors, Collcutt's first office, at Essex Street off the Strand, was below the premises then occupied by E. W. Godwin.

Another designer whose obvious debt to Street still awaits full clarification is Bruce Talbert. The available facts about his early career have been published by Sally Macdonald in *Furniture History* ('Gothic forms applied to furniture: the early work of Bruce James Talbert', vol. XXIII, 1987, pp. 39–66). While he was with Skidmore's, the architectural metalworkers in Coventry, Talbert worked on designs by George Gilbert Scott, and this may explain how he made contact with Street. Talbert dedicated to Street his *Gothic Forms Applied to Furniture, Metalwork and Decoration for Domestic Purposes* (1867), the book that was to establish his reputation as a designer, possibly in recognition of help in securing Talbert's first London job with the cabinet-making firm of Holland & Sons.

In 1855 Street published *Brick and Marble Architecture in North Italy*, and in the following year began his association with the Ecclesiological Society by contributing a number of designs to the second series of *Instrumenta Ecclesiastica*. He returned to London in 1856, with a substantial practice as a builder and restorer of churches, schools and parsonages. In 1868 Street began on his most important secular commission, the building of the Law Courts (PL. 174); it was to occupy him for the rest of his life. As at Cuddesdon, he showed extraordinary daring in the furniture for the Law Courts, achieving in the Klismos-type chair (PL. 176) the nearest to pure abstraction. Released in his secular models from the conventions of ecclesiastical Gothic, he played with an eclectic mix of historical forms, as in his fanciful 'Glastonbury' chair made for the Dublin Cathedral Chapter House (PL. 176) – a long way from Pugin's historically correct version for the Bishop's House in Birmingham (PL. 12).

Street had married in 1852 Mariquita Proctor, niece of the vicar of Hadleigh, whose church he had restored. She died in 1874, only a year after Street had completed the design and building of his own house, Holmdale, at Holmbury St Mary in Surrey. His second marriage took place in 1876, but his wife died in the same year. For Holmdale Street softened the powerful muscular Gothic of his earlier style. The L-shaped tile-hung and half-timbered house blends discreetly with its vernacular revival neighbours, Hopedene by Norman Shaw and Moxley by Basil Champneys. The church at Holmbury St Mary, which contains a handsome memorial to Jessie Street made by Holland & Sons, was a gift to the village from Street. It was his last, dating from 1879, only two years before his death.

Philip Webb entered Street's office in Oxford as senior clerk in 1852. He was joined there in 1856 by William Morris, who was to become his hero, his patron and his lifelong friend. In 1858 Webb left Street's office to set up his own practice. Red House for Morris at Bexleyheath (PL. 73) was one of his first independent commissions, and it marked the start of a career as a domestic architect. This house shows the influence of Butterfield and Street in that it is still essentially a Gothic Revival building, but the vernacular details, of sweeping tiled roofs descending almost to the ground floor, pierced with heavily gabled dormers, point the way forward. In contrast to his contemporary Gothic Revivalists, Webb built only one church and about sixty houses.

Under the influence of Dante Gabriel Rossetti Morris had already decided to exchange architecture for painting, and that in turn had been abandoned in favour of decoration, first of his rooms in Red Lion Square, then of his Red House and then on behalf of his own firm. The fruitful collaboration at Red House had inspired the setting up of Morris, Marshall, Faulkner & Co., a partnership remarkable in its concentration of artistic talent and almost total' lack of business direction.

It had been said, 'Morris was a pioneer in every field of his activity, he prepared the ground for the development which each of the branches underwent subsequently.' (Hermann Muthesius, *Das englische Haus*, 1904, English edn, 1979, p. 13.)

Morris's architectural training had lasted long enough to give him a professional understanding of the possibilities for the Red House. Here 'the theories of its owner and architect on domestic building and decoration were to be worked out in practice' (J. W. Mackail, *Life of William Morris*, 1899, vol. 1, p. 139). The interior was to be in the medieval style, and this involved the co-operation of Rossetti and Burne-Jones in the execution of the painted decoration of walls and furniture. His wife and sister-in-law were set to embroidering hangings. Some of the painted furniture from Red Lion Square was installed in the house, and Webb designed large built-in pieces for hall and dining room. The influence of Pugin is apparent, but Webb also looks forward to the type of roofed cabinet that was at this same moment emerging in the work of Burges and Richard Norman Shaw. Morris had realized his dreams for his personal 'palace of art', and was now testing ideas that became the basis of his decorating philosophy.

The Red House interiors were not universally admired, even in his own circle.

'[The house] was designed by Morris in what he called the style of the thirteenth century. The only thing you saw from the distance was an immense red-tiled, steep, and high roof; and the only room I remember was the dining-room or hall, which seemed to occupy the whole area of the mansion. It had a fixed settle all round the walls, a curious music-gallery entered by a stair outside the room, breaking out high upon the gable, and no furniture but a long table of oak reaching nearly from end to end. This vast empty hall was painted coarsely in bands of wild foliage over both wall and ceiling, which was open-timber and lofty. The adornment had a novel, not to say startling, character, but if one had been told it was the South Sea Island style of thing one could have easily believed such to be the case, so bizarre was the execution.' (William Bell Scott, *Autobiography*, ed. William Minto, 1892, vol. II, p. 61.)

For the moment Morris had succeeded in creating a supremely happy environment for his family and friends. Yet all too soon it had to be abandoned. In 1865 Morris returned to London and established his family and his firm in Queen Square.

The Red House interiors showed the team at a rough experimental stage and woefully betrayed the amateur attainments of the decorators; but practical skills came with application. Morris's touch of genius was to provide a unity of inspiration to the many separate components of interior decoration. The 'Morris look' was recognizable without being startling. It is a measure of his understanding of popular taste that many of his patterns have been available since they were first put into production.

All those furnishings that had still been wanting in 1865 would shortly be available from the firm. Mackail ruefully pointed out: 'No long time after Red House was given up, it became possible to have supplied it from the works at Queen Square with almost everything necessary to complete its decoration and furnishings. Such is the irony of human affairs.' (p. 175.)

Street had recognized a natural affinity between medievalists like himself and the Pre-Raphaelite painters: 'In truth what Pre-Raphaelites are doing for painting must be done for architecture – if at all – by the thirteenth-century men.' But it was Morris who brought the two strands into a practicable partnership. Morris spent only eight months in Street's office, but he acquired a lifelong respect for architecture as the central key to the arts, around which painting, sculpture and decoration must revolve. He also absorbed Street's ethos of perfectionism; Street was prepared to learn blacksmithing in order to design the dramatic ironwork for St James the Less, Pimlico (1859) and the Law Courts (1868; see PL. 174). The parallel is inescapable with Morris's own mastery of the skills needed in decorating. At this date Ruskin was evolving the same philosophy for the decorative arts. The following comes from *The Two Paths* (1859): 'No person is able to give useful or definite help towards the special applications of art, unless he is entirely familiar with the conditions of labour and materials involved in the work.' Morris could hardly have looked for a more powerful advocate.

Above PL. 71 A. W. N. Pugin: St Augustine's Grange, Ramsgate; 1852. Pugin's last house, still uncompleted at his death. He set the domestic style of Reformed Gothic with his asymmetrical brick building.

Right PL. 72 G. E. Street: All Saints', Boyne Hill, Berkshire; 1854. Now engulfed by the suburbs of Maidenhead, this house was part of a self-contained and compact grouping of church, vicarage, school, almshouses and other buildings.

Above PL. 73 Philip Webb: Red House, designed for William Morris, 1858–9. Muthesius believed the house to be 'unique in its time'; although this was demonstrably untrue in the purely architectural sense, it was a very rare example of a complete entity comprising the architectural envelope and all its contents. It is a house at the crossroads of nineteenth-century domestic design, looking back to Pugin and William Butterfield, with an inevitable debt to Street, and looking forward to Richard Norman Shaw and the vernacular revival.

Right PL. 74 Philip Webb: panel of painted glass quarries; for Red House, *c.*1859.

Above PL. 75 G. E. Street: table in oak; designed for Cuddesdon College, Oxford, *c*.1854. This table is an example of Street's most didactic application of straightforward and visible construction and the honest use of materials.

Below PL. 76 Philip Webb: trestle table; of the pattern for Red House. The two tables in the hall of the house were the first examples of an enduring model, described by May Morris as 'the first one'. The early examples of the table, including one for the Burne-Joneses at the time of their marriage in 1860, were made at Major Gillum's Boys' Club in the Euston Road. Morris approved of this solid joinery construction, disliking furniture that was 'so very light as to be nearly imponderable; it should be made of timber rather than walking sticks'.

Right PL. 77 Pine table; possibly designed by William Morris, *c*.1856, for his rooms at Red Lion Square. The table owes an obvious debt to Street's Cuddesdon design. The four plank-like legs with Gothic cutouts at the foot are related to the trestle design made by Webb for Red House (see PL. 76), which was to remain in the Morris firm's repertoire into the present century. Excursions by Morris into furniture design were exceedingly rare and it is likely that the furniture-making experiments at Red Lion Square were a collaborative effort with advice from Webb, who was already in Street's office at the time of the Cuddesdon commission and certainly witnessed the design of the table. The singular decoration of the Red Lion Square rooms was described by Lady Burne-Jones in her *Memorials* of her husband, the text being illustrated with a comic drawing by Burne-Jones which shows this very table – 'heavy as a rock' – in the background amid other more improbable pieces. The table came from the Morris family, but is undocumented before 1923.

Right PL. 79 William Burges: painted wardrobe; 1858. The first of a suite of painted pieces for Mr Yatman of Haslemere. Burges exhibited six items in 1859, but his painted furniture reached a large public in 1862 when he included three more pieces in the Medieval Court. This wardrobe consists of a simple case topped by a pitched and gabled roof, the painted decoration of figures symbolizing 'flax' and 'wool' referring to its use as a linen press or clothes cupboard.

Below PL. 78 Richard Norman Shaw: title page to *Architectural Sketches from the Continent*; 1858. Street's office was like a staging post between Pugin's principled Gothic and the eclectic Art Movement style of which Morris was a pioneer. The title page looks forward to Morris and back to Pugin in both its flowing acanthus margin and the roundels of medieval craftsmen at work.

The International Exhibition of 1862

*M*ay Day 1862, the eleventh anniversary of the inauguration of the Great Exhibition, saw the opening of the second International Exhibition in London. It had been intended to hold the exhibitions at five-yearly intervals, but caution in the face of the huge scale of the undertaking suggested that decennial exhibitions would be more feasible; the lapse of a further year was due to war between France and Austria which broke out in April 1861. The death in December 1861 of Prince Albert cast a pall over the preparations. The Queen was still in deepest mourning in May and was not present at the opening.

The site was adjacent to the new Royal Horticultural Society building and it was intended that the Exhibition building should eventually become part of a scientific and cultural complex. The Horticultural Society's architect was Captain Francis Fowke, a young artillery engineer of modest architectural attainments who was engaged on the new building for the South Kensington Museum. Fowke was no Paxton – though both were, in theory, amateurs, a condition favoured by Cole, who distrusted professional architects – and Crace, who was engaged to decorate the interior, no Owen Jones. Even a satirical magazine seems to have been quite uneasy at Cole's choices:

> It's a wonderful place is the Great International,
>   And – although discontent somewhat dashes our pride,
> Thanks to Royal Commissioners' conduct irrational, –
>   We justly may boast of the marvels inside.
>   And the things that are filled in,
>   And CRACE's fine gilding,
>   Make us pardon FOWKE's building
>   To some slight extent.
>   (from *Fun*, II, 19 July 1862, p. 173.)

Unlike the Crystal Palace the 1862 building disappeared without trace in little more than a decade, the financial surplus that would have ensured its future as a picture gallery not having materialized. Cole was aware of the inevitability of a financial loss, as the intended permanent structure cost far more than the temporary Crystal Palace. With the support of the Prince he argued its utility successfully, but Albert's death deprived him of a level-headed spokesman and the commissioners demolished the building in a panic. The site was eventually (1880) to be occupied by Alfred Waterhouse's Natural History Museum.

Crace's efficiency, at least, was to triumph, the elaborate scheme being completed in just four months, but the intricacy of the 'Raphaelesque' decoration and the too-great range of colours diminished its impact. Critics gave Fowke less than his due in that the much-derided domes over the transepts, at 160 feet (49 m) in diameter, were then the largest ever achieved in this country, but both he and Crace were attempting effects that were too fussy for so large a space. The history of Crace's decoration of the building is given in detail by Stephen Wildman in *The Craces, Royal Decorators 1768–1899*, ed. Megan Aldrich, 1990, pp. 146–55; a succinct account of the building can be found in the *Survey of London*, vol. XXXVIII, 'The Museums of South Kensington and Westminster', ch. IX. A more lasting monument to Fowke is the Royal Albert Hall (1863–71), with an even larger, elliptical dome whose iron frame spans 273 feet (83 m) in its longer diameter.

Whatever the shortcomings of the building (and the Crystal Palace was indeed difficult to surpass), in design terms many of the displays were of greater significance. The purpose of the exhibition was to demonstrate the improvements that had taken place in design and manufactures during the last ten years. Lessons had been learnt, as the 1851 Commissioners had intended, from comparisons with foreign competitors. The advance in British taste was partly due to notable publications, Owen Jones's *Grammar of Ornament* (1856), and Ruskin's *Stones of Venice* (1851–6). Pugin was dead, but his influence had been widely assimilated and his followers emerged as the most original exhibitors.

The Medieval Court at the 1862 Exhibition (PL. 80, 81) in spite of its ecclesiastical basis – it was set up as a showcase for the Ecclesiological Society, keen to extend its sphere of influence into domestic Gothic as well as church architecture and furnishing – again provided a focus for the progress of the Gothic revival. The display was a parade of works in a flamboyantly developed Reformed Gothic which had progressed far beyond the simple imitation of earlier forms. William Burges, deputed by the Society to organize the Medieval Court, remarked that 'all the principal and rising architects, and a very large proportion of the best manufacturers' were represented. The 1862 display, as Burges recognized, marked the confluence of two generations; Street's pupils and their contemporaries were to provide the foundations from which the Arts and Crafts Movement developed.

The momentum of Pugin's inspiration and drive survived the deaths of his most crucial collaborators, Herbert Minton in 1858 and John Hardman in 1867, partly because their heirs continued to use or adapt his ideas. J. G. Crace completed unfinished projects to Pugin's designs, though there was an element of intricacy and over-ornamentation that betrayed Pugin's commitment to simplicity and abstract structural principles. Pugin's own followers interpreted his ideas with less perfect understanding than more independent successors such as Street and Webb.

The 1862 Medieval Court (PL. 80, 81) brought together the young talent from Street's office; Philip Webb, Richard Norman Shaw and William Morris, as well as Street himself, with William Burges and John Pollard Seddon. Burges, initially destined to follow in his father's footsteps, had trained as an engineer before entering the office of Edward Blore; he worked subsequently with Matthew Digby Wyatt, and it was probably Wyatt's influence rather than Blore's that led Burges to the romantic medievalism that characterizes his work. Burges's strong sense of the interaction of mass and void, masked by his addiction to painted and gilded decoration, may reflect his early training in engineering.

Seddon's precocious publication, *Progress in Art and Architecture with Precedents for Ornament* (1852), shows his rapid assimilation of Gothic ornament on Ruskinian principles, the illustrations in particular betraying a debt to *The Stones of Venice*. In 1862 he had just arrived in London, having spent the previous decade in partnership with the Llandaff architect John Prichard, with whom he had built the French-Gothic Ettington Park (1858–60). The delicate polychrome tracery of Ettington shows the trend that Seddon would follow with his designs for inlaid and painted furniture. The strength and assurance of his furniture designs probably stems from his background in cabinet-making as a son of Thomas Seddon, head of the family firm founded in the mid-eighteenth century.

The Medieval Court is chiefly remembered for the first appearance in public of the newly founded Morris, Marshall, Faulkner & Co., but evidence of their contribution has proved surprisingly difficult to document. One reason was economic: to have wares illustrated in the catalogue published by the *Art Journal* cost money, and at this early stage in his commercial life Morris may have been cautious of spending on what was, in effect, advertising.

The combined talents of this remarkable group produced an exhibit of epic power. Street's contribution being exclusively ecclesiastical – a reredos executed by T. Earp, an altar frontal for the Ecclesiological Embroidery Society, and church plate in the Gothic taste for John Keith's prize-winning display – was overshadowed by the massive architectonic cabinets from Norman Shaw (a desk for his own use exhibited by the maker James Forsyth), Burges and Morris. The pieces by Burges were a fireplace and the inlaid table for C. L. Somers Cocks of Treverbyn Vean in Cornwall, shown by Crace; the 'Wines and Spirits' buffet; the 'Yatman' cabinet, by Harland and Fisher; the Great Bookcase; the 'Sun' and 'Metals' cabinets and the 'Bacchus' wine cooler. Those by Seddon were the 'King René's Honeymoon' cabinet; an inlaid roll-top escritoire; and a chair with painted back panels by Rossetti and an unpainted pair to it, as well as plain chairs without arms. For £25 Morris had taken two stands in the Medieval Court, one for stained glass and one for painted tiles, jewellery and furniture, including the 'St George's' cabinet; the 'Backgammon Players' cabinet; the 'English Life 1810–1860' bookcase; the 'Rossetti' japanned sofa and related chair designed by Webb; a chest; copper candlesticks; a red lacquer music stand; and a screen with stamped leather panels. There was also an iron bedstead and a washstand. Burges did not like the tiles, which were discreetly removed from the display. The firm sold £150 worth of goods at the Exhibition, a considerable feat since the 'Backgammon' cabinet was priced at only 30 guineas.

Burges's 'Wines and Spirits' cabinet was acquired for the South Kensington Museum at a cost of £40; Seddon declined to part with the 'King René' cabinet, which eventually entered the collections in 1927.

Summing up the contribution from the Medieval Court, *The Clerical Journal* sounded a cautiously optimistic note:

> 'A mere cursory glance is enough to reveal the extent of advance and improvement which has taken place during the last ten years; it further shows that we have not yet arrived at any resting-place, but are still pushing forward … and though we do not say that this century will witness the ripening of a new and durable style of English art, we are bold to say that we shall achieve – nay we have achieved – works which posterity will recognise as being among the great works of the artist mind and hand – works whose style may go out of fashion, but which will, nevertheless, be treasured by our descendants even as we treasure the great works of bygone schools of art.' (May 8, 1862, p. 421; quoted in J. Banham and J. Harris, *William Morris and the Middle Ages*, 1984.)

In contrast, the *Art Journal* expressed disillusion: 'The second Medieval Court has been decidedly inferior to the first.'

With hindsight, we can see that in the decade separating the two London exhibitions Pugin's successors reached the limit of pure Gothic; new ideas for furniture and domestic design in the next decade were to be eclectic, tempering medievalism with Japanese, Moresque and Egyptian motifs. E. W. Pugin's development of his father's style includes chairs with dramatic 'Klismos'-type backs and his continuation of Scarisbrick, a new commission negotiated after his father's death in 1852, which exploited the drama of Gothic in a frankly competitive mood. Commerical plagiarism of Pugin's ideas went on for decades but was mainly timid and lacking in architectonic force.

The early 1860s saw the apogee of flamboyant Neo-Gothic, with the strong lines of functional form married to a dramatic use of inlaid or painted polychromatic decoration. After this there was an inevitable decline. The influence of Gothic, so deeply rooted in the designers of Street's generation, lasted for many years, but in the case of furniture and the decorative arts mainly as commercial exploitation rather than in new perceptions of Gothic forms.

Burges was to design more painted cabinets, washstands, beds and chairs; Seddon's inlaid pieces were to be developed by Talbert (his *Gothic Forms* appeared in 1867) and continued by Charles Bevan; Webb's hooded 'reredos' dresser of 1862 for the Morris firm proved to be an enduringly popular type, still featured in the catalogue in the present century.

Gothic did not disappear, but it did not develop further. As ever, the fundamental reasons were financial. Morris realized that the way forward for him could not be with expensive painted pieces relying on individual patrons. Burges did not need to be constrained by such considerations, especially after he started his long association with a millionaire patron, the Marquess of Bute.

'Former worshippers of bright, original, intelligent vivacious Gothica, turned their backs on her, to grovel in the dust before Queen Anne.' So remarked J. Moyr Smith in *Ornamental Interiors Ancient and Modern* (1887, p. 68). In an engraved view of the Medieval Court can just be seen the neighbouring stand of Cox & Sons, a firm of metalworkers and church furnishers who in the 1870s were to emerge as the employers of most of the designers associated with the Art Movement. In 1862 their business was still largely in church metalwork. Cox & Sons' progression from ecclesiastical to art manufactures exemplifies the trend in domestic design that was to lead into the Art Movement. An early warning of the decorative trends in art applied to manufactures is exemplified in the woven hangings exhibited by the Scottish firm of Templeton, carpet manufacturers who moved into intricate jacquard weaving.

PL. 80 View of the 1862 Medieval Court from a stereoscopic photograph, arranged for the Ecclesiological Society by William Burges and William Slater. The popularity of the 1851 Medieval Court ensured enormous public attention for the 1862 display, which became and has remained the focus of interest in design reform at this date. The level of interest is attested by the large number of photographic views that were made of the exhibition. In the foreground can be seen the roll-top escritoire designed by J. P. Seddon and made by Seddon & Co. To the right is a Gothic armchair (PL. 83), and in the background a man leans on the back of a side chair, both pieces designed by Seddon. Behind him is part of the display of Cox & Son, church furnishers, who were later to play an important part as manufacturers of 'Art' furniture. In spite of the Ecclesiologists' wish to show their interest in the domestic market, the display is still dominated by religious art.

PL. 81 Another photographic view of the Medieval Court, showing four cabinets designed by Burges. On the right of the 'Sun' cabinet is the 'Yatman' cabinet, painted by E. J. Poynter, which was exhibited by the makers Harland & Fisher. On the extreme right towers the fireplace designed by Burges for Treverbyn Vean, the 'Manorial hall of Colonel Cocks, Cornwall'. The juxtaposition in the Medieval Court of the Treverbyn Vean fireplace and the chair (PL. 83) designed by Seddon and chosen by Birket Foster for The Hill at Witley in Surrey neatly encapsulates the breadth of mid-century patronage: from a Gothic Revival country house for a member of the aristocracy to an enlarged country cottage for a successful watercolourist. The font cover and an altar candlestick from G. E. Street's St James the Less in Pimlico dominate the foreground.

Below PL. 82 J. P. Seddon: roll-top escritoire in oak inlaid with various woods and with pitchpine facings, the brass drawer handles set with turquoise cameos and cabochons of malachite and ruby glass. This may also be seen in the stereoscopic view (PL. 80). The monogram 'JS' and the devices of architect's drawing instruments support the theory that this was made for the designer's own use. The *Civil Engineer* commented: 'Mr Seddon also had a large show of furniture, in style much akin to that of Mr Burges, and being less recondite in treatment, is consequently more intelligible and likely to be better appreciated.' (November 1862)

Above PL. 83 J. P. Seddon: walnut armchair with leather upholstery and panels of canework in the back; made by T. Seddon. This may also be seen in the stereoscopic view (PL. 80). A drawing by Seddon shows a version of this design, with back panels painted by Rossetti in the medieval style with figures of Pyramus and Thisbe. The painted chair was acquired by the artist Myles Birket Foster for his house, The Hill, at Witley in Surrey. As well as the Rossetti chair, the unpainted version with the canework panels and the plain chair seen in the background of the stereoscopic view were at The Hill, which was decorated by the Morris firm in 1864, one of its earliest domestic commissions.

PL. 84 J. P. Seddon: 'King René's Honeymoon' cabinet, oak inlaid with various woods to a design by Burges, the door panels painted by Rossetti, Burne-Jones and Madox Brown. The story of King René is taken from Walter Scott's *Anne of Geierstein*. The cabinet was shown by the Morris firm in the Medieval Court.

PL. 85 Philip Webb: chest of wood with silvered and painted decoration and wrought iron mounts and hinges; painted by Webb. This too was shown in the 1862 Medieval Court by the Morris firm.

PL. 86 Philip Webb: 'St George's' cabinet, with panels painted by Morris. Shown by the firm at the exhibition. Superficially from the same medieval inspiration as Burges's painted furniture, the subject matter of the panels on this and the other painted pieces from the Morris firm is purely romantic. The relationship with Pre-Raphaelite paintings is apparent.

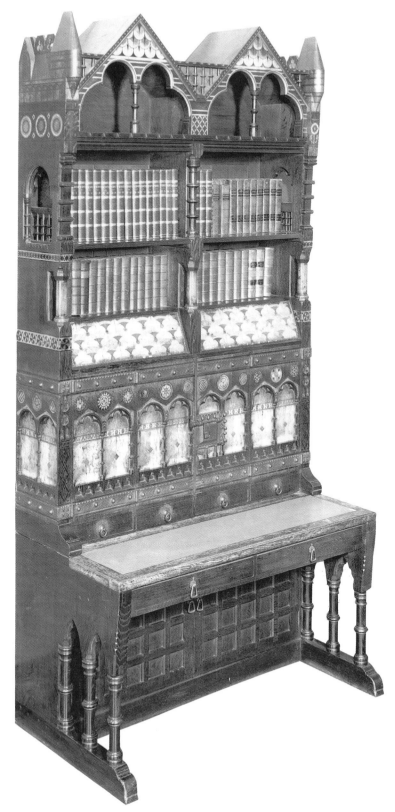

Above PL. 87 Philip Webb: 'Backgammon' cabinet, with figures painted after a drawing by Burne-Jones dated 1861, now in the Fitzwilliam Museum. Shown by Morris at the exhibition.

Right PL. 88 Richard Norman Shaw: writing cabinet and bookcase; 1861. The cabinet was shown in the Architectural Exhibition in that year. The same piece or a version of it featured in the 1862 Medieval Court, exhibited by the woodcarver James Forsyth. Small differences apparent in pictures of the cabinet suggest that there may have been more than one version. This piece owes a debt to the massive hall cabinet designed by Webb for Red House, *c.*1859.

Left PL. 89 William Burges: painted and gilded bookcase, with panels symbolizing Christian and pagan art. The scheme of decoration was entirely devised by Burges and the paintings executed by Burne-Jones, Poynter, Simeon Solomon, Albert Moore, Henry Stacy Marks and Frederick Smallfield, making a miniature picture gallery of advanced aesthetic taste. At nearly 11 ft (3.3 m) in height it must have made a striking impression at the exhibition.

Above PL. 90 William Burges: panel of stained glass based on the door panel 'Architecture'; painted for the bookcase by Simeon Solomon.

PL. 91 Stained glass panel, *c.*1864; taken from the 'King René's Honeymoon' subjects on the door panels of the 1862 Exhibition cabinet. The set of stained glass panels was made for the drawing room in Birket Foster's house at Witley.

PL. 92 William Burges: 'Wines and Spirits' buffet, painted by Edward Poynter. One of a pair showing Wine vanquishing Spirits and vice versa. The pair to this cabinet was acquired from the 1862 Exhibition for the South Kensington Museum. It was chosen in preference to any of the Morris pieces because it was considered more 'truthful', as the painted decoration made reference to the purpose of the cabinet.

Left PL. 93 William Burges: cabinet with painted panels by Poynter; made by Harland & Fisher for Mr H. G. Yatman of Haslemere. It was shown first at the Architectural Exhibition in London in 1859, and can be recognized in the view of the 1862 Medieval Court (see PL. 80). The base repeats the theme and decorative details of the two 'Wines and Spirits' buffets.

Above PL. 94 Philip Webb: chair in ebonized and painted wood; designed for the 1862 display. With a structural design and mixture of sources from Egyptian furniture and the vernacular and with a suggestion of the eighteenth century in the 'japanned' finish, this design attracted much criticism, demonstrating that its eclecticism was too advanced for this early date.

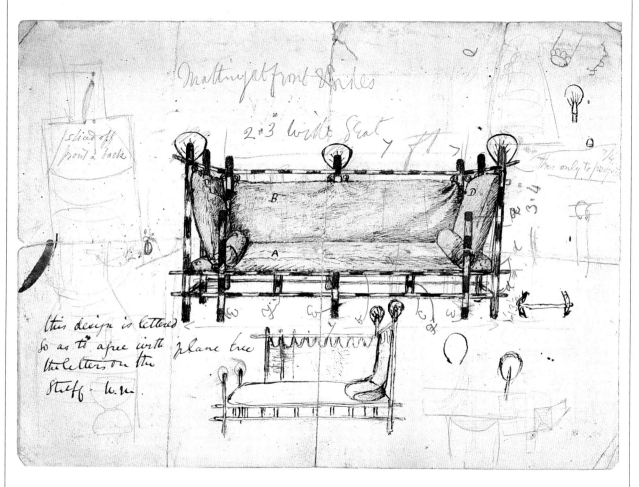

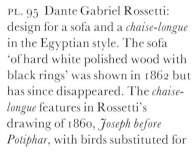

PL. 96 Philip Webb: copper
candlestick; designed for the
Morris firm and shown at the 1862
Exhibition.

PL. 95 Dante Gabriel Rossetti:
design for a sofa and a *chaise-longue*
in the Egyptian style. The sofa
'of hard white polished wood with
black rings' was shown in 1862 but
has since disappeared. The *chaise-
longue* features in Rossetti's
drawing of 1860, *Joseph before
Potiphar*, with birds substituted for
the palmette finials. Watercolours
of the dining room in Rossetti's
Chelsea house show that there was
also a large buffet or dresser *en suite*
with the sofa, the supports
terminating in the same manner
with palmettes. This too seems to
have disappeared.

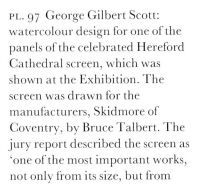

PL. 97 George Gilbert Scott: watercolour design for one of the panels of the celebrated Hereford Cathedral screen, which was shown at the Exhibition. The screen was drawn for the manufacturers, Skidmore of Coventry, by Bruce Talbert. The jury report described the screen as 'one of the most important works, not only from its size, but from the care with which it has been executed, and the successful endeavour to treat what is in fact a large architectural subject in metal alone.' This fragment of the whole design comes from an album once in the possession of Mr Bayne of the Heaton, Butler & Bayne decorating and stained glass firm.

PL. 98 Richard Norman Shaw: drawing on blue paper for the panel from the railing of wrought metal shown by Benham at the 1862 Exhibition. From the same album as PL. 97.

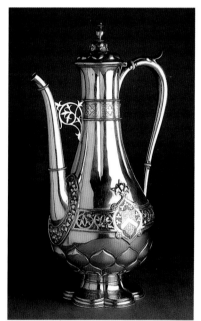

Above PL. 100 John Hardman Powell: flagon, ruby glass mounted in gilt metal with a handle in the form of a bird. Shown by Hardman & Co. at the exhibition.

Left PL. 99 Richard Norman Shaw: iron and brass firedogs; probably for Benham's. They are a variant of the pair shown by Benham's in 1862. The prototype is thirteenth-century from an old house in Vezelay. It is illustrated by Viollet in the first volume of the *Dictionnaire de Mobilier* (1858, p. 139).

PL. 101 John Hardman Powell: silver coffee pot; made by Hardman & Co., 1863, for Colonel Somers Cocks of Treverbyn Vean. Hardman's showed a tea and coffee service designed by Hardman Powell in 1862 with the same scale pattern on the lower body of the pieces. Pugin's legacy of influence on Hardman Powell, his son-in-law, may be detected here.

Left PL. 102 William Burges: octagonal table; detail of the top decorated with 'The Wheel of Fortune', inlaid in various woods. Made by J. G. Crace, using a Pugin design for the base. Dating from 1858, the table was made for Treverbyn Vean, the Gothic-style Cornish house of Colonel Somers Cocks, a Crimean veteran and connoisseur of old china.

Above PL. 103 Silk and wool jacquard-woven *portière* hangings; by J. & S. Templeton of Glasgow. The hangings were a triumph of weaving technology, being made in one piece rather than sewn together from separate elements. They were fashionable though expensive, and Templeton's were able to exploit this successful formula as interest in 'art' textile design expanded. Many accomplished designers, for example Bruce Talbert, Lewis F. Day, Walter Crane and C. F. A. Voysey later worked for the firm.

Left PL. 104 J. G. Crace: cabinet and writing desk of walnut, with carved and inlaid ornament in Puginesque Gothic style. Shown at the 1862 Exhibition. Described in J. B. Waring, *Masterpieces*, vol. iii, pl. 205: 'of ingenious construction, ornamented with carved panels, brass-work, and inlay of various woods, very tastefully combined', and favourably compared with the 'Medieval carved furniture of Belgium and Holland'.

Above PL. 105 Locks shown by Hobbs in the 1862 Exhibition: the designs attributed to Christopher Dresser on the basis of their similarity to Dresser's work for Benham & Froud in the 1870s (Waring, *Masterpieces*)

Morris, Marshall, Faulkner & Company

'The growth of decorative art in the country owing to the efforts of English Architects has now reached a point at which it seems desirable that Artists of reputation should devote their time to it.' (From the *Prospectus* of the firm, 1861.) The genesis of the firm is a story too well known to need further elaboration here: it can be traced step by step in a recent publication, *William Morris, Design and Enterprise in Victorian Britain*, by Charles Harvey and Jon Press (Manchester University Press, 1991) and in the many other books devoted to Morris. First and unsurpassed is Aymer Vallance's *William Morris, His Art, His Writings and His Public Life*, 1897. The magisterial *Life of William Morris*, 1899, by J. W. Mackail, Burne-Jones's son-in-law, paints an unforgettable picture of the man, poet and political visionary as well as supremely practical workman, mastering successively carving, modelling, joinery, embroidery, stained glass, tapestry weaving, textile dying and block printing, and – his last obsession – the hand printing of books.

As well as the named partners – Peter Paul Marshall, surveyor and sanitary engineer and amateur painter, and Charles Faulkner, mathematician and Oxford friend of Morris – Webb, Rossetti, Burne-Jones and Madox Brown were financially involved. Faulkner's sisters Kate and Lucy were indispensable, tirelessly painting tiles and gessoing pianos with Burne-Jones. Webb, as Rossetti remarked, was a key member of the group: 'our most active man of business as regards the actual conduct of the firm'.

It is possible that a remark of Street's provided the immediate inspiration for the founding of the firm: 'Before a Gothic house could be suitably furnished some attempt must be made to improve modern upholstery, and, following in the steps of Pugin, we must establish a Gothic manufactory.' (From a lecture, 'On the application of Gothic architecture to civil and domestic buildings', reported in *The Builder*, 19 May 1860, p. 308.) One of Morris's earliest preoccupations, the revival of embroidered hangings and tapestries for the decoration of rooms, was initiated by Street's medievally inspired designs for ecclesiastical embroidery. Significantly, the prosperity of the Morris firm at its inception was assured not by Street but by G. F. Bodley, who was responsible for getting the first stained glass commissions. The east window of his church of St Martin in Scarborough is Rossetti's *Parable of the Vineyard*, which had been exhibited in 1862.

William White, a Gothic Revivalist contemporary of Street and Bodley, both of whom he had encoutered in Gilbert Scott's office, was another early patron of the firm, commissioning glass for Lyndhurst Parish Church on which he had been working since 1858. The reredos wall in the church was painted in encaustic by Frederic Leighton and the decorations were carried out by John Hungerford Pollen. White was the son of the Revd Francis White, private chaplain to Sir Henry Dryden of Canons Ashby, and great-nephew of the naturalist Gilbert White of Selborne. He had entered Scott's office in 1845 and left in 1847, before Bodley and Street, to set up his own practice at Truro in Cornwall. During this phase he designed and furnished the Rectory at St Columb Major (*c*.1850), in which Puginesque details are magnified and exaggerated (see Gavin Stamp, *The English House, 1860–1914*, 1986, p. 56).

Stained glass was not only the greatest source of revenue, but the most important element in establishing the firm. Rossetti, Madox Brown and Burne-Jones had all been working with the glassworks Powell & Sons of Whitefriars, and this link was retained though they now designed principally on behalf of the new firm. Their pictorial skills ensured the reputation of Morris glass through an experimental period when the technical quality was still uncertain. Not all the glass was for ecclesiastical commissions, but the huge programme of church building in the mid-century was an important factor in sustaining the firm through the early years.

Webb's furniture for the firm in the 1860s fitted Morris's ideal of 'work-a-day' furniture on medieval principles: sturdy in workmanship, clear in structure and made of honest materials. Like the Puginesque hooded dresser of 1862, a version of Webb's trestle table (PL. 76), one of the first of which was made at Major Gillum's Boys' Home in the Euston Road in about 1860 and presented to Burne-Jones for his new married quarters, was to remain in the Morris & Co. catalogue into the present century. The first examples had many faults and bear the signs of attempts to cure them. Simplicity of construction for the benefit of untrained craftsmen is only arrived at with considerable difficulty, as Pugin had discovered. The Gothic Revival table at Kelmscott Manor is a more uncompromising piece, without the appeal in vernacular terms possessed by the trestle. These tables show clearly Street's part in forming Webb's ideas.

Major Gillum of Oakleigh Park, Barnet, was an important early patron. For him Webb designed furniture with Oriental overtones including a side table based on a Chinese or Japanese altar table (PL. 106), early examples of a style which was also seen in the

Japanese Court at the 1862 Exhibition. A walnut circular table of the same date makes use of turnings on the legs and stretchers which recall bamboo (PL. 108). A black-painted and gilded chair from Kelmscott Manor, formerly attributed to Rossetti, is one of the most exciting designs from this early group of Webb's work (PL. 94). In form, the chair is based on a traditional type, with the elements exaggerated and squared up. There is no one source for the complex articulation of the members, though some debt to Egyptian furniture is apparent. The attribution to Webb is due to A. R. Dufty, who has recovered the history of its conception and manufacture (see 'Kelmscott: exoticism and a Philip Webb chair', *Antiquaries' Journal*, 1986, pp. 116–20). The chair was exhibited in the Medieval Court in 1862 as a contribution from the Morris firm; inevitably the eclectic form posed problems for the critics. It probably stimulated a comment in *The Ecclesiologist*: 'Some painted and japanned furniture, exhibited by Messrs Morris, Marshall & Co., is simply preposterous.' (June 1862, p. 171.)

The chair is one of a group of experimental designs from the Morris circle. A drawing survives of Rossetti's 'Egyptian' sofa (PL. 95), also shown in 1862, and the connection with Webb's chair is obvious. Between 1855 and 1857 William Holman Hunt had designed a more picturesque 'Egyptian' chair (PL. 68), inlaid with ivory lotus motifs and with a slung leather seat based on a 'Thebes' stool in the British Museum, and made up by J. G. Crace. It is significant that this quaint design should have been taken up by Madox Brown, made for the firm in a plain undecorated version of which examples survive (PL. 69). A Liberty stool based on the design became a popular item in the shop's repertoire, whereas Rossetti's and Webb's pieces remained unique. The Victorian public were addicted to exotic novelties, not to abstract interpretation.

The relationship between Webb's architectural commissions and the decorative work of the Morris firm was intricate and interdependent. Red House, as a team effort between the architect and his artist-collaborators, was to be matched in an important early commission. The decoration of the 'Armoury' and 'Tapestry' rooms in St James's Palace (1866) marks a turning point in the firm's reputation. Mackail pointed out that Royal patronage could have ensured easy prosperity for Morris, had he been prepared to make any kind of commercial compromise, but this he was temperamentally incapable of doing: even the Office of Works balked at the huge cost of the hand-embroidered curtains proposed for the decoration of the Throne Room in 1880.

The 'Green Dining Room' in the South Kensington Museum (1867) followed the first St James's Palace commission; then came 1 Palace Green, London (1867, for George Howard, later Earl of Carlisle, himself a painter in the Pre-Raphaelite tradition), Rounton Grange in Yorkshire (1872, for Isaac Lowthian Bell), and Smeaton Manor, near Northallerton (1876, for Bell's son-in-law and daughter Mrs Ada Godman). Of the decoration at Palace Green Aymer Vallance remarked:

'It would be a rash statement to affirm of the decoration of any single apartment, that it was absolutely the best example of the style it obeyed. Yet if even it were safe to speak thus unreservedly, it might be concerning the beautiful dining-room at the Earl of Carlisle's House, Palace Green, representing as it does the united efforts of Burne-Jones, William Morris and Philip Webb.' (*The Studio*, 1898.)

Not every comment was so appreciative. Norman Shaw, in a moment of exasperation, exclaimed: 'William Morris was a great man who somehow delighted in glaring wallpaper.'

Webb's architectural commissions that came through the firm gave him an unusual measure of control over the final result. He may have resented the flamboyance of some of Morris's interiors because they obscured the details over which he took such pains, but his dictatorial attitude towards his patrons confirms the satisfaction that he derived from his position as total arbiter. The strength of the Morris team lay in the exceptional skills of the individual members. Webb's originality as an architect and designer was matched by the artistic talents of Rossetti, Burne-Jones and Madox Brown, and the capacity – amounting to genius – of Morris himself for flat pattern design.

Three early wallpaper designs for Morris & Co., 'Fruit', 'Trellis' (PL. 113) and 'Daisy', recall the Red House and its garden (PL. 73). 'Trellis' of 1862 with its birds by Webb, was inspired by the rose trellis enclosing an old-fashioned garden at the side of the house. The design for 'Daisy' wallpaper and matching tiles was based on embroidered hangings in coloured wools on blue serge devised by Morris for the principal bedroom at the Red House. These were derived from miniatures in a fifteenth-century manuscript of Froissart's *Chronicles*, in the British Museum but perhaps known to Morris through a publication by H. N. Humphrey, *Illuminated Books of the Middle Ages* (1844–9; see *William Morris and the Middle Ages*, Whitworth Art Gallery, University of Manchester, 1984, no. 56).

The 'Daisy' wallpaper was designed in 1862 and first issued in 1864, but was one of the most perennially popular. The simple but evocative pattern marked its owner as an aesthete without resorting to theatrical effects. The paper was often used in combination with the 'Sussex' (PL. 111) or 'Rossetti' (PL. 110) chairs of stained beech, or the bobbin-turned reclining chair named the 'Morris'. All these were to be staple products of the firm until it closed in the 1940s. Mackail, recognizing the crucial place of the vernacular revival in design reform, remarked: 'Of all specific minor improvements in common household objects due to Morris, the rush-bottomed Sussex chair perhaps takes first place. It was not his own invention, but was copied with trifling improvements from an old chair of village manufacture picked up in Sussex.' (p. 180.)

The 'Sussex' prototype was allegedly found by Madox Brown, who devised his own version with a distinctive round rushed seat and turned spindles in the form of a cross at the back. The 'Rossetti' chair is based on a provincial French model in common use in the early nineteenth century. The adjustable 'Morris' chair was devised from a traditional prototype, also found in Sussex by the firm's business manager George Warrington Taylor, in the Herstmonceux workshop of a carpenter named Ephraim Colman. He sent a description and sketch to Webb in about 1866, and the chair was in production from about 1870. It was susbsequently widely plagiarized, notably by the American Gustav Stickley, whose version of the 'Morris' was made at his Craftsman's Workshops in Grand Rapids, Michigan.

With the main elements of the Morris company now in place, the 1870s saw an expansion of the commercially important wallpaper range and the introduction of textile weaving and printing. Retail premises at 449 Oxford Street were acquired in 1877, by which time Morris was in control of the renamed Morris & Co. In the second stage of activities all imputations of amateurism were dropped. The high quality of production which Morris had extorted from his producers and strove so hard to maintain became an important element in the success of the firm.

Opposite PL. 106 Philip Webb: writing table of oak with brass handles; designed for the firm, between 1860 and 1868. The simple but sophisticated table was made for Major Gillum. Webb was still exploring abstract ideas, as in the 1862 japanned chair (PL. 94). The woollen tapestry hanging is 'Peacock and Dragon', and the rose-coloured carpet with patterned border is a version of the 'McCulloch' design (illustrated in the Morris & Co. catalogue), both from a later phase of the firm's production. Major Gillum had lost a leg in the Crimea, when he left the army he returned to lead a congenial life of patronage and philanthropy. He was Madox Brown's friend and patron, owning among other works the small version of *The Last of England*. Webb made designs for Gillum over a long period (see also PL. 76).

PL. 107 Philip Webb or Ford Madox Brown: oak swing toilet mirror, the position adjustable with a curved arm and pin; designed *c*.1862. A rare example of domestic furniture from a very early stage of the firm. Another mirror is shown at Kelmscott Manor on a dressing table by Ford Madox Brown, both of which are credited to him (see Newman and Watkinson, 1991, pl. 950). In character and manufacture it is close to the side table designed by Webb and made for Major Gillum (PL. 106) at about this date.

PL. 108 Philip Webb: circular table; designed in the 1860s to be made in walnut. Here Webb is still playing with turned stretchers in geometric arrangements. The table remained in production by the firm for a long period, and can be recognized in photographs of Swan House, Chelsea, designed by Norman Shaw for Wickham Flower, with decoration by Morris; and in a model with a circular stretcher for the library at Tangley Manor, where Webb made alterations and additions and Morris provided the decorations, also for Wickham Flower, in 1885.

PL. 109 Philip Webb: music stand or whatnot, ebonized and turned wood; designed for the firm, *c*.1864. The densely black panels are relieved by delicate turnings of great refinement. The piece is recognizable in one of the Birket Foster family photographs of The Hill, Witley, the house decorated and furnished by Morris from 1864, an early commission pre-dating the work on the Armoury in St James's Palace and the Green Dining Room at the South Kensington Museum. Other versions of the whatnot were made, with painted decoration on the side panels and shelf supports, and were used at The Hill for the display of a collection of antique china. Another type can be seen in photographs of the drawing room at Swan House. A photograph of the Morris premises at 449 Oxford Street, thought to have been taken in the present century, shows a further version in the window.

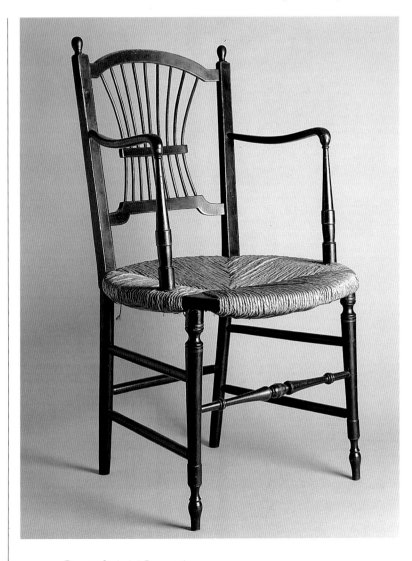

PL. 110 Dante Gabriel Rossetti: 'Rossetti' chair, ebonized wood with red painted details on the turning; designed for the firm, *c.*1865. Henry Treffry Dunn made a watercolour of Rossetti's sitting room in the house at Cheyne Walk which shows on the right a 'Rossetti' chair with red painted decoration. Although the chair was an enduringly popular model in the firm's production, red painted examples are uncommon and may have been made to special order.

PL. 111 William Morris: 'Sussex' chair, ebonized wood; the prototype was a country model of a 'Sheraton Fancy Chair', found in the workshop of a Sussex carpenter in 1865. The 'Sussex' chair was chosen by Birket Foster for The Hill at Witley, the rusticity fitting well with the idyllic rural atmosphere of the house, where Morris was again at work in 1866.

The 'Sussex' chair became a symbol for the Morris look. With the 'Daisy' wallpaper it remained in production throughout the firm's existence. The chairs retailed very cheaply – at 7 shillings (35p) around the turn of the century – and were in demand for institutional use, for example at Cambridge in the Hall of Newnham College and the Fitzwilliam Museum.

Above PL. 112 William Morris: *Geoffrey Chaucer Reading*; tile, painted 1864. Rossetti was the model for Chaucer, and the subject was used also for stained glass, for example in a window roundel at The Hill.

Right PL. 113 William Morris: design for the 'Trellis' wallpaper; 1862. Of this pattern Aymer Vallance wrote: 'The first wall-paper to be designed [Nov. 1862], though it came third in order of production, consists of a trellis, which gives its name to the pattern, intertwining roses, somewhat stiff in growth, and brown birds here and there among the branches, Morris diffidently refrained from designing the bird forms with his own hand, preferring to have them drawn by Mr Philip Webb.' (*William Morris: His Art, His Writings and His Public Life*, 1987, p. 87)

PL. 114 Edward Burne-Jones: two three-tile panels, from a set depicting Chaucer's *Dream of Good Women*; 1863. A version of the fireplace tile-panels used by Morris at The Hill, Witley. The pictorial tiles were painted by Lucy Faulkner; at this early date Morris was still treating tiles as pictorial space, not considering their geometric potential and ignoring the dividing lines as an irrelevance. He did not make use of the technical advantages of printing the outline, believing that the delicate brushstrokes of hand painting contributed to the effect he wished to obtain. At The Hill Morris was trying to create a modern version of a medieval painted interior. The pictorial themes were carried out in large tile panels, of which there were six throughout the house; Birket Foster's billiard room was decorated with a large overmantel showing scenes from *Cinderella* and inscribed: 'This is the Story of the Maid with Shoes of Glass and how she became Queen that was before called Cinder-Wench'; there were similar overmantels in the bedrooms. The same pictorial theme was continued in the stained glass 'King René' panels (see PL. 91) and in Burne-Jones's painted panels round the walls of the dining room telling the legend of St George.

Burges and Viollet-le-Duc

When an artist dies young, as Pugin did, there is inevitable speculation as to how he would have developed had he lived. The work of his followers offers some clues. Pugin's development was radical and rapid. In two decades he had gone from the delicate and fanciful Gothic of the Regency to the severest expression of the structural Reformed manner. It is difficult to imagine a further paring down of the elements than he had already achieved in, for example, the table designed for Crace to manufacture on behalf of 'poor vicars' (PL. 38). Street alone seems to have understood the rules; honest workmanship and materials combined with visible constructional elements and absence of all extraneous ornament are the characteristics of this trestle table and the circular Cuddesdon table (PL. 75). The line of Puginesque design in the next generation can be traced through Street's influence to Philip Webb.

Pugin's didactic and influential architectural publications of the 1830s show his progress at about midway. The 1851 Exhibition Medieval Court (PL. 59) organized only one year before his death does him less than justice. The clear thinking of his maturity is best exemplified in his pattern books, notably *Floriated Ornament* (1849), which influenced Dresser and Voysey. Burges became an ardent advocate of Pugin when he received a copy of *Contrasts between the Architecture of the 15th and the 19th Centuries* on his fourteenth birthday.

Burges's admiration was not unqualified. He recognized that Pugin had not solved the problem of adapting his Gothic sources to secular use. In 1868, when he was about to embark on his own most fully evolved medieval interiors, he remarked:

> 'We can all form a fairly correct idea of the interior of a Medieval church, but we find it much more difficult to realize the interior of a Medieval house, with its painted walls, its illuminated ceilings, its partially stained glass windows, its embroideries and its furniture, historiated in colours and gold. We have done one or two splendid churches; but none of the houses built in the Medieval style give us the faintest idea of the glories of a thirteenth-century domestic interior. I wish I could praise the Houses of Parliament on this head, but I cannot. In fact, the Medieval interior, or rather, the interior founded on Medieval Art has yet to be done.'

Burges was writing a blueprint for his own experiments.

Even in his earliest work Burges rejected the spare simplicity of Pugin's unornamented oak furniture. His 1856 competition design for Lille Cathedral features a great painted organ case, presage of painted cabinets to come. The public was to have a taste of these in the 1859 London Architectural Exhibition and in the 1862 Exhibition Medieval Court. Elaborated and enriched, the painted style eventually all but overwhelmed Burges's own Tower House in Melbury Road, London. Burges fulfilled several commissions as an architect, notably St Fin Barre's Cathedral in Cork, over which there were many arguments about money; but he was shielded from the full rigour of commercial reality by a private income and his relationship with his principal patron, the Marquess of Bute.

From 1865 until Burges's death sixteen years later he and Lord Bute were fellow conspirators. With a patron only eighteen years old and of legendary wealth, and an architect who himself had never grown up and to whom the word restraint was anathema, nothing very practical was to be expected. At Cardiff Castle (PL. 118) they created a fairy-tale palace, fantastic inside and out. Mixing Moresque detail with medieval painted decoration, carving, gilding, panelling, coffering and tiling in a bewildering cacophony of colour and pattern, Burges's eclecticism had many detractors when the drawing for the Great Staircase was exhibited at the Royal Academy in 1874. The critic in *Building News* was of the opinion that the design was 'one of the least happy that we have seen from Mr Burges's pencil'. His friend Godwin was appreciative:

> 'Mr Burges was accustomed to follow the bent of his genius sometimes rather eccentrically, and always without much regard to the decorative or architectural fashions of the hour, and hence he was not in the usual sense a popular man, but probably no one of his contemporaries understood so well what may be called the iconography of ancient buildings, or had a more fertile power of expression by means of decorative art. His house in Melbury-road is well known to artists, to whom it will probably long continue to be an object of interest. It was upon this house that he lavished his fortune, drawing hints from all styles, yet doing nothing in a fragmentary or piecemeal way, and infusing into the whole an intensely medieval spirit. His drinking cups of pure crystal, inlaid with rubies, and numberless other rare and beautiful objects, have perhaps furnished as much food for gossip of that kind which in other days was excited by the wonders of Fonthill.' ('The Late Mr William Burges', *British Architect*, 1881.)

The furniture was equally lavish, some of it ordered from Gillow's and some made to Burges's designs in a workshop set up in the castle by Lord Bute. The decoration was carried out by the recently founded firm of Campbell, Smith & Co. Meanwhile, Lord Bute had fixed on the ruined fourteenth-century Castell Coch, on an outlying

part of his Cardiff property, for further experiments in reconstruction. In 1872 Burges presented an archaeological report to Lord Bute, with a proposal to restore the property to provide 'a Country residence for your occasional occupation in summer'. At Castell Coch (PL. 116) the debt to Viollet-le-Duc is more apparent than at Cardiff Castle. Greater restraint in the reconstruction of the exterior and in the interior decoration make for an impressive and more legible idea of the potential of the romantic medieval style. Both castles survive, rare examples of the full panoply of flamboyant Gothic applied to domestic design.

The spirit of fantasy imbued all Burges's furniture and metalwork. He had no need to temper his ideas to utility or public taste and no ambitions in the commercial arena, and his work remained outside the mainstream of nineteenth-century design.

Left PL. 115 Eugène Viollet-le-Duc: Château de Pierrefonds; fireplace wall and segments of the vaulted and painted Salle de l'Imperatrice completed before the cessation of work in 1870. This chromolithographic plate shows the pointed vaults are decorated with trailing foliage and birds in cool Beaux-Arts tones, quite distinct from the consciously medieval colouring at Cardiff.

Above PL. 116 William Burges: vaulted ceiling at Castell Coch, painted with birds and trailing foliage, the ribs ornamented with butterflies; *c*.1879.

In a British context Burges's work for Lord Bute looks uniquely extravagant and irrelevant, working stubbornly against the grain of the highly regarded political theories proposed by Thomas Carlyle and John Ruskin that were shaping progress in architecture and design. However, the close parallels with Viollet-le-Duc's reconstruction and decoration of the French medieval castles at Pierrefonds and Roquetaillarde place Burges's work in a wider European context. In 1857 the restoration of the ruined late fourteenth-century Château de Pierrefonds, north of Paris, was ordered by Napoleon III. In 1863, with the exterior well advanced, the Emperor decided that the rooms should be made habitable. Viollet started to design interiors (PL. 115) and furniture that were intended to re-create the atmosphere of the late Middle Ages, using the knowledge gained while compiling his carefully researched *Dictionnaire raisonné du mobilier français de l'époque carolingienne à la renaissance*, which appeared from 1858. The work at Pierrefonds was unfinished at the outbreak of the Franco-Prussian War in 1870, and the fall of the Third Empire in the following year prevented the completion of a magnificent conception.

The Château Neuf de Roquetaillarde, near Bordeaux, one of the finest surviving early fourteenth-century structures in France, had been carefully surveyed by the historian Leo Drouyn, and it was he who in 1864 recommended its restoration by Viollet. The fabric of Roquetaillarde was better preserved than that of Pierrefonds, and Viollet's reconstruction was less doctrinaire. Coincidentally, the castle has similarities to nearby Villandraut, which was built on the same plan as the Welsh fortresses of the early fourteenth century, possibly by the same engineers. The Welsh connection cannot have escaped Burges as he laboured on the reconstruction of the fourteenth-century Castell Coch and the fifteenth-century Cardiff.

One of Viollet's pupils, Edmond Duthoit, was largely responsible for the decorative schemes at Roquetaillarde. He had trained as a sculptor in his family workshop, and then acted as a draughtsman on a long expedition to Syria and the Lebanon led by Comte Melchior de Voguë in 1861. He was in Viollet's office in 1864 when the work on Roquetaillarde began. The eclectic mixture of sources – medievalism spiced with Islamic references – can be directly compared with the interiors at Cardiff. The furniture, again based on the examples in Viollet's *Dictionnaire du mobilier*, was made by Tricot and Jeancourt of Paris, who encountered unforeseen difficulties in the finishing of the gilded and coloured pieces with their innumerable coats of lacquer. Painted furniture of this type was unfamiliar in France. Roquetaillarde is a valuable survival, the interiors, among the rarest of their date in France, giving an insight into the lost opportunities at Pierrefonds.

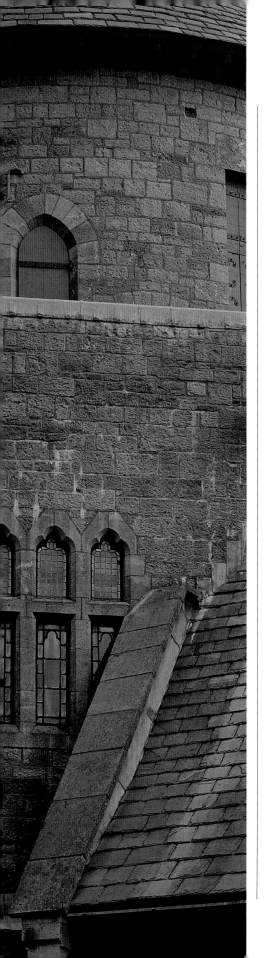

Left PL. 117 Castell Coch was a picturesque ruin, uninhabited since the late Middle Ages. Burges drew up a plan for its renovation in the early 1870s and the work started in 1875. Even though the exterior was completed in 1879, the intricate work on the interiors took a further twenty years. The interiors are reminiscent of the richly coloured splendours of Cardiff Castle, but the conception is more delicate, appropriate to a summer retreat. The result is strikingly similar to Viollet-le-Duc's restoration project for Napoleon III at the Château de Pierrefonds.

Right PL. 118 William Burges: the clock tower at Cardiff Castle; one of the most conspicuous features of a sensational essay in scenic architecture. The debt to Barry and Pugin's clock tower at the Palace of Westminster is unmistakable. In 1865 the eighteen-year-old Marquess of Bute retained Burges to report on the possibility of restoring the Castle. The main task was to bring order and a greater semblance of authenticity to the muddle of Georgian Gothick lodgings that Henry Holland had contrived in about 1776. The collaboration of these two men, separated in age by twenty years but with a consuming common passion for their medievalizing architectural projects, was to continue until the architect's death in 1881.

Above PL. 119 William Burges: detail from the crenellated wall at Cardiff Castle. W. H. Mallock, writing in 1920, remembers the completed Castle as it was when he had visited as Lord Bute's guest: 'Cardiff Castle, till late in the nineteenth century, was mainly, though not wholly, ruinous, and some decades ago it was, at enormous expense, reconstructed by the late Lord Bute. All the lore of the architectural antiquarian was ransacked in order to consummate this feat. Indeed the wealth of detail accumulated and reproduced by him will be held by many people to have defeated its own ends. Ornaments, carvings, colourings, of which ancient castles may severally offer single or a few specimens, were here crowded together in such emphatic profusion as to fill the mind of the spectator with something novel rather than of anything antique.' (W. H. Mallock, *Memoirs of Life and Literature*, 1920, p. 117)

Right PL. 120 Alfred Waterhouse: detail of carving from the entrance to the Natural History Museum, London, 1877.

PL. 121 William Burges: claret jug
and decanter; 1870. Chinese *sang-
de-boeuf* vase mounted in silver gilt
set with semiprecious stones in
filigree mounts; an inscription on
the foot reads WILLIELMUS:BVRGES:
EX:LIBRO:SUO:ANO:DNI:MDCCCLXX.
This was one of the pieces selected,
as requested in his will, by Lord
and Lady Bute after Burges's
death in 1881.

PL. 122 William Burges: Zodiac
tile panel, painted by Henry
Stacy Marks; from Eaton Hall,
reconstructed in the French
Gothic style for the Duke of
Westminster by Alfred
Waterhouse, 1870–2. The Zodiac
procession was first used on a settle
dating from 1869–71, for Burges's
rooms at 15 Buckingham Street.
The procession of grotesque
figures derives ultimately from
Dürer's *Dance of Death*.

THE ART MOVEMENT

The Art Movement merged Gothic with the Queen Anne Revival and the vernacular style, adding Japonisme, Egyptian Moresque and other exotic influences. It dominated avant-garde domestic design in the years after the 1862 Exhibition. This was a time of optimism and lavish patronage for architecture and design: 'There has assuredly never been since the world began an age in which people thought, talked, wrote and spent such inordinate sums of money and hours of time in cultivating and indulging their tastes.' (*Furniture Gazette*, vol. v, 1876, p. 76.)

The origins of the Art Movement pre-date the 1862 Exhibition. Designers who were to be identified with the Movement had already been playing with the elements of the style in the 1850s. William Morris was devising and making painted furniture for his rooms in Red Lion Square as early as 1856, and was soon encouraging his wife and sister-in-law to attempt large-scale embroideries (which he called tapestries, in medievalizing vein) for the embellishment of the Red House. At the Exhibition Morris's pieces were complemented by the remarkable group of large painted cabinets by Burges, who had already made a considerable impact in this area at the Architectural Exhibition in 1859. Painted furniture and 'Art' needlework were to be key elements in the artistic interior.

The Art Movement embraced all aspects of fine and decorative art, from painting and sculpture to fire grates and china bedroom sets. The most successful exponents, such as Godwin, had a breadth of artistic experience and appreciation that went far beyond mere professionalism. As well as architects, many were painters, for example, Burne-Jones and Walter Crane; and collectors, such as Burges and Rossetti. Artists' houses were among the first showcases of the Movement. Collecting, traditionally the prerogative of the rich connoisseur, had become the province of the artist-aesthete. It was this common interest that forged the eclectic language of the Art Movement.

In the work of Burges the synthesis was complete, his antiquarian interests merging with his romantic Gothic vision. The collector's find became the core of a decorative object that evolved from it. He enmeshed Chinese *sang de boeuf* pots or glass vessels in silver mounts studded with Greek coins, antique gems, Chinese jade and Persian seals (PL. 121) to evoke a romantic vision of the distant past. These objects were housed in cabinets whose painted panels told of their functions through allusion and a literary imagery far more subtle than the pictorial pieces in Morris's Red House.

With the groundwork of the Gothic Revival as a solid base, architecture expanded into the realms of 'Old English' and 'Queen Anne', with furniture and fittings to match. The architect Sir Thomas Graham Jackson wrote:

> 'It was not the letter, but the spirit of Gothic architecture which was of use to us: its frank conformity to circumstance, its glorious liberty from the fetters of dogma that oppressed its classic sister, its ready response to the calls of construction, its unaffected naturalism, and its welcome acceptance of fresh ideas and principles.' (Basil Jackson, *Recollections of Thomas Graham Jackson*, 1950, p. 121.)

Two young men exemplify this imaginative transition. At Ramsgate in September 1852, unnoticed in the crowd at Pugin's funeral stood William Eden Nesfield, aged seventeen, and his friend Richard Norman Shaw, aged twenty-one. Pursuing their homage to this great preceptor, the two young men then managed to obtain permission to climb the scaffolding of the still unfinished Palace of Westminster to take notes of design details. In just the fashion described by Jackson, Nesfield and Shaw made the imaginative leap into Queen Anne through discovering the vernacular. In September

1862 – coincidentally the tenth anniversary of Pugin's funeral – Nesfield and Shaw made a sketching tour in Sussex looking for vernacular subjects. Their sketchbooks survive, an invaluable record of the models that formed the vernacular vocabulary.

One page of Nesfield's 1862 sketchbook is a potent document of the Art Movement; juxtaposed are 'A curious Settle at the George & Dragon Inn' and 'Ancient Egyptian chairs from Der Styl' (Gottfried Semper's recently issued *Der Stil*, 1861–3). The Egyptian pieces are the celebrated Thebes chairs and stools from the British Museum. Eastlake thought the Gothic designs of Shaw and Nesfield 'too quaint and archaic . . . such work is too exotic and far-fetched for ordinary appreciation.' He noted the vernacular details of the building and the Japanese character of the interior ornament in Nesfield's 1862 Gothic Revival house, Cloverley Hall in Shropshire. This was to be the mixture that formed the basis of Art Movement architecture and design.

Awareness of Japanese art, a noteworthy novelty at the 1862 Exhibition, added new spatial dimensions to the structural language of Reformed Gothic – Godwin was to claim that he was inspired by Japanese architecture. The Egyptian finds from Thebes provided furniture types, a conspicuous lack in the Japanese domestic environment which boasted only low tea tables, headrests and altar tables. Other Eastern cultures provided pattern and fresh constructional materials, such as the fretted ironwork and tile-hung interiors of Alhambran or Moresque inspiration.

PL. 123 Panel of a screen; detail from PL. 156.

Professional Designers in the 1860s and 1870s

The Paris 1867 Exhibition had a mission, which had been outlined by Napoleon in 1863. It was to outdo the British, who in 1862 had shown disquieting advance in taste and technical capacity. On the return of the French exhibitors from London he had remarked, 'I congratulate you upon your energy and your perseverance to rival a nation which is in advance of us in certain branches of industry.' One of the reasons for the Emperor's unease may have been the enormous effort that the British manufacturers had put into rivalling the French on their own ground. For example, Jackson & Graham recruited expert French workmen to improve the quality of their gilt bronze furniture mounts, an area in which the French had previously been unsurpassed.

In 1867, with an exhibition three times the size of its predecessor in 1855 and Paris at the peak of prosperity and popularity, Napoleon expected no less than the overthrow of these aesthetic upstarts. The British still held their own; Holland & Sons showed a technically sophisticated cabinet by Bruce Talbert which incorporated enamel plaques and gilded 'galvano-plastic' relief panels, made by an electroplating process, subsequently featured in Talbert's *Gothic Forms Applied to Furniture, Metalwork and Decoration for Domestic Purposes* (1868). The exhibits were classified by type rather than by nationality, a departure from the original idea and one which paved the way for the trade-orientated exhibitions in the seventies.

As early as 1855 the Emperor's cousin, Prince Napoleon, as overall comptroller of the 1867 Exhibition, had foreseen the limited scope of successive International Exhibitions as popular public spectacles. In the early seventies the almost annual shows all over the world demonstrated only too clearly the law of diminishing returns. After the financial success of the Great Exhibition profits had been elusive, and now inspiration was running out. Commercial considerations dominated the displays, and the general tone of the jury reports reflected public disappointment. As a means of publicizing their wares, manufacturers were beginning to find that the increasingly numerous periodicals offered more useful publicity, and they ceased to support the exhibitions in sufficient numbers. After 1874 the annual shows specializing in different trades instituted in London by Henry Cole were discontinued. It would be wrong to suggest that the displays were devoid of interest. Individual objects of considerable distinction continued to be shown by good firms. The trade wars encouraged by Napoleon were waged without bitterness; in the early seventies British manufacturers offered the hospitality of their stands to their French counterparts during the Franco-Prussian War and in the impoverished years of France's subsequent economic collapse.

At the 1871 International Exhibition in London the emphasis was on the furniture and cabinet-making trades. Collinson & Lock Art Furnishers, founded in that very year by two of Jackson & Graham's former employees, showed T. E. Collcutt's ebonized cabinet with panels ascribed to Albert Moore (PL. 170), which was to be described by Charles Handley-Read as 'one of the most original, attractive and influential pieces of furniture ever designed by a Victorian architect' (*World Furniture*, 'England 1830–1901', 1965, p. 255). Certainly it was a pioneering example of the taste for ebonized and painted pieces.

It is perhaps a measure of the increasing scarcity of new designs that Collcutt's cabinet was repeated for the 1873 Exhibition in Vienna and for the 1876 Exhibition at Philadelphia. On Collinson & Lock's stand at the Vienna Exhibition there were also pieces of greater distinction designed by Godwin, including the 'Lucretia' cabinet with panels by Fairfax Murray. This, too, was repeated for Philadelphia. Talbert's 'Pet' sideboard, made for the Vienna Exhibition by Gillow's, was bought for the South Kensington Museum. The severe and structured form is enriched with carving of great refinement. Jackson & Graham contributed a spectacular cabinet – it has been suggested that at £4,000 it may have been the most expensive piece of Victorian furniture ever made – of ebony inlaid with ivory, lapis lazuli and other semi-precious stones forming monograms and armorial bearings. It was made for Thomas, Earl Bective, MP for the county of Westmorland, and is now known only from a description.

PL. 124 Charles Bevan: 'New
Registered Reclining Chair';
made under licence by Marsh
& Jones of Leeds, and advertised
in the trade press in 1865. The
chair embodies within a Gothic
framework the structural and
engineering precepts central to
design reform as envisaged by
Pugin in the 1840s.

PL. 125 Charles Bevan:
davenport, oak inlaid with various
woods; made by Marsh & Jones,
*c.*1864. It is strongly influenced by
Seddon's 1862 roll-top desk
(PL. 82). A design for a similar
piece was published in the *Building
News* in 1865. Bevan used
accessible sources such as Ruskin's
Stones of Venice to arrive at a
synthesis of Reformed Gothic
ideas suited to a marketable style.

Left PL. 126 Charles Bevan: detail from the door panel of an oak buffet with geometric inlay in various woods; made for Titus Salt by Marsh & Jones, 1865–6. Titus Salt Jr was Bevan's most important patron. His father, a textile magnate, had created Saltaire, a model works and village for his employees; the younger man's creation was Milner Field, built in the woods above Saltaire by Thomas Harris, 1872–3, its theatrical style an ideal setting for Bevan's flamboyantly ornamented 'Modern Gothic Furniture'.

Opposite PL. 127 Bruce Talbert: 'Pericles' Gothic cabinet, oak and fruitwood with marquetry inlay and brass hinges; made by Holland & Sons. This important Gothic piece was a Grand Prix winner at the 1867 Paris Exhibition, where the stature of the leading British manufacturers and professional designers was triumphantly confirmed. The Talbert Gothic cabinet made a great impact at the exhibition, and was widely illustrated and discussed. The *Art Journal* described it as 'certainly the most distinguished amongst competing Gothic works'.

Opposite, above left PL. 129 Charles Bevan: semi-grand piano by John Broadwood; case panelled and inlaid with various woods, by Gillow's of Lancaster, 1871. In 1867 Bevan designed a grand piano with inlaid decoration ornamenting the whole of the case for Titus Salt.

Left PL. 128 Charles Eastlake: oak cabinet with inlay and painted panels; made by Heaton, Butler and Bayne. Shown in the 1867 Exhibition. The panels, painted by Clement Heaton, show an early use of gold background, later a hallmark of 'artistic' cabinet decoration. The cabinet is illustrated as the frontispiece of Eastlake's influential *Hints on Household Taste* (1868), which consisted of proselytizing articles on domestic decoration and furniture originally written for the *Cornhill Magazine* and *The Queen*, recast and collected in book form.

Left PL. 131 Side table, possibly designed by J. P. Seddon; made by Gillow's. Seddon combined his architectural career with designing for his family firm and for other cabinet-making firms when the Seddon firm closed. A table of this pattern can be seen in one of the Birket Foster family photographs of The Hill, Witley. Even though the number of designers involved with the furniture at The Hill makes firm attributions difficult, there are documented Reformed Gothic pieces by Seddon, related to the 1862 Medieval Court.

Above PL. 130 Bruce Talbert: buffet, oak inlaid with various woods; made by Holland & Sons, *c*.1867. A version of this design is illustrated in Talbert's *Gothic Forms Applied to Furniture and Decoration for Domestic Purposes* (1867). This book set out for the consumer an achievable modernity, using furniture and decorations available from manufacturers. Talbert had trained as an architect in Glasgow but turned to designing furniture and metalwork in the 1860s, for Doveston, Bird & Hull of Manchester and for the Skidmore Art Manufactures Co. of Coventry. Working from a London base he set a pattern for the career of a professional designer.

Left PL. 132 Tile panel, possibly designed by Seddon; made by Maw & Co. Shown at the Paris 1867 Exhibition. The 'Peacock' motif appears as a chapter heading in J. Moyr Smith's *Ornamental Interiors* (1887); Moyr Smith was Dresser's pupil, trained in his studio from 1867 to 1871.

Below PL. 133 J. P. Seddon: jardinière, stoneware, in the form of a French Gothic capital; designed for C. J. Bailey's Fulham Pottery, 1877.

Above PL. 135 Bruce Talbert: flagon of parcel-gilt silver; made by Skidmore Art Manufacturers Co., 1866–7.

Right PL. 136 Bruce Talbert: large table clock, decorated wood and brass case with wrought and painted ironwork; made by Skidmore Art Manufacturers Co., *c.*1865.

Opposite, below right PL. 134 Bruce Talbert: triangular Gothic clock case of wrought brass; made by Cox & Co., or Hart, Son, Peard & Co., *c.*1870. A similar clock is included on a page of designs credited to Bruce Talbert in the Cox & Co. catalogue of 1871. A version of this model in the Museum für Angewandte Kunst in Vienna was purchased, according to the receipt, from Hart. Subcontracting among manufacturers was common in the nineteenth century.

Left PL. 137 Christopher Dresser: detail of a cast iron hallstand; designed for the Coalbrookdale Company. Shown at the 1867 Exhibition. The most complex of Dresser's many designs for iron furniture, this large hallstand re-creates the High Victorian Gothic used for painted and gilded furniture in terms of monochrome low-relief sculpture. A modified version of this pattern, the 'Gothic Hall Table', was illustrated in the *Furniture Gazette* in 1876. Jones's pupil and collaborator on the *Grammar of Ornament*, Dresser had a great natural aptitude for decorative design and pattern making.

Above PL. 139 Christopher Dresser: vase with coloured and gilded decoration; designed for Minton's, date marked 1866. Shown at the 1867 Exhibition.

Opposite, right PL. 138 Christopher Dresser: vase with coloured and gilded decoration on an ivory ground; designed for Minton's. Shown at the 1867 Exhibition.

Left PL. 140 Christopher Dresser: unglazed earthenware plant pot, decorated with an abstract design symbolizing 'Truth, Beauty, Power'; designed for Josiah Wedgwood & Sons, 1867. The motif was adapted for Plate 12 in *Principles of Design* (1873), where Dresser explains his sources of inspiration as 'the bursting buds of spring, when the energy of growth is at its maximum, and especially such as are to be seen in the spring growth of a luxuriant tropical vegetation; I have also availed myself of those forms to be seen in certain bones of birds which are associated with the organs of flight, and which give us an impression of great strength, as well as those observable in the powerful propelling fins of certain fish.' (p. 17.)

Right PL. 141 Christopher Dresser: abstract pattern for stained glass, c.1867–71; from an album assembled by Dresser from all phases of his design career. In a paper 'Ornamentation considered as high art' before the Royal Society of Arts, which set out views similar to those expressed in *The Art of Decorative Design* (1862), Dresser stated: '. . . that true ornamentation is of purely mental origin, and consists of symbolised imagination or emotion only. I therefore argue that ornamentation is not only fine art, but that it is high art . . . even a higher art than that practised by the pictorial artist, as it is wholly of mental origin . . .'

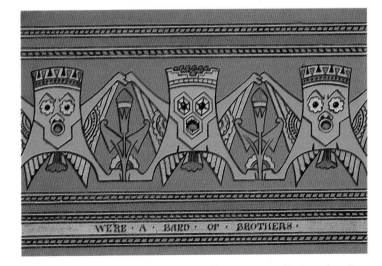

Above PL. 142 Christopher Dresser: 'Band of Brothers' frieze pattern for a Minton cylindrical vase shape; exhibited in London, 1871; from the same album as PL. 141.

Left PL. 143 Owen Jones: detail of mirror frame, ebony veneer with ivory inlays; made by Jackson & Graham. Shown at the 1867 Exhibition. The mirror and display cabinets of the same design furnished a room, which had been added to Alfred Morrison's country house at Fonthill in Wiltshire to house an extensive collection of Chinese porcelain. Described in *The Builder* as built, decorated and fitted up by Jackson & Graham 'from Mr Jones's designs in the Cinquecento style', the room contained many of the finest objects from the Summer Palace in Peking, which had been looted and burned at the end of the Second Opium War in 1860. Morrison's collection provided Jones with material for his *Grammar of Chinese Ornament* (1867).

Right PL. 145 Owen Jones: 'Stanhope' wallpaper design; for Jackson & Graham, *c.*1870.

Opposite, *right* PL. 144 Owen Jones: detail of arm of sofa, the frame inlaid with various woods; designed for Alfred Morrison, 1867; made by Jackson & Graham.

Opposite PL. 146 Owen Jones: 'Sultan' silk fabric; made by Warner's, *c.*1870.

Right PL. 147 Christopher Dresser: silk damask; for James W. & C. Ward, 1871.

The Revelation
of Japan

*I*f we can now perceive, with hindsight, that the Medieval Court at the 1862 Exhibition signalled the end of the Gothic Revival, we can also see that the decision to include a Japanese Court marked the beginning of significant new design initiatives. In the nine years since Commodore Perry had sailed into the harbour at Okinawa, trade with the West had enormously increased and interest in Japanese art and artefacts had spread beyond the group of collectors, many of them artists, who were the first enthusiasts. William Burges was one of the earliest collectors of Japanese prints; but the influence of these on his work is so subtle as to defy precise analysis. They taught him a 'horror of regularity', as we can readily appreciate, and he made no secret of his admiration for Japanese culture, writing of the display at the Exhibition: 'To any student of our reviving arts of the thirteenth century an hour or even a day or two spent in the Japanese Department will by no means be lost time, for these hitherto unknown barbarians appear not only to know all that the Middle Ages knew but in some respects are beyond them and us as well.'

The Japanese Court led to an outbreak of what amounted to Japanese mania. However, the public view of Japan was distorted by the fact that the exhibit consisted of lacquer, bronzes, netsuke and porcelain (PL. 148) from the personal collection of the first British Minister in Japan, Sir Rutherford Alcock, 'Her Majesty's Envoy to the Tycoon'. The emphasis on curiosities and items which the public were expected to find amusing augured ill for the inevitable 'novelties' to come. Commercial exploitation resulted in what can only be described as Japanese props, like theatrical scenery. Nevertheless, the thoughtful use of Japanese forms and pictorial ideas produced a new and exciting phase in decorative design.

On the July day in 1853 when four ships under the command of the American Commodore Matthew Galbraith Parry sailed into Tokyo Bay, Japan had been in political, cultural and commercial isolation for nearly 250 years. The tiny trickle of Japanese art that had already reached Europe by the Dutch trade routes, with their limited traffic through Nagasaki, had prepared an audience eager for more, an eagerness that did not diminish as the trickle became a flood. Siegfried Bing was to describe it in the first issue (1888) of his important periodical *Le Japon artistique*, with prescience, as 'art nouveau'; it was, he said, 'a fresh form of art, quite startling in its novelty'.

Japanese art had a dual appeal. Decoratively, it offered an exotic world depicted with an almost abstract formality that lent Japanese-inspired artefacts an instantaneous individuality; but an extra attraction came from the peculiar circumstances of Japanese development during the centuries of isolation, when cultural and artistic traditions had prospered at the expense of political and technological development. Native artists and craftsmen were seen as innocent of commercial exploitation and of the taint of industry, existing in a society that mirrored the idealized medieval world which haunted the writings of Carlyle, Ruskin and Pugin.

The temptation to be patronizing to these apparently innocent and backward people was irresistible. Taking their interest in the armaments of his ships as a good augury for future trading relations, Francis Hawks, chronicler of the American expedition, was confident 'of the comparatively easy introduction of foreign customs and habits among them, if not of the nobler principles and better life of a higher civilization' (quoted in Pat Barr, *The Deer Cry Pavilion*, 1968, p. 16). Commodore Perry presented his new trading partners with a demonstration model of a steam locomotive with a tender and carriage and 350 feet (107 m) of track of toylike proportions. When the first excitement of balancing on the roof of the carriage as it whirled round the track had worn off a little, the Japanese got down to the serious business of repairing the technological lacunae of centuries.

In a typically well-orchestrated operation the Japanese set about solving the problem of providing the West with desirable artefacts. Their new audience proved to be fascinated by intricate workmanship and complex techniques. Left without an occupation by the interdict on the weapons of the samurai, of which the sword and its furniture was traditionally a masterpiece of metalworking technique, the redundant craftsmen turned their talents to the making of *shakudo* (gold-copper alloy) ornaments which attracted many imitators in the West.

Looking to their accustomed mentors, the Chinese, for inspiration, they lighted in 1865 on the ancient technique of cloisonné enamel. This was to have an immediate and widespread impact in Europe. As early as 1867, European exhibitors at the International Exhibition in Paris were showing cloisonné pieces. By the early 1870s ceramic manufacturers, including Minton's, had devised a cloisonné style of decoration for ceramic wares (PL. 184).

The influence of Japan, which was to be crucial to the Aesthetic style, came intially through the works of art that had found their way to the West in the wake of Commodore Perry's expedition in 1853. In spite of continuing reluctance on the part of the Japanese authorities to open up completely to Western trade, from the mid-1850s a great variety of Japanese art objects were available in London and Paris. One of the first specialist shops was in Paris: La Porte chinoise, in the rue Vivienne. The dealer Murray Marks was active in London before 1862. Whistler and Rossetti were among his customers, and it was he who later assured the Pennells, Whistler's first biographers, that it was Whistler who had introduced the craze for blue-and-white china and Japanese art objects to London when he returned from Paris in 1859. Godwin is thought to have acquired the Japanese prints that decorated his walls at the auction of works of art that had arrived too late to be exhibited in 1862. W. E. Nesfield was a member of the circle, a Japanese enthusiast and collector; in his life of Nesfield, J.M. Brydon remarked that his room appeared like 'the studio of an artist rather than the business room of a professional man' (*Architectural Review*, i, 1897, p. 286).

To a large extent Western appreciation of Japanese art was to be of its quaintness at the expense of its subtlety. Entrepreneurs bought Japanese objects without any critical connoisseurship, but simply to satisfy the demand for items conforming to a preconceived idea of Japanese exoticism. Even Bing's *Le Japon artistique* was criticized for being simply a medium through which enterprising dealers inflated the demand for Japanese art: '*Artistic Japan* bids fair to be more mischievous than serviceable to the cause it espouses. Its letterpress is the work of men who substitute enthusiasm for knowledge. Instead of information we have rhapsodies; instead of research, vapouring.' (*The Japan Weekly Mail*, 30 March 1889.)

The Japanese were only too happy to provide this profitable export market with whatever was required, and, able to be patronizing in their turn, they developed a whole genre of decorative art devised specially to appeal to the West. Designers looking for inspiration were hampered by their lack of direct knowledge, but with the succession of the more enlightened and outward-looking Meiji regime (1868–1905) visitors from the West were welcomed.

PL. 148 The Japanese Court at the 1862 International Exhibition in London. A group of enamelled wares from the collection of Sir J. Rutherford Alcock, illustrated in Waring's *Masterpieces*.

Left PL. 149 J. McNeill Whistler: *Symphony in White II*, 1864. This painting, also known as 'The Little White Girl', was exhibited at the Royal Academy in 1865. It was one of a series of subjects suggested by Japanese prints, in which Whistler was feeling his way towards increasingly abstract composition – the title, with its musical allusions, confirms the artist's abstract conception. Joseph Pennell remarked: 'Now there was no masquerading in foreign finery. . . . The room was not littered with his purchases from the little shops in the Strand and the Rue de Rivoli.'

Above PL. 150 W. Eden Nesfield: *Medieval Architecture*, 1862; detail of binding. The embossed gilded patterns in an abstract transitional style illustrates the shift from archaeological Gothic to Japanese inspiration. These patterns reflect the subject matter of the books, for which the characteristic asymmetry of full-blown Japonisme would not have been appropriate.

Left PL. 151 Albert Moore: *Pomegranates*, 1866. A number of Moore's figure compositions at this date incorporate artistic furniture of medieval or Japanese inspiration.

Below PL. 153 Félix Bracquemond: dish from the 'Hokusai' service; designed for Rousseau, 1867, and presented to the South Kensington Museum by Rousseau himself after the service had been shown at the Paris Exhibition in 1867. The decoration was derived from Hokusai's *Mangwa*, an influential source of Japanese decorative motifs.

Right PL. 152 W. Eden Nesfield: figures copied from Japanese prints; a page from a sketchbook in use in the early 1860s. The two dated drawings in this book were made in 1862.

Above PL. 155 W. S. Coleman: jardinière, decorated with a Hokusai-inspired design, made by Minton & Co., 1869. Minton's commissioned designs from Coleman in emulation of the Rousseau-Bracquemond service (PL. 153).

Left PL. 154 E. J. Poynter: tiled Grill Room for the South Kensington Museum; detail of the grill, iron with brass fittings, made by Hart, Son, Peard & Co., 1866. The blue-and-white tiles with a chequered pattern and the pictorial tiles showing the Months and Seasons that line the walls were painted by the female students of the museum's porcelain class, and from 1871 by Minton, Campbell & Company's Art Studio in Gore Lane. The decoration was completed in 1873.

PL. 156 Screen of ebonized wood in six sections inset with panels of Chinese painting on silk, fretted and gilded decoration incorporating inscriptions and dedication; 1867. The design of the screen is attributed to William Eden Nesfield; it was a wedding present to Richard and Agnes Norman Shaw from James Forsyth, the sculptor who was responsible for making the writing cabinet designed by Norman Shaw in 1861 (PL. 88). At this date Nesfield was Norman Shaw's partner and Forsyth's chief patron and friend – Forsyth's son was given 'Nesfield' as his middle name – but the most cogent argument in favour of his authorship of this bold pioneering example of Japanese inspiration is stylistic. Motifs comparable with those used for the screen feature in the decoration of Cloverly Hall and at Farnham Royal (see C. L. Eastlake, *A History of the Gothic Revival in England*, 1972 edn, p. 345).

Left PL. 157 Set of fruit knives and forks, silver-gilt with agate handles, decorated with sunflowers and the initial 'A' for Armstrong. Designed for Sir William (later Lord) Armstrong of Cragside in Northumberland by Norman Shaw or Nesfield, *c.*1868. Norman Shaw was Armstrong's architect, but the delicate Japonisme is more characteristic of Nesfield.

Right PL. 158 Model of a Japanese house, '*Maison d'habitation de classe inférieure*'; from a group illustrating different levels of domestic architecture sent by the Japanese government to the Paris Exhibition, 1867. The models were in startling contrast to the fanciful Japanese Pavilion with its exaggeratedly curving roofs and hanging paper lanterns in the Galerie des Machines. Models and reconstructions of actual Japanese buildings supplemented with authentic detail the information derived from prints and block books.

The Revelation of Japan

PL. 159 The Golden Temple, Kyoto, Japan. This type of view would have been known to the Victorians through the work of Felice Beato, one of the first European photographers to work in Japan, who took a series of pictures between 1862 and 1868.

A collection of his photographs, published in Japan in 1868, was certainly known in Europe, and achieved wider circulation through engravings based on the photographs which were used by Aimé Humbert in his _Japon Illustré_ (1870).

PL. 160 E. W. Godwin: oak desk for the Earl of Limerick, Dromore Castle, Ireland, 1869 (see also PL. 161–3). The drawing for this advanced, abstract design survives.

Above PL. 161 E. W. Godwin: sofa from a design for Dromore Castle, Ireland, 1869. Dromore, a romantic Gothic castle for the Earl of Limerick, was the most ambitious of Godwin's domestic commissions. Godwin's drawings, headed 'Art Furniture', demonstrate the gradual subsuming of oak Gothic pieces into schematic Japonisme.

Right PL. 162 E. W. Godwin: dressing table for Dromore Castle; detail of the upper section with candle-holder.

Above PL. 163 E. W. Godwin: oak armchair with gold-stamped leather upholstery for Dromore Castle; designed 1869 and made by William Watt in 1870.

Opposite PL. 164 E. W. Godwin: buffet of ebonized wood with silvered fittings; a version of the buffet or sideboard designed for Godwin's house in Bristol, *c*.1867. The design featured in William Watt's *Art Furniture* catalogue (1877), and was in production with minor variations for a number of years.

PL. 165 E. W. Godwin: cabinet, ebonized wood with silvered fittings; designed for the Revd W. H. Lane, 1869. A large related cabinet is illustrated in William Watt's *Art Furniture* catalogue (1877, pl. 14).

Art Manufactures and the Queen Anne Revival

The brief but intense two-decade vogue for 'Art manufactures' was the result of a considerable upheaval in the relative positions of the architect-designer and the manufacturer. In the Regency period fashionable furnishers such as Morel & Seddon had wielded great power, dispensing commissions to artists and architects. A. W. N. Pugin had been in their employ when they were decorating Windsor Castle in the 1820s; but it was he who altered the hierarchy, by himself becoming the employer of the specialists in each branch of the decorating work on his architectural projects. The same system was operated by a number of architects, for example by E. W. Godwin at Dromore Castle, in Limerick. The larger pieces for Dromore may have been made locally; but William Watt was contracted to execute Godwin's designs for the smaller furniture. In a significant reversal of roles Godwin subsequently became Watt's employee, and also made designs for a number of other firms, including Gillow, Collinson & Lock and William Smee.

The manufacturer's influence increased in direct ratio to the level of public interest in the Art Movement. The prerogative of the rich patron to commission decoration and furnishings from leading architects and designers gave way to the demands of the market-place. It is fruitless now to speculate whether Godwin or the other architects directly involved with manufactures would have evolved differently had they remained at the exclusive bidding of a single patron, but we can begin to evaluate the popularity of certain of their designs from surviving examples. Many of the pieces of furniture and decorative objects once thought to be unique or very rare are now known to have been produced in some quantity. Even if the numbers are not large, the fact that Godwin's Japanesque sideboard (PL. 164), said to have been designed for his own use, should have found a public, however small, alters popular misconceptions about Victorian taste.

The Art Movement developed in two distinct directions. One of these was an exploration of abstraction and asymmetry and disposition of mass and void without pandering to fashionable taste for costly materials and finish. This was largely the province of avant-garde designers such as Godwin and Christopher Dresser – both of whom, incidentally, had strong views about materials and surface effects – and was marketed initially through mainly short-lived 'Art' manufacturing ventures. The unforeseen critical success of many of these designs led to their exploitation by the more adventurous trade manufacturers who relied mainly on career designers such as Bruce Talbert, T. E. Collcutt, Charles Bevan and Henry W. Batley. Warner's wove fine silks and Jeffrey's manufactured wallpapers to designs by Owen Jones, Talbert, Godwin and Dresser.

The complementary strand, initiated in the trade, and more preoccupied with the 'quaint' side of Japonisme and other exotic cultures as well as the 'Jacobethan' and eighteenth-century revivals, was generally distinguished by complex and immaculately executed technique. This rough demarcation line was constantly overstepped: for example, Collinson & Lock managed to combine daringly abstract and attenuated forms with fine cabinet-making techniques without apparently violating the integrity of Godwin's designs. Collcutt was responsible for the major part of the furniture in Collinson & Lock's first catalogue of 1871, and in 1872 Godwin entered what was supposed to be an exclusive arrangement to supply designs for the firm. Until 1874 it was paying a substantial monthly retainer to Godwin as well as fees for individual designs.

Experimental 'Art' ventures interacted with the trade to produce the daring eclecticism which characterizes the best of Art Movement architecture and decoration. Godwin's designs for the co-operative Art Furniture Company were successfully commercialized by the trade manufacturer William Watt, with a range of Jacobean and 'Anglo-Japanese' style furniture. Dresser's revolutionary design ideas, exemplified in his *Art of Decorative Design* (1862), were eagerly adopted by firms such as Wedgwood, Minton, Elkington and Coalbrookdale, as well as wallpaper manufacturers, such as Jeffrey & Co., and textile firms. His perceptions were radically altered by his trip to Japan in 1876, but the manufacturers, now joined notably by Hukin & Heath, Dixon's and Perry's, kept faith with his vision. In his monograph on Dresser, Widar Halen lists more than sixty firms who employed him as designer. Dresser's artistic directorships in, for example, Dresser & Holme (1878–82), Linthorpe's Art Pottery (1879–82) and the Art Furnishers' Alliance (1880–3) permitted a greater measure of control by the designer; but these were short-lived, possibly because commercial factors were insufficiently controlled. However, he had established an unprecedentedly commanding position as a designer, with many firms using his name or a facsimile signature as a marketing device.

The divergence of designer and trade manufacturer, exemplified in the retreat to craft workshops of the Arts and Crafts Movement, spelled the end for the Art Movement; a collapse from which only a few firms – notably Morris & Co. and Liberty's – emerged unscathed. The position in the trade of the designer had so deteriorated by the 1890s that A. L. Liberty was able to insist upon anonymity for the designs made for his store in Regent Street. The rule was waived, as a great concession, so that Archibald Knox could exhibit his work with the Arts and Crafts Exhibition Society, an absurd situation since Knox was far too talented a designer to be treated in this fashion.

Although his principal interest was in Isnik pottery, Joseph-Théodore Deck later made Japonisme an aspect of his varied experiments in ceramics. His intensely coloured dish of about 1870 with Japanese-style decoration, now in the Victoria and Albert Museum, came from the reference collection started by Herbert Minton, and continued by his successor Colin Minton Campbell, to inspire the Minton artists and technicians.

The celebrated dinner services for the Rousseau and Haviland firms were designed by Félix Bracquemond to incorporate Japanese motifs from Hokusai's ten-volume *Mangwa* (PL. 153), consisting of prints of Japanese everyday life. Minton's answer to Bracquemond, in 1870, was to commission Hokusai-inspired designs (PL. 155) from the artist W. S. Coleman. French Japonisme, with its emphasis on natural ornament, was one of the principal routes towards Art Nouveau, which was to provide an important showcase for the French luxury trades.

The leading British manufacturers of Japanese-inspired objects were Elkington's, Royal Worcester, Minton, Wedgwood, Doulton, and Thomas Webb. As well as their celebrated enamel, Elkington's made some of the finest mixed-metal pieces and – most ambitious of all – some rare experiments with the complex technique of *komai*, intricate geometric patterns in relief covering the surface of the object (PL. 223). There is evidence that Japanese craftsmen were employed by British silverware manufacturers.

These same *komai* patterns were used in a complex and technically outstanding exploitation of transfer printing for the decoration in gold of Worcester porcelain dishes. The director R. W. Binns had amassed an enormous assortment of Japanese ceramics for his employees to study; the whole collection, numbering some 10,000 pieces, was sold after his death.

In response to the growing importance of the Art Movement, Colin Minton Campbell initiated, with the co-operation of Léon Arnoux, the manufacture of boldly coloured ornamental 'Persian' enamelware and Chinese and Japanese 'cloisonné' wares at the Minton works, some to designs by Christopher Dresser. Campbell

also established Minton's Art Pottery Studio in Kensington in 1871. The two most distinguished artists associated with the Art Pottery venture were Edward Poynter and W. S. Coleman. Poynter's pictorial tiles for the Grill Room at the South Kensington Museum (1866), which had been executed by lady students at the National Training School, provided the inspiration, and Coleman was appointed art director of the studio, which enjoyed a great *succès d'estime* among distinguished society, and even royal, patrons. Coleman's plaques (PL. 180) found a ready sale at what were then very high prices of £30 to £50. The pictorial tiles and plates, and flasks and other holloware, hand-painted by a group of students from the South Kensington Schools, were unusual and attractive but the venture, having missed an important opportunity to provide tiled decoration for the Criterion Theatre, lost money and after a serious fire in 1875 was not reopened.

Although this venture was a commercial failure, it had long-term implications as the first of the Art Potteries, which were later to play such a dominant role in the Arts and Crafts Movement with its basis in small-scale Guild workshops.

The development of the Art Pottery movement in France, Britain and the United States was rooted in the experience of Japanese ceramics. Its place in the cult of hand craftsmanship and in the Arts and Crafts Movement has never been completely lost to sight. When the popular success of Art Nouveau as a decorative style necessitated a commercial scale of production this was successfully exploited by British firms such as Martin Brothers at Southall, Moorcroft (for Liberty in London), Pilkington (Lancastrian) and Minton's with their Secession ware; Zsolnay in Hungary; American firms such as the Grueby Faience Co. in Boston and the Rookwood Pottery Co. in Cincinnati; and many others in France and Scandinavia.

James Robertson and his sons, who founded the Chelsea Keramic Art Works in 1872, came from a dynasty of more than five generations of British potters. Robertson had brought his family to the United States in 1853. The basis of the Chelsea works was terracotta flowerpots; from 1872 the focus was on art pottery on the British model. The Japanese porcelains at the 1876 Exhibition inspired experiments with glazes. The firm lasted until 1889, when it was incorporated into the Chelsea Pottery.

Another outstanding name in this field is that of William H. Grueby, who was responsible for the introduction of matt glazes around the turn of the century. A former Rookwood decorator, Artus Van Briggle, who had trained in Paris from 1893 to 1896, established his own studio in Colorado in 1901. His ceramic work has the greatest affinity with the leading Continental potters of the Art Nouveau school.

In the United States Tiffany & Co. led the experiments with mixed-media effects on metalwares, and Louis Comfort Tiffany and his Associated Artists with stained and painted glass; John La Farge, who, like Dresser, had travelled in Japan, also designed and made Japanese-influenced ornamental glass; the Chelsea Keramic Works had notable success with moulded terracotta and coloured glazes; the Art Tile Works is self-explanatory. Herter Brothers made exquisitely inlaid and carved furniture with Japanese motifs or forms. As in France, the American Japanese style led into Art Nouveau.

The Art Movement came late to the United States. Its rise coincided with a period of mounting prosperity, and the style was the particular province of firms with patrons among the new millionaire class. They avoided the decline so noticeable in the 1880s in British 'Art' manufactures, and the movement lived on beside the utopian and essentially provincial American Arts and Crafts.

PL. 166 Philip Webb: sideboard, panelled with horizontal mouldings; of late seventeenth-century inspiration, 1864–6. The design for this sideboard, inscribed 'Cabinet in teak (by Webb)' is mounted in an album made up in 1874 (see Jill Lever, *Architects' Designs for Furniture*, 1982, no. 63) but it was probably designed some years earlier. A sideboard of this form may be seen in Birket Foster family photographs of the dining room at The Hill, Witley, where the Morris firm was active in 1864 and 1866. The built-in furniture for Major Gillum's Kensington house, dating from *c*.1873, is also of this early 'Queen Anne' type. Versions of the sideboard remained in the firm's catalogue in the twentieth century. Writing to E. R. Robson in the early 1860s, the firm's manager, Warrington Taylor, wondered: 'Is not Queen Anne furniture more suited to our wants, constructional but light ...?' This piece may have been Webb's response, not copying actual Queen Anne examples, but borrowing essentials from architecture and woodwork.

Left PL. 167 Richard Norman Shaw: cabinet and stand, pine stained red, the door panels decorated with leaves and branches in gilded gesso by J. Aldam Heaton; *c.*1875–7. The reeding and mouldings on this cabinet are similar to Webb's for the sideboard (PL. 166). Spanish seventeenth-century cabinets on stands provided the model for this piece, and for many later examples from Arts and Crafts designers, for example C. R. Ashbee and Ernest Gimson (PL. 310).

Above PL. 168 Bruce Talbert: Queen Anne-style library table, mahogany with intricate mouldings and turned legs and stretchers. The table is illustrated by Talbert on a page of suggested furnishings for the 'Study and Library' in *Fashionable Furniture*, 1881.

Opposite, left PL. 169 Bruce Talbert: detail of the 'Pet' sideboard, oak and carved boxwood; made by Gillow's, a version of the model shown in the London International Exhibition in 1873 which was bought for the South Kensington Museum. Fine carving had been a much admired, but generally over-prominent feature of exhibition furniture since 1851; here it is successfully integrated into Talbert's design.

Right PL. 170 T. E. Collcutt:
cabinet in ebonized wood with
painted and gilded decoration;
designed for Collinson & Lock.
Exhibited for the first time in
London in 1871, the present
example, with panels ascribed to
Albert Moore, is now in the
Victoria and Albert Museum. A
version was shown at the
International Exhibition in
Vienna in 1873 and bought by the
Prince of Liechtenstein. Another
was shown at the Philadelphia
Centennial Exhibition in 1876,
and illustrated in *Masterpieces of the
International Centennial Exhibition*
(1877), 'Industrial Art', vol. 2, p.
168. The ebonized finish
combined with painted panels and
gilding became the hallmark of
'Aesthetic' furniture.

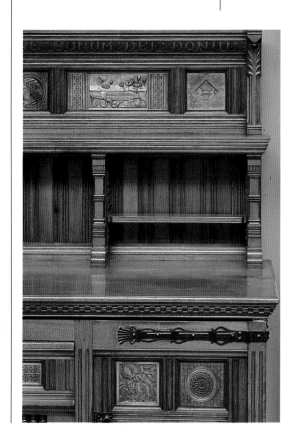

PL. 171 Bruce Talbert: cabinet in walnut with ebonized turnings and inlays of various woods; made by Gillow's. The piece is illustrated in *Fashionable Furniture*, Talbert's posthumously published book of designs, issued by the *Cabinet Maker and Art Furnisher* in 1881.

PL. 172 Edward Welby Pugin: oak chair; *c.*1858. In this early design the structural form shows the continuing influence of the elder Pugin.

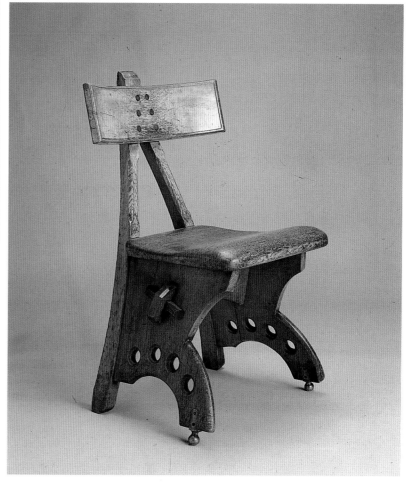

PL. 173 Edward Welby Pugin: oak chair, the 'Granville'; a registered design of 1870 manufactured by Pugin's own company. With the passage of twelve years Pugin's design ideas have become much more extreme. The chair combines a 'Klismos' back with a purely decorative Gothic revival base.

PL. 174 G. E. Street: the Law Courts, London, entrance front on the Strand; from 1868. Street was an admirer of Ruskin, and has here adapted English Gothic details to interact with the flat, patterned layout of Ruskin's favourite Venetian Gothic for this important secular commission. The Law Courts commission came midway in Street's career. In 1861 Godwin had employed the Venetian Gothic style for his first important architectural scheme, when he won the competition to design Northampton Town Hall. His dependence on Ruskin's inspiration is apparent from the use of details taken from the illustrations to the *Stones of Venice*. Superficially similar, the two show a crucial difference of approach; Northampton is principled and compact, while Street's building is eclectic and stylized.

PL. 175 John Henry Chamberlain: detail of Gothic-style cabinet, oak inlaid with various woods; *c*.1870. A passionate Ruskinian, Chamberlain adapted natural ornament to an architectural design. He made furniture designs for the Warwick firm of Collier & Plucknett.

PL. 176 G. E. Street: (right) oak chair with a 'Klismos' back, designed for the Law Courts and made by Gillow's, 1881–2; (left) oak chair with buttoned leather upholstery, using the 'Glastonbury' shape in a square, abstract design (see PL. 12, for Pugin's historically correct version). Made for the Synod Hall at Christ Church Cathedral, Dublin, 1877–8.

PL. 177 Ebonized cabinet, the upper arch-topped panel painted with a peacock on a gold ground, the lower panels with other birds in roundels, incised gold decoration and brass hinges. Another example of the finest quality of painted furniture, made to complement an expensive scheme, the cabinet is similar in style to the decoration of the Berkeley Square house of Frederick Lehmann, carried out by George Aitchison and Albert Moore. Peacocks trailing their tails formed the drawing-room frieze, painted by Moore.

Above PL. 178 Egyptian-style upholstered chair, ebonized wood frame decorated with coloured and gold incised motifs; made by Cox & Co. This model appears in the Cox catalogue of 1871.

Above PL. 180 William Coleman: circular plaque; for Minton's Kensington Gore Art Pottery Studio, *c.*1870. The subject is allusive, showing a young woman in a Greek chiton decorating an ornamental vase, just as the female students from the South Kensington Museum painted the pots in the studio in Gore Lane.

Right PL. 179 Daniel Cottier: stained glass panel, 'Flora'; from a set of the Seasons, *c.*1870. Cottier had studied glass painting in Glasgow in the early 1860s, and he worked in Edinburgh for the firm of Field & Allan in a style influenced by Morris. He moved to London in 1870 and was briefly in partnership with Bruce Talbert. In his later career, E. W. Godwin was his principal inspiration. When he set up his business in the United States in 1873, he relied initially on marketing furniture and decoration in Godwin's Anglo-Japanese style.

Left PL. 181 Tile panel, a standing crane on the branch of a flowering tree, painted in the Japanese style, on a rust background; made at Minton's Kensington Gore Art Pottery Studio, 1870–74.

Below PL. 182 Large ovoid vase, painted with a fish eating a prawn on a celadon green ground; made at Minton's Kensington Gore Art Pottery Studio, 1870–74.

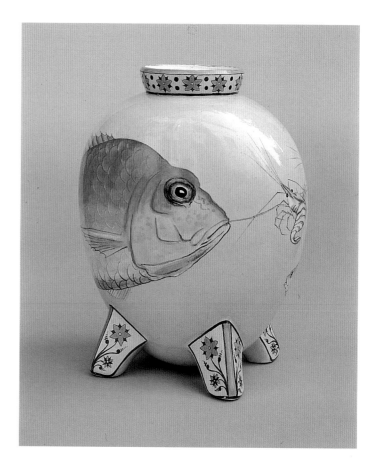

Left PL. 184 Christopher Dresser: two-handled vase in 'cloisonné ware'; for Minton's, *c.*1871.

Above PL. 183 Christopher Dresser: 'Beetle' vase in 'cloisonné ware'; for Minton's, 1873.

Right PL. 185 Plant trough, by Minton & Co.; a Japanese bronze form in majolica ware, *c.*1873.

Edward William Godwin

'In common with a few (I am sorry to say a very few) others in my profession, I look upon all my work as Art Work. A building to me is as a picture to a painter or a poem to a poet.' (E. W. Godwin, 1873, in correspondence with a client.) Godwin set up as an architect in his native Bristol in 1854, aged twenty-one, but his first conspicuous success came in 1861 when he won the Northampton Town Hall competition with a Ruskinian Reformed Gothic design. The furniture was massively Gothic already showing the signs of the abstraction that was to mark all his subsequent work. Godwin had made the acquaintance of William Burges in 1858, and they became close friends. Godwin's designs for the Earl of Limerick's Dromore Castle mingle Gothic with Japanese decorative motifs and newly assimilated Japanese constructional principles, in defiance of the rules formulated for the 'archaeological' Gothic of the design reformers. At Dromore Godwin came close to Burges's extravagantly decorated style, but his own taste was for the austerity and geometry of Japan.

A versatile and original architect, he ranged from the quirky and romantic vernacular of Beauvale Lodge (1871 for Earl Cowper, who referred to this addition to his many residences as 'my new cottage') to striking proto-modernistic town houses for Whistler and his fellow artist Frank Miles. The severely simplified and deliberately composed 'White House' (1877 [PL. 186]; demolished and replaced with a Palladian pastiche) and Miles's studio house (still extant in Tite Street, Chelsea) both fell foul of the Metropolitan Board of Works and ended up with decorative features that Godwin had not intended. The Miles house survives in the 'Queen Anne' disguise that finally passed muster with the board. The exaggerated gable and the close glazing bars cannot mask completely the originality of the composition and its Japanesque origins.

Godwin was to become one of the leading designers of the Art Movement. In common with Dresser, but with few others, he responded intellectually, rather than in a purely decorative manner, to Japanese influence. Godwin's Japanese-style furniture and decoration was evolved from study of Hokusai's *Mangwa*, which he acquired in the 1850s, and of Japanese architecture and building methods. He wrote in 1875 of his researches in Japanese source books:

> 'There is lying on the table as I write a Japanese book: for all I know it may be quite a common collection of prints, or it may be out of print and rare; whatever it is, I have not as yet met with another copy, and as the illustrations are specially devoted to construction, some account of them may perchance interest some of your readers in the architecture of a country from whose artists and art-workmen we have learned so much.' (*Building News*, February 1875.)

Godwin never went to Japan and he was forced to assimilate an exotic culture from printed sources and exhibition displays. Yet his appreciation of the Japanese approach to composition and pattern-making was remarkable. His understanding of pattern placed him in the forefront of reform in the design of wallpapers, initiated by Metford Warner in collaboration with Jeffrey & Co.

In 1862, when he moved into a tall stone-built eighteenth-century town house at Portland Square in Bristol, Godwin came as close as was conceivable at that date to employing the simplicity of Japanese taste in his own living quarters. On the plainly painted walls he hung Japanese prints. Persian rugs were the only adornment of bare boards and the carefully selected furniture was antique. Ellen Terry remembered this beautiful scheme and remarked on 'its sense of design in every detail'. But for the average observer such austerity could only be equated with poverty; the spare elegance was not often successfully imitated.

The application of Japanese principles to the construction of furniture was first exploited by Godwin in the furnishing of his London house in the mid-1860s. These pieces were made by the aptly named Art Furniture Company, trading at 25 Garrick Street, Covent Garden, in 1867. According to their advertisement they were 'prepared to supply at ordinary trade prices, domestic furniture of an artistic and picturesque character, designs by C. Eastlake, A. W. Blomfield and W. Godwin and other architects'. The Art Furniture Company did not survive long, but the manufacture of Godwin's Anglo-Japanese and other furniture designs was taken over by William Watt, a collaboration that continued until Watt's death nearly twenty years later.

Godwin's breadth of reference was impressive. Although the Anglo-Japanese designs had the widest currency, thanks to the commercial efficiency of Watt and Collinson & Lock, and their exploitation for the American market by Daniel Cottier, his work in the 'Egyptian' and 'Greek' idiom is perhaps even more excitingly abstract. The 'Greek' chair (PL. 190), inspired by the Parthenon Marbles, is so far removed from Regency Neo-Greek, and the 'Egyptian' pieces from the Napoleonic Egyptian Revival, that their inspiration must have come from a totally fresh aesthetic experience. The conclusion must be that severely reformed Gothic combined with the discovery of Japanese art had so attuned Godwin's ideas to abstraction that he was able to apply its principles to all aspects of design. He experimented with a bold Tudor and simplified Neo-Renaissance; he was also involved with stage design and with the dress reform movement, designing for Liberty's dress department, which he managed from its inception in 1884. However, he had grown disillusioned. When he was redecorating in 1876 he considered various options, even revision of his own furniture models.

'The third course was to hunt up secondhand shops for eighteenth-century mahogany work inlaid with strips of satinwood. Whether it was that I had grown a trifle weary of modern designs in general, and my own in particular, or that I longed for more colour than was to be found in plain oak or American walnut, or that the cost of the eighteenth-century work was so much below the least expensive of the specially made goods of the present day, or whether – as is most likely – it was from a concretion of these three thoughts, the eighteenth century won the competition, and my dining room was furnished with a bow-fronted sideboard, Chippendale chairs, flap tables, cabinets, bookcases, and a little escritoire, all of admirable colour, design and workmanship.' (*The Architect*, July 1876.)

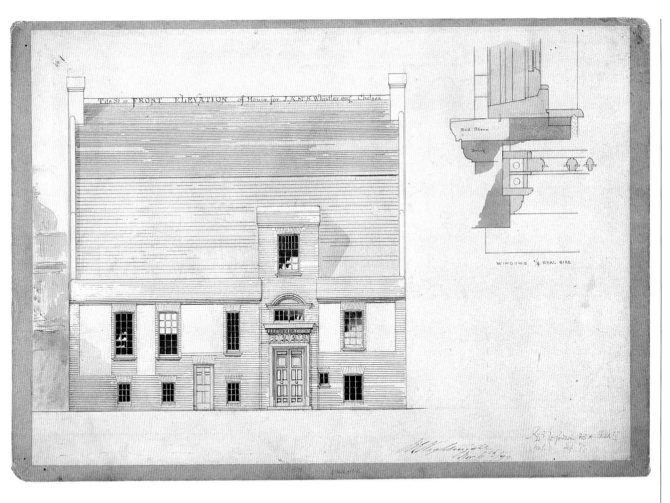

PL. 186 E. W. Godwin: front elevation of the White House in Tite Street, Chelsea; for J. McNeill Whistler, 1878. This is the first version before the decorative requirements of the Metropolitan Board of Works had eliminated the purely abstract arrangement of the façade. Even in the form in which it was eventually built, its white brick walls, stone facings, green slate roof, blue door and woodwork were thought as 'fantastic' and 'eccentric' as the artist himself. Quarrels with Frederick Leyland over payment for the 'Peacock' room, and the notorious court case brought by Ruskin, reduced Whistler to penury and his tenancy of the house was brief. In bitter memory of Leyland's part in his troubles he made a savage caricature, *Filthy Lucre*, in which the devil – Leyland – is shown seated on a model of the house, running a shower of golden guineas through his fingers.

Opposite PL. 187 E. W. Godwin: circular eight-legged table with radiating turned stretchers, walnut veneer; version of a design for William Watt dated 1876, illustrated in the 1877 catalogue of his Art Furniture Warehouse at 21 Grafton Street. This example was invoiced to the original owner by the decorator Aldam Heaton in 1885. The table is without extraneous ornament, its decorative qualities coming purely from the interplay of the structural elements; as Godwin remarked, 'It is essential that the common objects of everyday life should be quiet, simple and unobtrusive in their beauty.'

Right PL. 188 E. W. Godwin: drop-leaf table with shelf, in mahogany with lacquered brass braces, the stretchers in an asymmetrical Japanese fret pattern; *c*.1872. A table of this design belonged to Ellen Terry, with whom Godwin lived from 1868 to 1874; it is now in the Ellen Terry Memorial Museum at Smallhythe in Kent. This design exemplifies Godwin's precepts, set out in a newspaper article in 1872: 'We require first that furniture be well lifted from the floor (thereby eliminating dust-catchers) and that it be as light as is consistent with real strength.'

Above PL. 190 E. W. Godwin:
Greek chair, ebonized oak, the
distinctive turned legs being
inspired by a stool depicted on the
East Frieze of the Parthenon
Marbles in the British Museum.
Godwin's sketch of the stool dates
from *c*.1883. The chair was
illustrated in *Building News* (18
December 1885) as an example of
inexpensive furniture 'executed by
representatives of the late William
Watt'. The more elaborate version
of the 'Greek' chair, of which full
details are shown in *Building News*,
has scrolled arms and a row of
turned spindles in the back.

Left PL. 189 E. W. Godwin:
cabinet, satinwood with brass
mounts, the upper doors inset with
painted and gilt panels of the
'Seasons'; 1877. The central doors
are formed of arched panels and
frets taken directly from Japanese
architecture.

PL. 191 E. W. Godwin: chair, birch with a caned seat. The elements of the 'Greek' chair have been simplified still further to produce a stripped-down abstract form, modernist before the fact. The historicist references have been eliminated, though some relationship with the structure of Egyptian furniture is still apparent.

PL. 192 E. W. Godwin: ebonized chair, designed for William Watt, 1877, to go with a table for the 1878 Paris Exhibition.

PL. 193 E. W. Godwin: gong in the Japanese style. One of Godwin's most unequivocally Japanese-influenced designs. A drawing for it is in a sketchbook dating from about 1870.

PL. 194 E. W. Godwin: tile panel with figures of the Seasons.

PL. 195 E. W. Godwin: design for the 'Butterfly Brocade'; for Warner & Son, 1874, to be woven in silk damask exclusively for Collinson & Lock.

America: From Design Reform to Philadelphia 1876

French ideas had dominated decorating taste in America until the design reforms first proposed by Pugin, developed by Ruskin and Carlyle and then given a more practical form by Eastlake, began to take a hold on the public imagination. It was left to the artistic and intellectual middle class to follow the stylistic advice offered by a growing number of publications devoted to the artistic domestic interior. These inclined towards Reformed Gothic with a judicious admixture of Japonisme interspersed with genuinely antique pieces. From the 1870s, through Eastlake's writings, to Morris's contacts with the Craft Revivalists in the nineties the thread of American aestheticism can be traced to Britain. American provincial 'Carpenter's Gothic' is a curious anomaly, derived from the eighteenth-century pattern books issued by Batty Langley and the Halfpennys.

The 'Eastlake' style came initially from his *Hints on Household Taste*, promoting a Puginesque Gothic, first published in Britain in 1868, and issued in an American edition in 1872. American designers had been aware of Eastlake's ideas since the critical reports of the original edition in 1868. However, the so-called 'Eastlake' style was also taken from the published designs of one of Pugin's most accomplished followers, Bruce J. Talbert, circulated in *Gothic Forms Applied to Furniture, Metalwork and Decoration for Domestic Purposes* (1867) and *Examples of Ancient and Modern Furniture, Metalwork, Tapestries, Decorations, &c.* (1876). The chapter on the 'Eastlake' style in *Decoration Applied to Furniture* (1877), by Harriet Prescott Spofford, is illustrated with plates taken, without acknowledgement, from Talbert's *Gothic Forms*.

She had recognized the practical value of *Hints*: 'The book met a great want,' she wrote. 'Not a young marrying couple who read English but were to be found with "Hints on Household Taste" in their hands, and all its dicta were accepted as gospel truths. . . . The book occasioned a great awakening, questioning, and study in the matter of household furnishing.' However, she preferred the refinement of Talbert's forms. By the mid-seventies Daniel Pabst of

Philadelphia, Kimbel & Cabus in New York and the Boston Household Art Company were all making furniture that owed a clear debt to Talbert. Less obviously plagiaristic, Christian Herter's echoes of Talbert came from contact with the designer himself.

When the Glasgow-born designer Daniel Cottier, a former partner of Talbert's, established his firm in the United States in 1873 he took with him a repertoire culled from Talbert himself as well as from Godwin, Collcutt and J. Moyr Smith. The results feature in Clarence Cook's *The House Beautiful* (1878), which has a fine embossed and gilded cover designed by Cottier, an exquisite frontispiece by Walter Crane and a number of plates showing Godwinesque furniture which is credited to Cottier. Cottier claimed that furniture imported from Britain could not stand up to the American climate, so he set up his own workshop, thus creating still unresolved problems of authorship for the designs. One of Godwin's most striking wallpaper designs, the Japanese-style 'Bamboo' of 1872, was used for the dining room of a house in Hartford, Connecticut, *c.*1873, and may have been supplied by Cottier.

Collinson & Lock featured prominently at the Philadelphia Exhibition in 1876, and may have played a significant part in the dissemination of Talbert's, Collcutt's and Godwin's designs; but it is Cottier's entrepreneurial role that is documented. In 1881 Godwin's former partner, Robert W. Edis, published his *Decoration and Furniture of Town Houses* in London and New York. The frontispiece shows his own sitting room furnished with Godwin's designs.

The importance of the Philadelphia Exhibition, in inspiring the newly established decorative design ventures and in stimulating American ambitions to supply their own domestic market, can hardly be overstated. The moment was propitious: American architecture and decoration were discovering an individual character; and coincidentally the balance of economic power altered. On a wave of prosperity American architecture surged forward. Reporting on 'Industrial Art', Bing recalls the impact on Tiffany's display at the 1878 Paris Exhibition:

> 'Many of those amateurs whose interest extends to all areas of art will still remember their surprise on seeing, at the Exposition of 1878, several examples of metalwork of the most extraordinary quality. Although not intrinsically original in concept – their decorative principles were taken directly from the Japanese – the borrowed elements were so ingeniously transposed to serve their function as to become the equivalent of new discoveries.' (*La culture artistique*, p. 121.)

Tiffany's had unveiled their Japanese-style silverware (PL. 220, 221) at Philadelphia; in two years they had come far enough to impress the French on their own ground.

The 1876 Centennial Exhibition in Philadelphia saw the emergence of a distinctive American design culture. Tiffany's had come of age, throwing off the dependence on French example that had hitherto inhibited the creation of a distinctive personality. Kimbel & Cabus were commended for the 'harmonious' arrangement of their drawing room in the 'Modern Gothic' taste. The stylistic co-ordination of the interior was still at a relatively undeveloped stage. A trade card of this date shows that they were familiar with Dresser's *Principles of Design* (1873); Dresser's distinctive sugar bowl (fig. 149) is shown on a Talbert-inspired dresser. (See *In Pursuit of Beauty*, exhibition catalogue, Metropolitan Museum of Art, New York, 1986, p. 257.)

Herter's had already found an individuality that transcended the decorative devices so apparently derived from Talbert. But the displays also demonstrated the extent to which American design was still dependent on European inspiration. One critic regretted that Herter's

'... did not make an exhibit of some of the beautiful work with which the house has been credited during a few years past. Had the work of their able designer Mr A. Sandier been seen in comparison with that of the English designers, it would have been less easy to concede to them the superiority which their designs in the main portrayed.'

(*American Architect*, 2, 6 January 1877, p. 3.)

Alexandre Sandier made a number of the drawings for *The House Beautiful*; his own designs show echoes of Eastlake and Talbert, severely plain with inconspicuous carved panels and simple turnings. He was able to transmute his Reformed Gothic into a Godwinesque Anglo-Japanese style, the type of decoration for which Herter Brothers was to be famed in the 1870s and 1880s. Herter's Japanesque furniture, in contrast to Godwin's, was richly ornamented with carved and inlaid panels, gilding and painting.

It was ironical, in view of the fact that it celebrated the centenary of the successful – for the United States – outcome of the American War of Independence, that the Exhibition should have provided an invaluable showcase for British design. The ironwork Japanese-style pavilion designed by Thomas Jeckyll for Barnard, Bishop & Barnard (PL. 196) was a conspicuous centrepiece. Collinson & Lock's stand was a feast of British Aestheticism, with a large Neo-Renaissance cabinet by Talbert, an intricately Japanesque cabinet by Godwin partnered by Batley's delicate Japanesque chair with its laced bolster (PL. 203), and a third version of Collcutt's celebrated ebonized cabinet. Talbert also created a beautiful bird- and flower-patterned silk for the occasion (PL. 202). For Walter Crane it was a moment of triumph: his great portière executed by the Royal School of Art Needlework framed the entrance to a display to which he had contributed more embroidery designs; and for Jeffrey & Co. he had designed award-winning wallpapers.

Morris, too, was featured, his wallpaper designs vying with Crane's for first place in popularity. The products of Morris & Co. were already widely known in the States and greatly admired. Papers such as the 'Willow' and 'Marigold' were very popular, some surviving in American houses of the 1870s, notably the Newport mansion, Château-sur-Mer. Both Morris's and Crane's designs were imitated by American manufacturers. In another field American manufacturers were quick to profit by the interest shown in the British exhibits. The Ohio potteries began using the multicoloured local clays to produce encaustic tiles in the manner of Minton's. In the 1890s the American Encaustic Tile Company produced transfer-printed tiles with illustrations from Cranes' *The Baby's Own Aesop* and from Morris patterns.

Dresser arrived in America in 1876 en route to Japan where he was to act as agent for various firms, including Londos of London and Tiffany of New York, in addition to his mission to advise the Japanese government on design and manufactures. Seeing the impact that British wallpapers had made at the Exhibition, he took the precaution of registering fifteen designs with the United States patent office, to be manufactured by Willson and Fennimore of Philadelphia. While he was in Philadelphia he lectured at the Pennsylvania School of Industrial Art, confirming the avid professional interest in his work that had already been stimulated by his publications. The furniture made by Daniel Pabst to the designs of Frank Furness underwent a revolutionary change after 1876, showing most clearly the impact of Dresser's ideas. The Philadelphia architect Frank Furness knew the work of Talbert and William Burges as well as that of Dresser.

Assimilation of the British-derived Aesthetic taste produced an American style with a recognizably individual character. Just as the development of American Gothic and vernacular had been determined by different cultural and social conditions, so the American Aesthetic movement evolved in response to the demands of affluent patrons: Rockefeller, Vanderbilt, Marquand; millionaires all. For them the eighties were a time of prosperity and economic expansion. The picture of Aestheticism that emerges from *Artistic Houses* (1883–4), and Edward Strachan's *Mr Vanderbilt's House and Collection* (1883–4) reveals the masterpieces of Herter and of L. C. Tiffany's Associated Artists glittering with mosaic, marble and coloured panels of glass, with furnishings of marquetry and ivory inlay and ornaments of silver encrusted with gold and enamel. The liberal and intellectual middle class continued to prefer the vernacular and its logical derivative, the utopian Arts and Crafts Movement.

Opposite, above left PL. 196 Thomas Jeckyll: Japanese Pavilion for the Philadelphia Centennial Exhibition of 1876; built by Barnard, Bishop & Barnard. This was the first showing of the pavilion, which was based on traditional temple architecture. It was dismantled and taken to Paris in 1878. It was then returned to Norwich, where it had been made in Barnard's iron and brass foundry, and erected in the park; it is shown there in this turn-of-the-century photograph. In 1944 it was dismantled and sold for scrap, having been judged to be derelict and a danger to the public.

Opposite, below left PL. 197 Gatehouse of the Kiyomizu temple in Kyoto. This was the traditional Japanese architecture that inspired Jeckyll's Pavilion.

Opposite, right PL. 198 Thomas Jeckyll: one of a pair of 'Sunflower' andirons, gilded bronze; motif taken from the railings surrounding Barnard's 1876 Japanese Pavilion. The andirons were shown in the pavilion, and proved popular in America. A pair can be seen in old photographs of David L. Einstein's library and the hall of the Long Island house of Samuel P. Hinckley (both in *Artistic Houses*, 1883–4). They featured in the decoration of the 'Peacock' room, now installed in the Freer Gallery in Washington. Barnard's also made fire grates using motifs from the brackets supporting the roof of the pavilion, Japanesque designs of birds and flowering branches.

Right PL. 200 Thomas Jeckyll: cast-iron single seat; made by Barnard, Bishop & Barnard. The Japanese cloud motif was used for the pavilion benches at the exhibition. This exotic design was chosen for seating on the platforms of Cambridge station.

Left PL. 199 Gates made from the Japanese Pavilion railings; designed by Jeckyll.

Above PL. 201 Walter Crane: screen consisting of four panels of Japanese-style embroidery; executed by students at the Royal School of Art Needlework, *c.*1875–6. Shown in Crane's pavilion for the School at the Philadelphia Exhibition.

Opposite PL. 202 Bruce Talbert: silk brocade; designed for Cowlishaw, Nicol & Co., *c.*1875. Shown at the exhibition. The design was illustrated by Talbert in *Examples of Ancient and Modern Furniture* (1876). In 1868 the South Kensington Museum bought over fifty designs by Anna Maria

Garthwaite (1690–1763) for Spitalfields silk, dating from about 1736 to 1746. This provided a pool of patterns appropriate to the eighteenth-century revival style, and the similarity in character and technique between these designs and Talbert's cannot be coincidence.

Left PL. 203 H. W. Batley: mahogany side chair with embossed velvet upholstery; designed for Collinson & Lock, *c.*1876. The chair is recognizable in the photograph of the Collinson & Lock stand at the 1876 Philadelphia Exhibition (see Elizabeth Aslin, *E. W. Godwin, Furniture and Decoration*, 1986, pl. 40). Also prominently displayed are a large Jacobean cabinet by Bruce Talbert and an elegant Anglo-Japanese cabinet by Godwin. The chair caught the imagination of the American decorator Constance Cary Harrison, who featured it in the frontispiece illustration for *Woman's Handiwork in Modern Homes* (New York, 1881). The design was used by Herter Brothers in the furnishing of Thurlow Lodge, as well as inspiring a side chair used by the firm for a number of decorating commissions.

Opposite, left PL. 206 Théodore Deck: Persian-style tulip vase, *c.*1871. One of these vases can be seen on top of the Talbert cabinet in the photograph of Collinson & Lock's stand at the 1876 Exhibition. This decorative variant of Deck's vase, also produced in the celebrated *Bleu Deck* glaze, was shown in London in 1871, when a number of British firms offered French manufacturers the hospitality of their stands. The bands of daisies bordering the panels of decoration show a community of taste with Talbert, one of the most successful professional designers of the period and a prominent exhibitor in Paris in 1867.

Left PL. 204 Albert Willms: two vases with separate bases in gilt bronze, cloisonné enamel of birds and flowers; made by Elkington & Co., 1875. A group of Elkington's cloisonné ornaments was shown in Philadelphia in 1876, and much admired. The French designer Albert Willms had worked with Christofle, pioneer of the cloisonné revival, in Paris. Willms became head of Elkington's design department in the early 1860s, and it was under his influence and with the advice of Dresser that the firm began experiments with Oriental techniques. Its earliest known cloisonné work dates from *c.*1865.

Above PL. 205 Walter Crane: tile depicting 'There was a lady loved a swine'; made by the American Encaustic Tile Co., after 1876.

Above PL. 207 George Tinworth: birds on a nest, high-relief plaque; made by Doulton's Lambeth pottery, from a pulpit exhibited at the 1878 Paris Exhibition. At the London International Exhibition of 1872 Doulton's exhibited an 'Art' furniture cabinet in ebonized wood mounted with stoneware reliefs by Tinworth. Doulton's were substantial prize-winners at the Paris Exhibition, a silver medal being awarded to Tinworth himself.

Paris 1878 and the End of an Era

In 1880 Pugin had been dead for nearly thirty years; on the foundations that he laid had arisen a great edifice, the unassailable reality of British design. However, the financial collapse that had been threatening for some time now became a fact. The 1880s recession struck on two fronts; the value of agricultural land dropped critically and the apparently unstoppable momentum of industrial development was checked. To take one instance, as the world supplier of steel the British were overtaken by Germany and the United States, a great blow to Britain's lead in industrial innovation; in many other ways market supremacy was threatened. The result was bankruptcies, retrenchment and realignments, noticeably in the luxury trades that had so vastly expanded in the prosperous sixties and seventies.

The Paris Exhibition of 1878 was of importance to the furnishing trade. The British presence was very strong, with a dazzling array of Queen Anne schemes carried out by Collinson & Lock. France needed the exhibition to demonstrate that the financial problems of the years following the war were at an end, but the country had existed in an artistic time-warp unable to break out of the architectural and decorative traditions imposed by Beaux-Arts training. Intricate exhibition pieces were increasingly out of step with public taste. Jackson & Graham showed Talbert's 'Juno' cabinet, (PL. 210), a relatively restrained and classical piece. The centrepiece of William Watt's stand provided a tantalizing echo of James Whistler's fabulous 'Peacock' room, in the form of a fireplace and overmantel designed by Whistler in collaboration with E. W. Godwin (PL. 211).

The 'Jacobean' sideboards in pale oak pointed to an increasingly commercial tone to the displays. George Augustus Sala had enunciated a great truth among his comments on the Paris Exhibition of 1867:

> 'As a rule the Exhibition displays only the appurtenances of the palaces of kings and the garniture of the mansions of millionaires. There must be a section of the people and a very vast section too, whose requirements are not comprised in carved bedsteads, inlaid cabinets, damascened bookcases and lacquer work billiard tables.'
> (*Notes and Sketches of the Paris Exhibition*, London, 1868.)

Increasingly department stores were to play the role in middle-class life that the exhibitions had once performed.

Also significantly came the purchase by self-made millionaires of land from the breaking up of ancestral estates. Mark Girouard has studied the phenomenon of the *nouveau riche* style in *The Victorian Country House* (1979 edn, ch. 22, pp. 291–304). The focus of taste was French and the architecture in the historicist Beaux-Arts style. This was not a movement that was of much benefit to avant-garde British designers and manufacturers.

A critically different realignment occurred in the economically important textile trades. Cotton exports, comprising 80 per cent of the market, held up during the depressed years, but the buyers shifted from Europe to the Empire; from being an internationally competitive industry it came to rely on Britain's captive market. Certain designers retained their foreign contacts – for example, Morris and Dresser in America – but in the long term reliance on the Empire had poor implications for quality and innovation.

In 1860 a treaty with France had removed the protection of the British silk industry, which was quickly stifled by competition from the factories in Lyons. In 1891 Arthur Lazenby Liberty took a leading part in the attempt to revive a native industry, in collaboration with Thomas Wardle, with whom he must have come to an agreement after the closure of Wardle's decorating venture. Liberty again emerges as an enigma; his large imports of silk from Japan and India must have done much to undermine the very industry which he was now so prominently promoting.

By lamentable coincidence the 1880s saw the death of a whole generation of Pugin's successors. These could hardly be regarded as inevitable; most were in their forties or fifties. Street, Burges, Talbert and Jeckyll died in 1881; Rossetti in 1882; Christian Herter in 1883; Godwin and the American architect H. H. Richardson in 1886; Nesfield in 1888; Sedding and Daniel Cottier in 1891.

The failure in quick succession of many – even most – of the 'Art' manufacturers may have been attributable to the recession. The facts were mundane: the exotic was out of fashion, and the purely aesthetic did not satisfy a new desire for moral justification and other preoccupations, such as health, domestic convenience and cleanliness. Significantly, the London exhibitions in the 1880s dealt with Health (1884) and Inventions (1885). In *Decoration and Furniture of Town Houses* (1881) the architect Robert Edis shows a strong preoccupation with cleanliness; for the International Health exhibition he wrote *Healthy Furniture and Decoration*. The understated elegance of the eighteenth-century revival was reassuring to a public wary of display.

A significant manufacturing failure was the takeover in 1885 of

Jackson & Graham by Collinson & Lock; this was particularly cruel as the founders of Collinson & Lock had trained in Jackson & Graham's workshops. Jackson & Graham had been in financial trouble since 1882 but had contrived to stay afloat, staving off creditors with hollow assurances, for three more years. From their foundation in about 1838 until the end of the 1870s Jackson & Graham, leading luxury furnishers in London, must have looked impregnable. The firm's workshops occupied a vast site on the north side of Oxford Street, in the cabinet-making triangle bounded on two sides by Oxford Street and Tottenham Court Road, where Heal's now stands a lonely monument to a massive concentration of furnishing manufacturers and retailers.

In order to survive, the firms that had taken advantage of the vogue for 'Art' furniture changed tack in the eighties. Cox & Son, ecclesiastical furnishers and prominent exhibitors in the Medieval Court at the 1862 Exhibition, had taken up a number of the Art Movement designers but by the late seventies were again prudently concentrating on church commissions. From 1884 Collinson & Lock turned to historicist pieces designed by Collcutt and a newcomer, the sculptor Stephen Webb.

The furniture by Stephen Webb was in a hybrid Queen Anne-Georgian style inlaid with intricate ivory intarsia 'in the manner of the late Renaissance'. Webb was one of the very few who managed to bridge the gap between cabinet-made furniture and the workshop productions of the Arts and Crafts Guilds. He was an early member of the Art Workers' Guild and an exhibitor with the Arts and Crafts Exhibition Society. Collinson & Lock were themselves taken over in 1897 by Gillow's, who had since the 1860s been making good quality mass-market reproduction furniture.

Holland & Sons were forced to contract, disposing of their Pimlico workshops to William Morris in 1890. With the departure of Wright & Mansfield, leading 'Adam Revival' manufacturers, Morris & Co. now dominated the business of fine cabinet-making, which it had entered some five years earlier with a limited range of eighteenth-century style 'rich inlaid cabinets and suites of fine construction and design' (Aymer Vallance, *Life and Work of William Morris*, 1897, p. 123). This was the very area of the market which Holland had failed to hang on to. It seems likely that they had been subcontracted by Morris to make the fine furniture, and the consequent loss of identity precipitated the disposal of the workshops.

This rapid and widespread decline was surprising after the many successes of the British manufacturers in Paris in 1878. Conspicuous among the prize-winners were the ceramic manufacturers: G. A. Sala had remarked complacently, 'In that section of the Exposition Universelle where British pottery makes so opulent and interesting a

display, wheresoever one turns there is reason for congratulation.' (*Paris Herself Again*, 1882, p. 154.) Sala traced the revival of the ceramic trade in Britain to the introduction by Minton's in the 1840s of encaustic tiles for Sir Charles Barry's Reform Club and Pugin's Neo-Gothic interiors in the New Palace of Westminster.

As Eastlake had noted, Pugin's enterprising collaborator Herbert Minton was an inspired innovator, resolving one after the other the problems of creating a secular Gothic Revival interior. The technical quality of all his products, not only the encaustic tiles, but the stoneware dishes, the brilliantly coloured 'Della Robbia' majolica ware and the 'Henri Deux' pieces with their intricate inlaid decoration, were to make his reputation as an outstanding ceramic manufacturer.

In spite of his successor Colin Minton Campbell's affinity for the Art Movement, it is evident from reports of the Paris Exhibition in 1878 that the firm was still producing special showpieces rather than modest domestic wares suited to a profitable mass-market. The display was dedicated to 'Henri Deux' ware and *pâte-sur-pâte*, as well as the more adventurous 'Japanese' cloisonné and turquoise-ground 'Persian' ware. Minton's had ignored the sound basis of holloware production at their peril. Campbell retired in 1880 and died in 1887. From 1886 Minton's started to make losses and continued to do so. In 1900 a record loss of £16,000 was announced.

Minton's suffered the fate of many luxury manufacturers, but the decline was inevitable in their case. Without their own London retail premises – their wares were sold by Thomas Goode and Mortlock's – they were dependent on business generated at the exhibitions, for which their technically sophisticated pieces were ideally suited. As interest in exhibitions diminished this essential prop was removed. Léon Arnoux and L. M. Solon, who had been responsible for some of the finest prize-winning productions, were both elderly, and adapted poorly to the new trends. Arnoux retired in 1892 but went on advising the firm until his death ten years later. Solon did not leave the firm until 1904; he died in 1913. His son joined Minton's in 1900, and it was he who designed Minton's commercial Art Nouveau range of 'Secessionist Wares'.

The Royal Worcester Porcelain factory had also scored a brilliant success in 1878, winning a gold medal for a display dominated by the Japanese-style porcelain vases and jardinières which they had been making since the early 1870s. However, the most important objects were a pair of vases in the Renaissance style 29 inches (74 cm) high, modelled in high relief with scenes of a medieval potter's workshop by James Hadley, backed by a large production team of the finest Worcester craftsmen. Only two pairs were made and, probably greatly to the relief of the firm's owner R. W. Binns, one was bought by an American visitor to the exhibition. The other pair belongs still to the Royal Worcester Porcelain Factory.

The Worcester factory had been rescued by Binns between 1861 and 1862 from almost certain oblivion. Although the extent of the difficulties in the eighties and nineties was well hidden, it is a documented fact that there was a severe scarcity of orders and many of the finest painters had to accept lower pay for their work. (For a detailed history of the factory see Henry Sandon, *Royal Worcester Porcelain*, 1973.)

Of all the luxury trades metalwork is the most susceptible to recession because of the intrinsic value of the material. This had been demonstrated repeatedly throughout the century by the difficulties in the French jewellery trade following each revolutionary or political upheaval. The same was equally true for enamelling and silversmithing. The enormously lavish production of silverwares by the New York firm of Tiffany & Co. from the mid-seventies throws the decline of firms such as Elkington's in Birmingham into unwelcome relief.

Elkington's situation mirrored that of Minton's in many ways. In the mid-century they had built on an aggressive policy of scientific experimentation, racing with Christofle in Paris for supremacy in the valuable electroplating business. Expansion followed development in the expensive and difficult techniques of champlevé and cloisonné enamelling. They poached designers and craftsmen from their principal rivals, among them Antoine Vechte, Léonard Morel-Ladeuil and Albert Willms. Elkington's had also shared the talented Pierre-Emile Jeannest with Minton's. With a reputation built on almost incredible technical virtuosity their dependency on exhibiting was critical, but the part played by exhibitions in shaping public taste was diminishing rapidly. Morel-Ladeuil died in 1888 but Willms continued working through the next decade, increasingly out of step with modern developments.

British manufacturers had stolen designers from the French, but they did not adopt the commercial acumen of their rivals. Christofle was careful to make his most extravagant productions only on commission, whereas Elkington's 1879–80 silver-gilt *komai*-patterned teaset, an extravagant example of Japonisme, was not sold until 1906. In the 1870s Hart, Son & Peard made an ambitious piece in the style of Burges, an épergne base in the flamboyant Gothic style (PL. 219); it may never have found a purchaser and survives only in truncated form.

Another factor, not easy to quantify economically, was the growing realization among a socially responsible middle class of the high cost in human terms of industrial development. Henry Mayhew's *London Labour and the London Poor* (1851–62) revealed urban working-class conditions of unprecedented squalor, which were now widely regarded as unacceptable. Artists and writers confronted the issue with considerable impact; Dickens's *Hard Times* (1854) inspired a generation of artists such as Luke Fildes and Hubert von Herkomer – both, coincidentally, owners of Aesthetic houses – whose works appeared as black-and-white illustrations for *The Graphic*, a publication notably willing to confront social problems unflinchingly. George Bernard Shaw described *Hard Times* as 'a passionate revolt against the whole industrial order of the modern world', and, while possibly overstating the case, he gives a measure of the strength of moral outrage.

This art was peculiarly British. When Van Gogh was in London he was profoundly inspired by this movement, notably through the *Graphic* illustrations. Ironically, both Fildes and Herkomer gave up these moving subject paintings in mid-career and turned to portrait painting to fund their Aesthetic style of life.

A glimpse of other problems is provided by J. Diblee Crace; outlining his reasons for winding up the family decorating firm in 1899 he cited 'the harassing anxiety attached to the employment of men, particularly by Trades Union action, and finally the Employer's Liability Act'. The survival of the firm until this time is explained by the fact that Crace was immensely versatile, with a line in rich Neo-Renaissance which ensured the firm a succession of wealthy patrons who sustained the business through the eighties and nineties.

PL. 208 T. E. Collcutt: mahogany cabinet with glazed doors on a stand; made by Collinson & Lock. A version was shown at the 1878 Paris Exhibition. The architectural form of the cabinet derives from bow-windowed façades of the early eighteenth century.

PL. 209 Richard Norman Shaw: Queen Anne-style house; designed as a jury house for the British pavilion at the Paris Exhibition. 'It is a ghost of an old English town house of the first years of the eighteenth century, with its red brickwork – showing the alternate courses of "headers" and "stretchers" of the "English bond" – its white stone balcony, fluted pilasters, elaborately moulded panellings, and ornate cornices; but instead of being built of the old-fashioned bricks, it is entirely constructed of cubes of Mr Lascelles' patented red cement, which are truer, harder, and quite impervious to wet, and to which he has succeeded in imparting the cheerful red tone characteristic of the epoch.' (G. A. Sala, *Paris Herself Again*, 1882, p. 363.) The house was constructed by W. H. Lascelles to publicize his recently (1875) patented 'Cement Slab System'. The house was awarded a gold medal.

Opposite PL. 210 Bruce Talbert: 'Juno' cabinet, ebony inlaid with ivory, mother-of-pearl, abalone shell and various woods, made by Jackson & Graham. Shown at the 1878 Exhibition where it won a Grand Prix. This cabinet is the most prodigious example of a technique of which Jackson & Graham was one of the supreme exponents. It was bought by the Viceroy of Egypt. In Talbert's obituary in the *Cabinet Maker and Art Furnisher* (1881) it was described as 'the finest object in cabinet work exhibited in Paris'.

Right PL. 211 An illustration of furniture from the William Watt stand at the 1878 Exhibition in Paris. The centrepiece of the stand is the butterfly fireplace and overmantel, part of a room scheme, a 'harmony in yellow and gold', designed by J. McNeill Whistler and E. W. Godwin in 1877. Whistler painted the dado and the panels of the overmantel and Godwin designed the furniture, including the chair and table, abandoning his usual ebonized finish in favour of a light mahogany. The scheme may have been commissioned by Watt in homage to the 'Peacock' room, which had been completed in 1877.

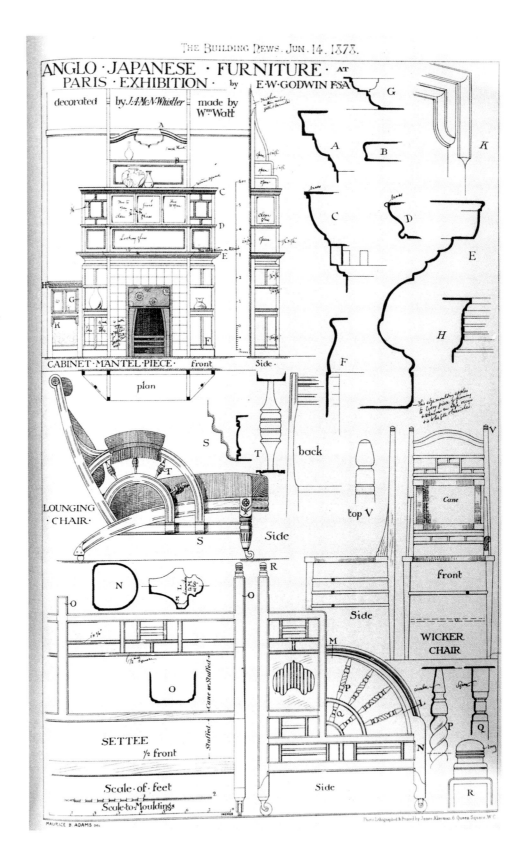

PL. 212 Thomas Harris: bracket clock, ceramic face and painted 'Vanitas' panel; made by Howell, James & Co. of London. One of two bracket clocks by Harris shown by the firm at the 1878 Paris Exhibition. Thomas Harris was the architect of Milner Hall, 1872, for Titus Salt.

PL. 213 R. Davey: 'Anglo-Moorish' buffet, oak with bands of inlaid decoration; made by William Walker. Part of a dining-room suite shown at the exhibition.

Opposite PL. 214 Jacquard-woven portière, attributed to Bruce Talbert; made by Templeton & Co. Like Watt, Templeton made a speciality of 'Art' manufactures, by leading designers.

Above PL. 215 Paul Avisse: *Coupe de Cybèle*; Sèvres porcelain. A version of the tazza shown at the 1878 Paris Exhibition. Fifteen examples of the tazza '*fond bleu au grand feu, décoration couleurs et or*' were made for sale in 1879.

Above PL. 216 Dessert plate of 'cloisonné ware'; made by Minton & Co. Shown at the 1878 Paris Exhibition in the Prince of Wales pavilion.

Left PL. 217 Three Japanesque vases by the Royal Worcester Porcelain Co. The company won a gold medal for its ceramic display at the 1878 Paris Exhibition, the Japanese-style porcelains with raised decoration in gold and bronze being particularly commended.

Right PL. 219 Centrepiece, enamel and parcel gilding on bronze; by Hart, Son, Peard & Co., possibly after a design by William Burges. Shown at the Paris Exhibition. The high Gothic style still fascinated Burges, who was at this time involved in the medieval-style decoration of Cardiff Castle and Castell Coch for Lord Bute, and of his own Tower House in Kensington.

Above PL. 218 Moon flask with Japanese-style cloisonné decoration by Minton & Co. Shown at the 1878 Paris Exhibition in the Prince of Wales pavilion designed by Norman Shaw. The cloisonné and majolica pieces were admired, and escaped – unlike the porcelain in the eighteenth-century taste and Solon's technical masterpieces of *pâte-sur-pâte* – the inevitable comparisons with the wares of the government-supported Sèvres Manufactory.

Left PL. 220 Coffee pot, silver, copper and brass, designed to imitate Japanese *mokume* work; Tiffany & Co., *c.*1879. Tiffany's had been invited to exhibit the Japanese-style silverware, developed under the influence of Edward C. Moore, in Paris in 1878.

Above PL. 221 Tankard, oxidised silver, 1874–6; and waiter or tray for visiting cards, hammered silver with an applied swimming frog of silver inlaid with gold and copper with black patination, dated 1880; Tiffany & Co. Edward C. Moore was Tiffany's chief designer and a director of the silver works from 1868. His own collection included a strong representation of Far Eastern metalwork. The firm produced Japanese-style metalwork until Moore's death in 1891. An inscription on the reverse of the tray records its ownership by the Vanderbilt family.

Left PL. 222 Silver and three-colour gold overlay jug; Elkington & Co., 1879.

Above PL. 223 Biscuit box, silver with geometric *komai* engraved decoration; Elkington & Co., 1881.

The American Renaissance

The 'American Renaissance' has been dated as lasting from 1876 to 1910 (in the catalogue of the exhibition of that name, held at the Brooklyn Museum, New York, in 1979). One of the best documented monuments to the style of the period is the William H. Vanderbilt House in New York, fully described in four sumptuously illustrated volumes by Edward Strachan (*Mr Vanderbilt's House and Collection*) which appeared in 1883 and 1884, paid for by William Vanderbilt himself. In 1877 Vanderbilt inherited $90 million from his father. By the time of his death in 1885 he had increased his inheritance to more than $200 million. In 1879 he commissioned Herter Brothers to design and furnish a vast palace on Fifth Avenue, on a site that he had purchased for $700,000, stretching for a whole block between 51st and 52nd Streets. In 1911 Vanderbilt's artistic pretensions were summed up by Gustavus Myers (*The Great American Fortunes*): 'With the expenditure of a few hundred thousand dollars he instantly transformed himself from a heavy-witted, uncultured money hoarder into the character of a surpassing judge and patron of art.' This was frequently the motive, and by no means the most ignoble, for lavish patronage of decorative design.

Herter's completed the house and its opulently appointed interiors in the very short space of two years, partly by some discreetly concealed short cuts. The furniture, however, was of unsurpassed quality, gilded, carved, inlaid and lavishly upholstered in silk and cut velvet.

Artistic Houses, which was issued in parts from 1883 to 1884, constitutes the most valuable record of rich American patronage in the 1880s (reissued as *The Opulent Interiors of the Gilded Age*, New York 1987). The emphasis in the text (probably written by the art critic George Sheldon) is on the paintings and *objets d'art*, but there are reminders of the British presence at the 1876 Philadelphia Exhibition, in the form of wallpapers by Morris in the sitting room of the Hovey House in Massachusetts (vol. II, pl. 167); of Dresser with the frieze in William L. Singerley's Philadelphia office (vol. I, pl. 173); and of Jeckyll, with his sunflower firedogs in the library of David L. Einstein's New York house. The rooms in the Einstein House were decorated in the styles of different historical periods, the library in the supposed manner of Louis XIII, an incongruous location for the firedogs – especially as the house also had a Japanese boudoir.

Included as well as the Vanderbilt House are all the most admired domestic interiors of this early period of the American decorative renaissance. Herter is notably represented, with the Pierpont Morgan House as well as the Vanderbilt House, and further uncredited but attributable interiors. The Furness-Pabst partnership is much featured in the Philadelphia houses: for example, in the Clara Jessop Moore House, the house of the President of the Philadelphia Academy James L. Claghorn, and that of the millionaire art collector Henry C. Gibson. Furness's own taste, as exemplified by the smoking room added to his Philadelphia house, could not be a greater contrast. He had spent summers in the Rockies and collected souvenirs of trapper life; the rustic furniture facing a raw stone fireplace is covered with bearskins, and the walls and ceiling are lined with rough-hewn planks.

Louis Comfort Tiffany trained as a painter and followed this career with a considerable degree of success – his paintings were shown at Philadelphia in 1876 and Paris in 1878 – until, in 1880, encouraged by his father's partner Edward C. Moore, he took up interior decoration. In the previous year he had written to Candace Wheeler: 'I have been thinking a great deal about decorative work, and I am going into it as a profession. I believe there is more in it than in painting pictures.' (*In Pursuit of Beauty*, Metropolitan Museum of Art, 1986, p. 474.) With Candace Wheeler, his friend Samuel Colman and Lockwood de Forrest he founded Associated Artists; the partnership was dissolved in 1883, but Candace Wheeler continued to use the name for her textile designs. Louis C. Tiffany & Company continued as the decorative design firm, and Tiffany Studios specialized in the glass and metalwork, Tiffany's main preoccupation from the 1890s.

Henry Gurdon Marquand's Newport House provided a showcase for the work of John La Farge, a noted stained glass artist and principal rival to Tiffany's Associated Artists. Marquand's New York music room was furnished to designs by the painter Sir Lawrence Alma-Tadema. Alma-Tadema's ivory, ebony and mother-of-pearl inlaid pieces have obvious affinities with the Herter furniture for Vanderbilt but, bearing in mind his position in the artistic élite of 1870s London, the inspiration may have come from Owen Jones's furniture for Alfred Morrison. Like Marquand, Alma-Tadema had one of La Farge's 'peony' windows in his London house.

Taking a lead from British Aestheticism, American decorative taste of the period takes Japan and the East (exemplified by Islamic and Indian culture) as its leitmotiv. Interiors were ornamented with

PL. 224 Fall-front desk, ebonized, inlaid, carved and gilded woods; by Herter Brothers, New York, *c*.1880.

objets d'art of Japanese and Moresque inspiration; silver from Tiffany & Co.; porcelain from Ott & Brewer of Trenton, New Jersey; Isnik-pattern pots from John Bennett of New York – the British-born Bennett had previously worked for Doulton's – and glass from the New England and Mount Washington works in Massachusetts. English ceramics were still prized: Royal Worcester under protective glass domes, intricately embossed Wedgwood Jasperware, and *pâte-sur-pâte* pieces by Solon were conspicuous in the rooms featured in *Artistic Houses*. But American manufacturers had learned quickly, and by the mid-eighties were able to supply a network of domestic consumer outlets, reducing the need for large-scale importation.

While French and Italian 'Renaissance' palaces were fulfilling the artistic fantasies of the railroad barons and millionaire industrialists, American architects were inventing the modern city. One of the great engineering achievements of the nineteenth century, John and Washington Roebling's Brooklyn Bridge (begun in 1867) was completed in 1883, the year that William Vanderbilt occupied his newly decorated Fifth Avenue mansion. New York's distinguished public and commercial buildings of the 1880s have the same massive presence as the industrial architecture of Britain's northern manufacturing towns. The small area of Manhattan Island and its solid rock base allowed buildings to reach skywards in a way unprecedented in Europe. Visiting downtown Manhattan in 1893, the French writer Paul Bourget reflected: 'As soon as one feels oneself undergoing the total ensemble of these buildings, one experiences again and again this impression of Babylon, which indeed is splendid and, I must admit, puts a spell on you.' (*Outre-mer*, *Notes sur l'Amérique*, 1895, vol. 1, p. 39.)

PL. 225 Mahogany table, inlaid with metals and mother-of-pearl, brass braces and finials, in the Anglo-Japanese style influenced by E. W. Godwin; by A. & H. Lejambre, Philadelphia, *c.* 1880.

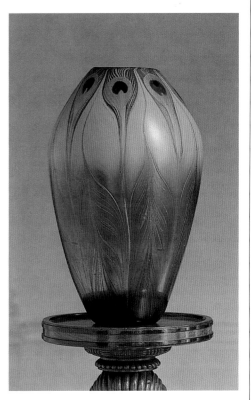

Left PL. 226 Cabinet, ebonized, inlaid and gilded woods, with Japanese panels; by Herter Brothers, New York, *c.*1880.

Above PL. 227 L. C. Tiffany: 'Favrile' glass vase, with peacock feather and trailed decoration. In 1892 Tiffany developed for his Tiffany Studios a new type of blown glass for ornamental bowls and vases, named 'Favrile' and patented in 1894. The satiny texture is enlivened with iridescence and patterns, organic or abstract, in jewelled colours.

Christopher Dresser

Dresser enrolled in the Government School of Design in London in about 1847. Here he studied under Richard Redgrave, at that time the tutor in botanical drawing. Dresser's special subject was 'art botany', and its application to design can be traced throughout his career which began in assisting Owen Jones with botanical drawings for *Grammar*. This training was to form the perfect preparation for an understanding of Japanese art and design. Having been a great enthusiast since the exhibitions of Japanese wares in London in the 1850s, Dresser had written on the beauties of Japanese art and design in a number of his early publications. As a result of his already established reputation he was invited to visit Japan in 1876 as a private guest of the Japanese government, to report on the development of modern Japanese industry. On his return he published *Japan, its Architecture, Art and Art-Manufactures* (1882). The experience of Japan marked his artistic maturity and ensured him a place at the forefront of the avant-garde in nineteenth-century industrial design.

The Japanese theme is very fully developed in Dresser's work from early in his career, but his approach altered significantly after he returned from his travels. A jardinière for Minton of 1873 deriving from a bronze form has none of the plasticity of Japanese ceramics he had assimilated for his later designs of the 1880s for the Linthorpe Art Pottery (PL. 247). One of his electroplated teapots, in the form of a hollow circle (PL. 237), was apparently based on a 'remarkable wheel-formed Japanese teapot' sold at Sotheby's in 1879, which was described in *The Times* (15 July 1879) and attracted much attention. Full appreciation of Dresser's Japanese forms comes only with an understanding of his sources, some of which remain difficult for a Western audience even today.

Dresser outlived his mid-life success, and had to retreat from Tower Cressy, his grandiose Kensington mansion, to the consoling pleasures of his garden and his conservatory in Sutton. With most of his contemporaries, he was forgotten for much of the first half of the present century. When his work was rediscovered, largely due to Sir Nikolaus Pevsner, it seemed so outlandish in the context of the conventional idea of Victorian taste that it was assumed very few of the pieces had been made in any quantity. Modern research has completely reversed this judgement. Examples of his work in every sphere of his activity except wallpaper and textiles are far from rare; but this evidence of his mass-market appeal, rather than diminishing his importance, has revealed the significant design innovator only dimly sensed half a century ago.

As well as his small number of architectural commissions and some furniture designs, Dresser experimented with a great variety of decorative materials including metalwork, glass and all kinds of ceramics from porcelain to pottery and redware. His wallpaper and textile designs run parallel with his influential publications and probably formed the bulk of his output in the 1870s when he is listed as an 'ornamentist'. He wrote a great many articles on design and decoration, but his important pattern books, *Principles of Decorative Design* (1873), and *Studies in Design* (1875–6), contain the essence of his ideas.

The extent of Dresser's commercial appeal in his own time has gradually become clear as more of his works appear on the market. The Japanese-style polyhedral designs, were too difficult for the mass market. A lozenge-shaped teapot with a central lozenge-shaped void (PL. 239, in a private collection) and a rectangular teapot (PL. 238, now in the British Museum) both appear to be unique.

PL. 228 Christopher Dresser: upholstered chair, ebonized, with incised gilt decoration; designed for the Art Furnishers' Alliance and made by Chubb's, 1880–83. The chair frame is made up in strict mathematical modules of 12 inches (30 cm), the seat being 24 inches square and 12 inches high.

Below PL. 229 Christopher Dresser: side chair, ebonized and turned frame; designed for the Art Furnishers' Alliance, *c.*1880. The chair appears in the illustration accompanying the description in the *Cabinet Maker* (1 July 1881) of the opening of the Art Furnishers' Alliance in New Bond Street.

Above PL. 230 Christopher Dresser: hot-water jug, copper with an insulating sleeve of compressed paper, bearing a facsimile signature of the designer; Richard Perry, Son & Co. of Wolverhampton. Perry specialized in japanned and tinned iron, and Dresser designed a number of coloured pieces as well as brass and copper for the firm between 1876 and 1883.

Right PL. 232 Christopher Dresser: planter, brass and copper; designed for Benham & Froud and made *c*.1882–5. Benham & Froud were suppliers to the Art Furnishers' Alliance, and a number of mixed metal pieces were made for exhibition in 1882. Dresser had been designing for the firm since at least 1878.

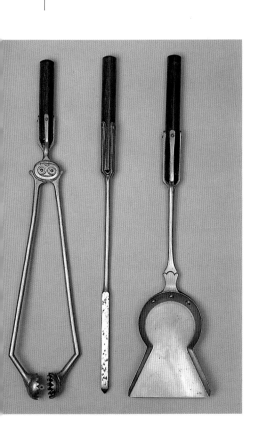

Above PL. 231 Christopher Dresser: fire irons in brass and steel with wood handles; designed for Benham & Froud.

PL. 233 Christopher Dresser: silver-plated bowl; made by Elkington & Co., date mark for 1885. The design was roughly sketched in 1864 and illustrated in *Principles of Design* (1873), where Dresser explains the rationale of his design: 'If we propose to ourselves the formation of a sugar-basin of semi-circular shape, of what thickness must the metal be in order that it may not bend when lifted? It is obvious that the vessel must not yield its shape to ordinary pressure, nor be subject to alterations of form when in ordinary use; but if it is to be formed throughout of metal of such thickness as will secure its retaining its shape, it will be costly and heavy, and an amount of metal will be used in its formation sufficient for the manufacture of two or three such articles. Instead of forming the vessel throughout of thick metal, we may construct it from a thin sheet of silver; but in order that it possess sufficient strength we must indent one or more beads on its side ... or we can form an angle by having a rim projecting into the basin ... or extending from it, and thus give strength; but the two beads are more desirable, as the one gives strength at the top and the other at the lower portion of the vessel.' (pp. 135–6.)

PL. 234 Christopher Dresser: conical electroplated bowl; made by Elkington & Co. Variants of the design were roughly sketched in 1864 and a more exaggerated form was illustrated in *Principles* (p. 139). With the passage of time Dresser's reason for using the zig-zag form for the legs – that they should also serve as handles – seems to have been overlooked.

PL. 235 Christopher Dresser: silver claret jug decorated with incised bands; made by Elkington & Co., 1885.

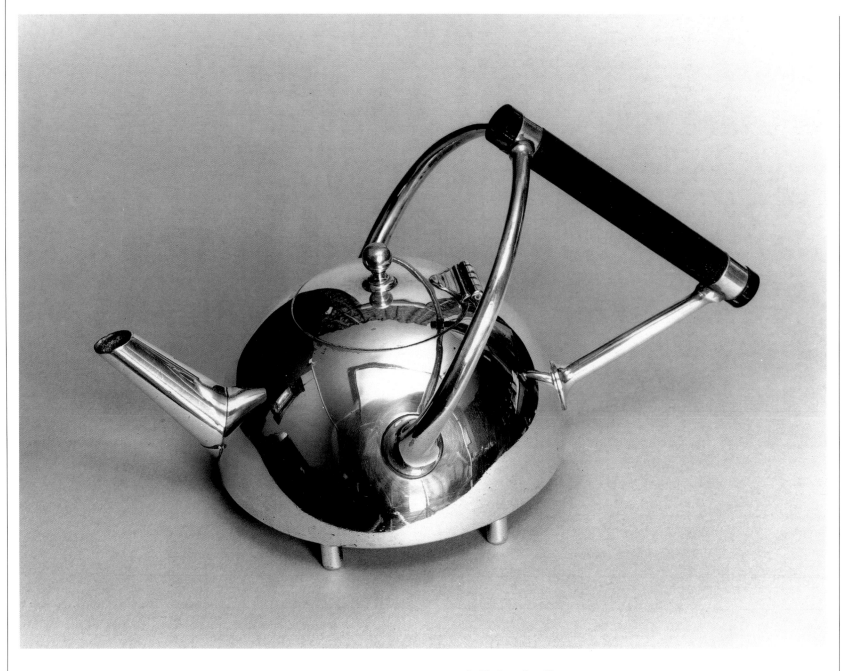

PL. 236 Christopher Dresser:
electroplated hemispherical
teapot, supported on six feet,
ebony handle; made by James
Dixon & Sons, 1880.

PL. 237 Christopher Dresser:
circular electroplated teapot with
cylindrical central void and ebony
handle; made by James Dixon &
Sons, 1879.

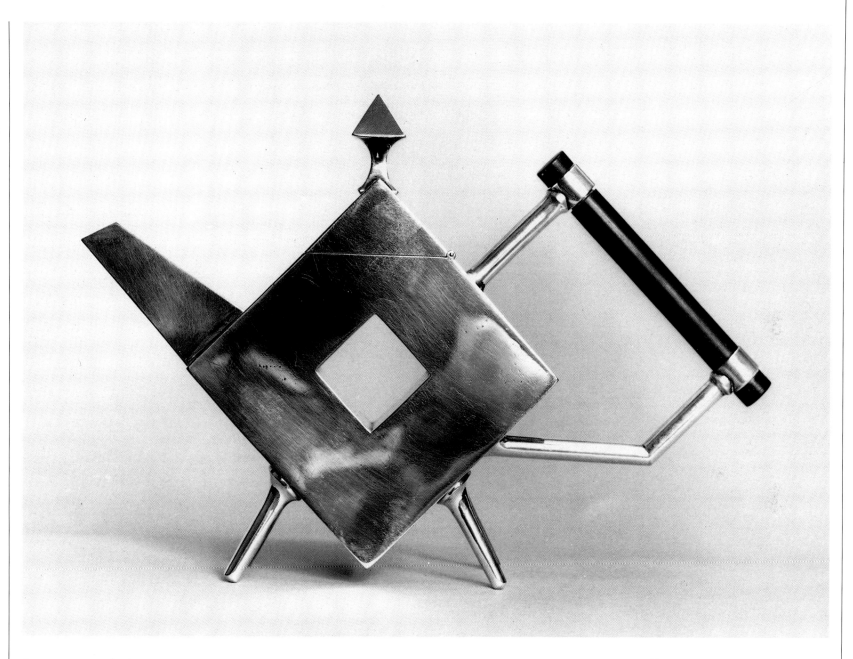

Opposite PL. 238 Christopher Dresser: rectangular teapot, electroplated, with ebonized wood handle, stamped with facsimile signature 'Chr Dresser'; made by James Dixon & Sons, 1879. Inspired by Chinese eighteenth-century metal teapots of this form.

Above PL. 239 Christopher Dresser: electroplated teapot; designed for James Dixon & Sons, 1879. The radical Japanesque polyhedral designs supplied to Dixon from 1879 to 1882 were made in very small numbers. They seem revolutionary still.

Left PL. 240 Christopher Dresser: electroplated cruet set; made by Elkington, 1885.

Above PL. 241 Christopher Dresser: electroplated cruet stand with two glass bottles; Hukin & Heath, design registered 1878.

Right PL. 242 Christopher Dresser: electroplated toast rack, double cantilever shape; made by James Dixon & Sons, 1880.

Below PL. 244 Christopher Dresser: electroplated toast rack, consisting of a flat plate and plain rods of metal; made by Hukin & Heath, 1878. Hukin & Heath were taking a risk with such severely simplified forms, but they were marketing the designer as much as the design, and many of their pieces bear the inscription 'Designed by Dr C Dresser'.

Below PL. 243 Christopher Dresser: Japanese-inspired electroplated toast rack; made by James Dixon & Sons, 1880.

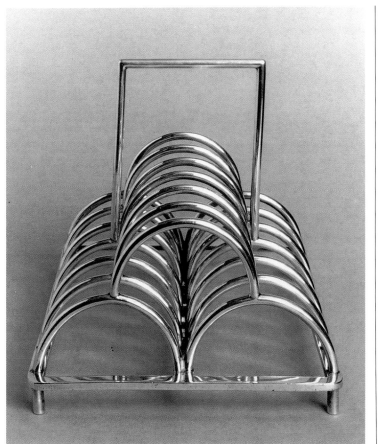

Left PL. 245 Christopher Dresser: two-handled vase, pottery with drip-glazes; made by Ault & Co., *c.*1887.

Above PL. 246 Christopher Dresser: vessel with trumpet-shaped spout, pottery with drip-glazes, impressed facsimile signature of the designer; made by Ault & Co., *c.*1887.

PL. 247 Christopher Dresser: three vessels, (left) Ault & Co., (centre) Linthorpe Art Pottery, (right) Ault & Co., showing the similarity of treatment. After his visit to Japan in 1876, Dresser's ideas about ceramic design became more sophisticated. He was influenced by the Japanese respect for the 'living' clay, making a virtue of its malleability. The small piece on the right is inspired by a Japanese inkpot.

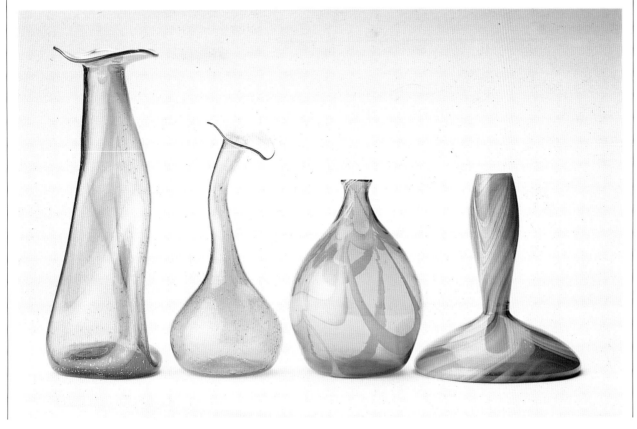

PL. 248 Christopher Dresser: four vases of 'Clutha' glass; made by James Couper & Sons. In spite of the Celtic-sounding name, these pieces were inspired by ancient Roman, Persian and Venetian glass.

NEW BEGINNINGS AND THE
ARTS AND CRAFTS MOVEMENT

When considering the re-decoration of his house with eighteenth-century furniture in 1876, Godwin as ever showed an almost uncanny appreciation of coming trends. At that date the eighteenth-century revival in furniture already established in the trade – a natural complement to the fashionable 'Queen Anne' style in architecture – was beginning to attract the attention of the Art Movement designers. Predictably, Norman Shaw was one of the first to try the 'Queen Anne' style for furniture, judiciously mixing seventeenth-century forms with eighteenth-century details. With W. H. Lascelles, his preferred builder, he was responsible for the British decorative message at the 1878 Paris Exhibition. As well as the English Jury House (PL. 209) 'built entirely of concrete bricks' on the rue des Nations – a gold medal winner, and admired by the French as 'construite dans un style très charmant et surtout très aimé des anglais, le style de la reine Anne' – Norman Shaw devised stands for the British exhibitors. His cabinet of 1878 is still massively structural in the Gothic Revival tradition, but the delicately naturalistic decoration by J. Aldam Heaton and the use of heavy, seventeenth-century architectonic mouldings bridges the jump from the Webb-Morris side cabinet of 1865 (PL. 166) to the next phase of Morris & Co. and the younger generation of designers and architects.

Eighteenth-century revival architecture suited the mood of the 1880s since it was both reticent and safe, rather than flamboyant like Neo-Gothic and Renaissance, or avant-garde like Anglo-Japanese and Egyptian. The choice of 'Queen Anne' was the result of a search for a style without associations, as distinct from ecclesiastical Gothic or academic classicism. The evolution of a fully secular Gothic vocabulary had not really worked and many of the buildings were either ornately historicist or featureless and dull. The early eighteenth century was perceived as the last moment of pre-industrial society, still an important consideration with artistic patrons. The new style encompassed a variety of possibilities, the 'Old English' or free-style vernacular, the Hanseatic or Dutch gabled style taken from North European urban architecture, and the mid-eighteenth-century Adamesque. Aspects of this hybrid have never entirely disappeared from British architecture: this was the type of 'English house' admired by Muthesius and, as Sir John Summerson remarked to Gavin Stamp, is 'the only sort which has never been laughed at' (Gavin Stamp, *The English House 1860–1914*, 1986, p.13).

By the late 1860s the choice for most domestic commissions was 'Old English', built of red brick with stone dressings and white-painted woodwork. The danger of accepting 'vernacular' as a style rather than as a local tradition is that its essentially materials-based aesthetic will be bastardized. This had produced the anomalies of brick building in stone-bearing country, and contributed to the rootlessness of much suburban ribbon development. The early examples of the vernacular revival were carefully researched. George Devey (1820–86) was one of the first adherents of the new rustic style, employing a convincing local vernacular for a series of cottages and lodges in Kent. The village houses constructed from old materials in Penshurst date from 1850, and it is now difficult to tell the mid-nineteenth-century houses from their earlier neighbours. Devey had a considerable influence on the younger men, such as W. E. Nesfield and Norman Shaw, whose sketchbooks show their serious pursuit of authenticity.

Vernacular, being the product of master builders whose design solutions were rooted in a strict regard for function, provided a logical extension of the principles of reformed Gothic as evolved by Pugin. The pragmatism of Japanese buildings exploited the same ideas, and inspired the simplicity and asymmetry of Art Movement architecture in the 1860s and 1870s. Vernacular is the bridge between the internationalism of Gothic Revival and Japonisme and the insular Arts and Crafts Movement. Other Art Movement architects who used the vernacular style were Godwin, Philip Webb, T. E. Collcutt and Ernest George, Norman Shaw's main competitor in the domestic field. In the next generation Shaw's pupils, including W. R. Lethaby and Sidney Barnsley, took the vernacular into Arts and Crafts. All these men designed furniture, and their inspiration came from the Queen Anne period or the later eighteenth century.

Others included Lewis F. Day, a stained glass artist who had set up as an independent designer in 1870. His contribution was in the field of textiles, wallpapers for Jeffrey & Co., and tiles for Maw's, Craven Dunnill and Pilkington. A cabinet dating from 1879 is like Norman Shaw's of the previous year, but more refined in form and with inlaid decoration incorporating elements from the designs of Robert Adam. By 1882 Day's decorating manual *Everyday Art* was recommending a restrained classicism in preference to Japonisme. Maurice B. Adams devised an elegant Adamesque style for fashionable imitation eighteenth-century pieces. These were so perfect for exploitation by the trade that it is now difficult to see him as a pioneer. Through his position on the staff of *Building News* Adams had interesting contacts with, for example, Godwin and Bruce Talbert; he was also associated with Norman Shaw through his work at Bedford Park. His most important patron was the wealthy philanthropist Passmore Edwards, for whom he designed a number of public and institutional buildings.

Bedford Park, the first 'garden suburb', sited beyond Hammersmith on land bought for development in the 1870s by Jonathan Carr, a rich cloth merchant, initiated the small architect-designed Aesthetic house. The architects involved included Godwin, Norman Shaw and C. F. A. Voysey. The utopian community was colonized by a homogeneous group of cultured residents, and took Art Movement values and artefacts to a wider public than that provided by the upper-class patrons on whom the architect-designers had formerly relied. Bedford Park was well publicized, the house plans being featured by Maurice B. Adams in *Building News,* and their long-term influence was greater than that of many more ambitious schemes. Muthesius approved of Bedford Park because of its implications for future suburban development. As he pointed out: 'The problem facing house building in the world of today is that of the middle-class house'; he believed that in his Bedford Park houses Norman Shaw had solved this problem. The greatest accolade for English domestic architecture came from Viollet-le-Duc, in his *Habitations modernes* of 1877.

The development of Bedford Park coincided with the fashion for books on 'taste in the home'. Since its publication in 1868 Charles Eastlake's *Hints on Household Taste* had led the field; now it was challenged by Rhoda and Agnes Garrett, *Suggestions for House Decorating* (1876); Harriet Prescott Spofford, *Art Decoration Applied to Furniture* (1878); the *Art in the Home* series (1878), with contributions from Mrs Orrinsmith on 'The Drawing Room' and Mrs Loftie on 'The Dining Room'. *The House Beautiful* by Clarence Cook, with its celebrated frontispiece by Walter Crane, appeared in 1881. Mrs Haweis took over as the arbiter of artistic taste in the eighties, producing in quick succession *The Art of Decoration* (1881) and *The House Beautiful* (1882). The home envisaged by these writers is closely akin to the garden suburb type, an impression reinforced by an obsession with health and hygiene. The beneficiaries of this combined initiative were decorators, textile designers, wallpaper manufacturers and modestly priced furnishers. The efforts of the new generation of designers – Crane, Voysey, Lewis Day, Mackmurdo and Heywood Sumner – were concentrated in this field.

It was on this wave of interest in home decoration that Liberty's, among others, rose to heights of prominence and prosperity. Closely bound up with Liberty's fortunes was the design studio founded in 1880 by Arthur Silver. One design that might be said to epitomize this phase of the Aesthetic movement is the 'Peacock Feather' of 1886, again in production today.

The Century Guild

The Guild, founded in 1882, gave a notable individuality to the Georgian revival. It was set up principally by A. H. Mackmurdo and Herbert Horne. Another member better known in his own right was William De Morgan. Influenced by the example of Ruskin and Morris, this was the first of the Guilds which later became the backbone of the Arts and Crafts Movement in Britain and America. Although the Guild lasted only until 1893 and produced relatively little in the way of furniture, its exhibits at the Health (1884), Inventions (1885), Liverpool International (1886), and Manchester Jubilee (1887) exhibitions made a considerable impact. A table by an evident disciple, C. E. Horton, was shown by Lamb of Manchester at the 1887 Manchester Exhibition (PL. 252). 'New Art' furniture, designed by G. M. Ellwood for J. S. Henry & Co. shows a clear debt to Mackmurdo as well as an affinity with his contemporary George Walton.

The Century Guild stand at the Liverpool International Exhibition of 1886 incorporated many features, both in the structure itself and in the exhibits, that were to become the hallmarks of British Art Nouveau. In particular this display emphasized the square plinth set on columns that was later to become almost a cliché in Arts and Crafts furniture, notably on pianos, sideboards and settles. The craftsmanship was of impressively high quality, not by any means a *sine qua non* of Arts and Crafts production, the pieces being executed by E. Goodall & Co. of Manchester.

With the short-lived but impressive Kenton & Co., a furniture venture involving Lethaby, Mervyn Macartney, Ernest Gimson and Reginald Blomfield, and the strikingly similar new direction at Morris & Co., immaculately executed mahogany pieces of eighteenth-century inspiration briefly dominated the avant-garde in furniture design. Blomfield's patterns of moulded panels take Webb's architectural details into furniture design. Macartney, a knowledgeable connoisseur of the eighteenth century who used his editorship of the *Architectural Review* to promote the furniture of the period, was associated with Morris & Co. in the 1890s. Century Guild links with Morris may have been closer than those of teacher and admiring pupils. It is thought that Morris & Co. sold the remaining stock after the closure of the Guild in 1893.

While William Morris was actively involved with the furniture designs his firm avoided making actual reproductions, but in the 1890s straight copies of Chippendale were made for commissions such as Standen in Sussex. Meanwhile in W. R. Lethaby and George Jack – respectively from the offices of Shaw and Webb – Morris & Co. had masterly interpreters of the eighteenth century. An impressive sideboard of 1887 (PL. 249) designed by Jack uses, but refines, Mackmurdo's signature of the column support topped with a flaring plinth. A more conventional display cabinet has the subtleties of detail that distinguished Morris furniture from the run of commercial eighteenth-century pastiche. The firm's most exquisite piece in this genre is the mahogany table (PL. 269) with swirling stretchers gathered into a central delicately carved daisy flower. For Stanmore Lethaby devised a form of English Renaissance style for the staircase, five chimneypieces, panelling, cupboards, doors and some furniture. The table was included in the Morris & Co. catalogue. Lethaby's table for Avon Tyrell is in a bold eclectic design with no obvious historical precedent.

Although he paid due respect in his study of contemporary architecture and design to the Gothic and Japanese phases of nineteenth-century furniture, Muthesius had a distinct penchant for the eighteenth century. His own quarters in London were furnished with good plain mahogany pieces: an architect's table of *c.*1740, a Chippendale chair, a *demi-lune* console and an urn stand with a fretted gallery. Speaking in *Das englische Haus* of 'The Period of Aestheticism' he draws attention to furniture design:

> 'Most importantly, there now came a revival of taste for the old furniture of the eighteenth century. The delicate art of Chippendale and Sheraton was rediscovered at this time. The graceful little cabinets and little tables with spidery legs were brought out of store and were found to fit the present mood excellently, for they were as slender and delicate and light as anyone could wish.' (p. 161.)

Predictably, he illustrated the revivalist interpretations of Walton and Baillie Scott, but the many examples of domestic furniture reproduced in the text come from the commercial sphere. Muthesius particularly applauded Gillow's mahogany furniture, remarking that 'Gillow deserves great credit for upholding at least moderately good taste during the battle of the styles in the nineteenth century.' That this was a widely held view is evidenced by the enduring popularity of reproduction or eighteenth-century style furniture. Mahogany furniture from firms such as J. S. Henry were admired abroad and items were purchased from exhibitions for the newly established decorative art museums, notably in Vienna and Trondheim.

PL. 249 George Jack: sideboard, mahogany with marquetry inlay; made by Morris & Co., *c.*1887. This is a version of the sideboard shown by the firm at the Manchester Jubilee Exhibition in 1887. The trend away from simple vernacular forms was characteristic of late Morris & Co. production.

Left PL. 250 A. H. Mackmurdo: mahogany cabinet on a stand; made by Goodall's of Manchester for the Century Guild stand at the Liverpool Exhibition in 1886.

Above PL. 251 A. H. Mackmurdo: mahogany chair in a stylized interpretation of eighteenth-century revival; made by Goodall's of Manchester for the Century Guild stand at the Liverpool Exhibition in 1886.

Below PL. 252 C. E. Horton: occasional table, mahogany; designed for Lamb of Manchester. One of the few contemporary designs to link with Mackmurdo's sinuous, flowing forms.

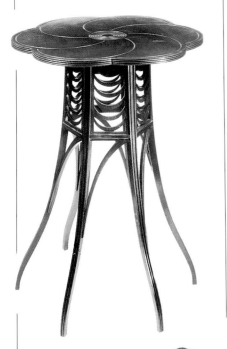

Right PL. 254 Heywood Sumner and W. A. S. Benson: music cabinet, mahogany and boxwood with wax inlaid decorations, on a mahogany stand; *c.*1889. The decorative design of the cabinet doors showing Orpheus charming the animals with the music of his lyre was made by Heywood Sumner, and Benson was responsible for the cabinet itself and the stand. A music cabinet using this unusual technique of decoration for the same Orpheus subject was shown at the Arts and Crafts Exhibition Society in 1889. This may be the exhibited example, though another version was made, and is now in the Kunstindustrimuseum at Trondheim in Norway. Heywood Sumner was a founder member of the Art Workers' Guild and one of the early Masters (1894). Benson was already designing furniture for Morris & Co.

PL. 253 C. F. A. Voysey: 'swan' chair in oak; for W. Ward Higgs, 1887. An important patron, Ward Higgs was the owner of Voysey's 'Chaucer' cabinet, designed to hold a copy of William Morris's *Kelmscott Chaucer* (1896). Voysey did not repeat this free-form style, the closest he ever approached to Art Nouveau.

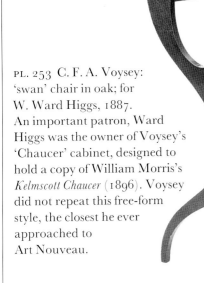

201

PL. 255 Philip Webb: seal design, a phoenix rising from the flames; made for A. A. Ionides, *c*.1880.

PL. 256 A. H. Mackmurdo: title page to *Wren's City Churches*, 1883, now widely recognized as a seminal influence on the development of Art Nouveau. Mackmurdo was one of the few Arts and Crafts designers to achieve the organic structure characteristic of Continental Art Nouveau furniture and pattern designing.

Right PL. 257 Edward Burne-Jones: 'Pelican' design for embroidery, pastel; 1881.

PL. 258 Mark V. Marshall:
massive stoneware vase, with fish,
water plants and ripples
naturalistically coloured with
glazes and modelled in high relief
in imitation of contemporary
Japanese pottery; *c.*1885. A
baluster pot made in about 1870
at the Miyagawa Kozan workshop
in Yokohama, on a similar scale
and with raised and glaze-
coloured decoration, was bought
for the South Kensington Museum
in 1879. Marshall's vase is a
sophisticated example of
sculptural pottery dating from the
earliest emergence of Art Nouveau
in Britain.

Morris and Company

The fact that William Morris had a private income was an important factor in encouraging him in the bold step of setting up his own business as a decorator. It allowed him to adopt an uncompromising stance on quality, eventually to be a great asset to the company, and permitted the endless experiments that he made with methods and materials. Morris's business manager George Warrington Taylor constantly made complaints such as: 'You may be certain that you will charge £9 for that which costs you £10. I *Know* your ways of calculating profits.' (Paul Thompson, *The Work of William Morris*, 1967, p. 23.) The firm was to exact considerable financial sacrifices from its founder, its annual deficits using up all his available funds, and after the sale of all his shares from the Devonshire copper-mining company which had provided him with his income he was forced to make the most stringent economies. In the end his work and persistence paid off, and by the 1880s Morris had begun to make a good income from the firm.

In the early years the firm had been supported by stained glass work and the relatively few decorating commissions associated with Webb's architectural work. Morris realized that the long-term profitability of a successful house decorator would depend on the production of wallpapers and fabrics on a commercial scale. The three wallpaper designs of 1862 were put into production by Jeffrey & Co. in 1864, and the 1870s saw the significant expansion of the firm's activities in this area. The hand printing of wallpaper – an uneconomic experiment which he soon abandoned – and textiles, and the weaving of silk and woollen cloths and tapestries, were undertaken initially by Morris himself, first at Queen Square and then at the Merton Abbey works, acquired in 1881. Some of the burden was taken for a while by contractors such as Thomas Wardle of Leek in Staffordshire, and Alexander Morton & Co. of Darvel in Ayrshire. Morris fell out with Wardle, whose quality and consistency could not be relied upon, and thereafter concentrated textile production at Merton. Carpet weaving began after 1878 at Kelmscott House in Hammersmith; hence the name 'Hammersmith' for the hand-knotted carpets. Machine-made Axminster, Brussels and Wilton carpets were produced by the Wilton Royal Carpet Factory; and Kidderminster by the Heckmondwike Manufacturing Co. in Yorkshire. (For a detailed study of all Morris's textile products see Linda Parry, *William Morris Textiles*, 1983.)

In 1861, anticipating the need for a choice of stock to tempt potential customers, Philip Webb designed a range of table glass in plain blown shapes to be manufactured at Powell's Whitefriars factory. Interest in this Venetian-type glass had been revived in the 1850s by the publication in 1849 of Aspley Pellatt's *Curiosities of Glassmaking*, which gave precise instructions for many of the Venetian processes, the only publication in the nineteenth century to provide such detailed technical information. Coincidentally, genuine Venetian glass became available when the Salviati firm set up in London following their success in the 1862 International Exhibition. Powell went as far as to introduce the use of soda glass in preference to lead glass to achieve paper-thin vessels decorated with trails or threads of coloured glass in the Venetian style. These Webb glasses formed a part of Morris & Co.'s stock into the present century. A service in green of the Morris-Powell glass survives at Wightwick Manor near Wolverhampton: Powell's own set is in the British Museum.

With the reorganization of the firm in 1875 the cumbersome original title of Morris, Marshall, Faulkner & Co. was dropped, official acknowledgement of Morris's sole responsibility for design decisions in all departments. Morris became the director, and in 1877 showrooms were acquired at 449 Oxford Street. New associates joined and the emphasis of the production changed, with pattern design predominating; the firm now sold comparatively few pieces of Webb's furniture, relying on the 1860s chair designs for stock. The former *ad hoc* production of hand-painted tiles was transformed by William De Morgan's association with the firm. The advent in 1880 of George Jack as Webb's assistant saw an injection of new ideas, and when he became chief furniture designer to Morris & Co. in 1890 he established the firm's later style. Technically, a great shift in the character of the furniture came with the addition in about 1890 of one of the Pimlico workshops of the cabinet-making firm Holland & Sons. From 1880 W. A. S. Benson was designing furniture and wallpaper for Morris while running his own metalworking business, which supplied lights and other accessories for the firm's decorating commissions.

Still Morris clung to his ideological integrity: in 1882 he wrote, 'On the whole one must suppose that beauty is a marketable quality and that the better the work is both as a work of art and in its technique the most likely it is to find favour with the public.' He gave a misleading impression of being dogmatically opposed to technological advances; but Morris, like Pugin, was a pragmatist.

The Merton works could not be mechanized because the firm had no network of outlets other than the Oxford Street premises and a shop in Manchester, so that production was too low to make it economic. The furniture was uncompetitively priced and could never be put into serial production. It was widely recognized that Morris had left decorative design better than he had found it and that his influence on the domestic interior had been beneficial; but in 1893 J. D. Sedding wrote: 'Let us not suppose that machinery will be discontinued. Manufacture cannot be organized on any other basis. We had better make life square with the facts, rather than rebel against the actual and inevitable, in striving for the ideal.'

Sedding was, in effect, speaking against the Arts and Crafts Movement. Morris, too, had had grave doubts about the chances of success of a return to hand craftsmanship and studio-workshops. He knew from experience all the practical realities of hand production and that quality could only be maintained by great sacrifices of time and money. The craftsmen became as much slaves to their products as any machine minder in a factory. In the event, the way in which life was made to square with the facts was through the Design and Industries Association and the highly professional Workshop Co-Operatives on the Continent.

The profitability of the Morris firm in the 1880s and 1890s was on a solid basis of quality production and of providing a particular public with the materials of the 'artistic' interior, but prosperity was assured also by immensely lavish commissions: for state rooms at St James's Palace; from the Hon. Percy Wyndham – for the decoration of 'Clouds' his large Webb house in Wiltshire – and from two Australian millionaire industrialists, William Knox D'Arcy and George McCulloch.

Morris decorated Stanmore Hall for Knox D'Arcy between 1888 and 1896, the central feature being a series of tapestries recounting the legend of San Graal. The house featured in *The Studio* in September 1893, and the author concluded that the effect was of 'sumptuous decoration kept within proper proportion. One has but to compare Stanmore Hall with houses of equally elaborate adornment to feel that in this respect it has no rival.' The walls of the small dining room were hung with the 'St James' damask, one of the most expensive of the firm's silk designs devised for the Palace commission. The large dining room where the tapestries were hung had a variant of the celebrated 'Clouds' carpet even larger than the original and in other rooms were versions of the 'Holland Park' and 'Swan House' carpets.

George McCulloch, a friend of Knox D'Arcy, lived in a very large London house at 184 Queen's Gate. A Scot who had made his way to Queen's Gate via the gold mines of Australia, he had become interested in collecting contemporary art and he commissioned from Morris a set of the San Graal tapestries in 1898. The panels were slightly larger than the Stanmore set, and were awarded a Grand Prix when they were shown in the Paris Exhibition in 1900. A very fine carpet was designed for the room in which the tapestries were to hang; by Dearle and named the 'McCulloch' it has been described as a masterpiece of its type (Parry, 1983, p. 97).

To dwell too much on expensively commissioned schemes misrepresents the ideology of the architect-designer movement. The theme of environmental and cultural improvement for the working class was not his alone, but was reiterated throughout the nineteenth century. Morris had by no means forgotten his original socialist ideals. He joined the Social Democratic Federation in 1883, and when this split – as such movements so often do – the following year, he founded a Socialist League of his own. The middle class was, relatively speaking, not large. A vast proportion of the population of Britain in the second half of the nineteenth century still belonged to the labouring classes, with incomes so small that they could barely afford necessities, let alone indulge in shopping for non-essentials. There was a feeling that it should be possible to design an environment specifically for their needs.

In 1884 Morris was persuaded into an experiment by Thomas Coglan Horsfall, a Manchester merchant and philanthropist. Horsfall wished to stimulate the critical faculties of the local working population by incorporating into the newly opened Manchester Museum two 'model rooms' furnished by Morris and his associate, W. A. S. Benson, cheaply and with good taste. Morris was rightly dubious about the project; as well as a well-founded fear that he would not be able to provide the furnishings cheaply enough, he remarked, 'Until smoke, filth and over-work are put an end to, all other measures are merely palliative.'

The two rooms were austerely but charmingly furnished with country-style pieces, a dresser of pine, a 'Sussex' chair and matching settee, a plain table and a Benson table lamp – what Morris termed 'the necessary workaday furniture' – bearing out his belief that the utilitarian could be decorative. He remarked in *The Lesser Arts of Life*, his 1877 lecture on decoration, 'The kitchen in a country farmhouse is most commonly a pleasant and homelike place, the parlour dreary and useless.' Of course the experiment was doomed. The bill for the construction and furnishing of the two rooms, a bedroom and a living room, was far too high. (See Sally Macdonald, 'For "Swine of Discretion": Design for living: 1884', *Museums Journal*, vol. 86, no. 3, December 1986, pp. 123–9.)

Morris was certainly making a serious effort to bring sound principles of decoration and furnishing within the compass of the working man, and it is ironical that this scheme by a pioneer of the vernacular revival in furniture was to be outmanoeuvred economically by banal mass-manufactured 'art furniture' aping his ideas.

The 'Model Artisan's Cottage' of 1887, commissioned from George Armitage for the Manchester Jubilee Exhibition by Neville Clegg, appears entirely frivolous by comparison. The description in the *Altrincham Division Chronicle* suggests 'greenery-yallery' decoration ordered by a well-to-do resident in a garden suburb. The furniture, consisting of simple Windsor chairs, a high-backed settle and fitted cupboards with leaded glass in the upper sections, was of green-stained ash. The wide chimneybreast accommodated 'an old Gothic fireplace'; the walls were distempered Indian red to the dado and yellowish-green above, with stencilled friezes at dado and cornice. (See Rosamund Allwood, 'George Faulkner Armitage, 1849–1937,' in *Furniture History*, vol. XXIII, 1987, pp. 67–87.) Morris knew that he was condemned to cater for 'the swinish luxury of the rich', and he deplored the state of things that made this inescapable, but he could not bear to relinquish his high quality work so his products, like those of his associate William De Morgan, were expensive.

William De Morgan studied painting at the Royal Academy Schools before his association with Morris, which started in 1863 with designs for tiles and stained glass. In 1869 he expanded his activities into the decoration of pottery; from 1873 production was based at his own Orange House Pottery in Chelsea. In 1882 he joined Morris at Merton Abbey, where he stayed until 1888 when he set up in partnership with the architect Halsey Ricardo (1854–1928) at Sands End in Fulham. The partnership with Ricardo ended in 1898 and De Morgan's partners from that date until he abandoned pottery for novel-writing in 1907 were Charles and Fred Passenger and Frank Iles. These three continued the business at Sands End until 1911.

De Morgan is celebrated for his part in the revival of lustre decoration for pottery. Among his contemporaries interested in the same field he admired particularly the French artist-potter Clément Massier and the Cantagalli firm in Florence. In the 1890s, for the sake of his health, De Morgan spent the winters in Florence, and his exchange of ideas at the Cantagalli factory bore fruit in the form of collaborative pieces.

'Lustre plates' had formed part of the Morris myth from the early days. Writing to Burne-Jones in 1865 regretting the failure of their plan to live all together at Red House, he said: 'I shan't always have the rheumatism, and we shall have lots of jolly years of invention and lustre plates together I hope.' (Quoted by Mackail, *Life of William Morris*, 1899, vol. I, p. 164.) De Morgan's lustrewares added richness to the sombre medieval tone of the 'Morrisean method' as described by Walter Crane: '. . . you might have gold and lustre (the choice ware of William De Morgan) gleaming from the sideboard, and jewelled light in the windows, and the walls hung with arras tapestry.' (*The English Revival in Decorative Art*, 1911.)

For Lord Leighton's exotic Leighton House in London De Morgan made brilliant blue tiles for the staircase hall as well as additional Isnik-pattern designs to complete the Arab Hall, devised by George Aitchison in 1877 to house the artist's collection of very fine Islamic tiles. The mosaic frieze above the tiled walls was designed by Walter Crane. For the Morris scheme at Membland, the Baring house in Devon, De Morgan provided large tile panels to Morris's design, with a predominantly green meandering 'acanthus' pattern (PL. 264). The partnership with Ricardo produced some of the most magnificent tiled interiors in this country – at Addison Road in London, for example. On a purely commercial level his tiles were produced in quantity for the side panels of fireplaces, one cornflower design being known as 'B.B.B.' from its use by the ironfounders Barnard, Bishop & Barnard. De Morgan's ideas continued to reflect his association with Morris as well as his interest in early Italian majolica and in Persian pottery. The full range of his inspiration can be appreciated in his designs, 1,248 original drawings bequeathed to the Victoria and Albert Museum in 1917 by his widow. (See M. Greenwood, *The Designs of William De Morgan*, 1989, published to accompany an exhibition at the Museum.)

Like Morris, W. A. S. Benson was brought up in affluent circumstances. His father was a wealthy barrister who sent his sons to Winchester. Benson read Classics and Philosophy at Oxford while dreaming of becoming an architect. In 1877 he was articled to Basil Champneys; he met Burne-Jones at this time, and Morris in 1878. Encouraged by Morris and with financial assistance from his father, Benson embarked in 1880 on a career as a designer and manufacturer of metalwork. From modest beginnings in the North End Road, Fulham, he soon progressed, in 1882, to a foundry at the old malthouse on Chiswick Mall. His first showroom was in Campden Hill Road; with the need to expand he moved to a new factory in Hammersmith and acquired a larger showroom at 82–3 New Bond Street.

The primitive equipment in his first workshop dictated the simple shapes of his early pieces, executed in a distinctive combination of brass and copper. More sophisticated machinery enabled him to develop the forms and individual elements, many of which were interchangeable. He took the precaution of patenting some of his more striking shapes. The spread of domestic electric lighting opened up a valuable market, and in 1897 he circulated a catalogue of electrical fittings and wiring. These fittings were chosen by Morris and Webb for a number of decorative commissions in the nineties.

While at Oxford Benson had shared rooms with George Heywood Sumner, who was to become his brother-in-law and a founder member of A. H. Mackmurdo's Century Guild. One of Benson's predecessors in Champney's office had been Halsey Ricardo, his exact contemporary. Through Ricardo Benson met William De Morgan and collaborated with him on some experimental lamp designs in about 1887. De Morgan and Benson were both drawn in to the Morris team but, while De Morgan retained his independence, Benson became director of the Morris firm after the founder's death in 1896. The full effect of these team efforts under the auspices of Morris & Co. can be judged at Standen in Sussex, and, in contrast, in the model rooms devised by Morris for the newly established Manchester Museum. In 1899 Benson's light fittings were shown at the Hermann Hirschwald Gallery in Berlin in a display of Morris's work.

Apart from the successful metalwork venture Benson continued sporadically to practise architecture, and made furniture designs for Morris & Co. Neither of these had the influence of his metalwork, in which he was an important innovator.

Benson's metalwork was noticed favourably in a number of publications, for example, *The Studio*, the *Magazine of Art* ('palpitatingly modern', 1896), Walter Crane's *The Bases of Design* (1898) and Muthesius's *Das englische Haus*: 'Benson was the first to solve the problem of design in metal in the more modern spirit when he created lamps that were later to have a revolutionary effect on all our metalware.' (1904; English edn, 1979, p. 199.) Benson's impact on the Continent was increased by his metalwares being shown from 1896 in Paris by Siegfried Bing at the Maison de l'Art Nouveau. This ensured him valuable exposure in *Art et Décoration*, where his light fittings were shown with furniture and fittings by such leading designers as Henri Van de Velde and Eduard Colonna, thus

confirming his position in the mainstream of the avant-garde in Paris. As a result his work was bought as part of the pioneering design collection being formed by the Kunstindustriemuseum at Trondheim in Norway.

George Washington Jack (1855–1932) was born in New York and came to live in Glasgow as a boy. He was articled to a Glasgow architect, Horatio K. Bromhead, but made his way to London in about 1875 and by 1880 had become Philip Webb's assistant. He took over the practice after Webb's retirement in 1900. He designed furniture for Morris & Co., as well as embroidery, stained glass, mosaics and cast-iron fireplaces, but his special talent was for woodcarving, which he taught at the Central School of Arts and Crafts. For W. R. Lethaby, head of the school, he wrote *Woodcarving, Design and Workmanship* (1903), in the 'Artistic Arts and Crafts' series. He was a lifelong adherent of the teachings of Ruskin, Morris and Webb, and he included a perceptive appreciation of their place in the reform of nineteenth-century design in his book.

Jack's furniture for Morris & Co., like Benson's, is in a freely developed Queen Anne revival style, using mahogany with intricate inlaid patterning and rather fussy metal mounts. It is instructive to compare Jack's suave 'Saville' chair with the 'Morris' reclining chair from the 1860s. In his choice of materials there is an affinity with the contemporary Kenton & Co. furniture, as well as Mackmurdo's designs for the Century Guild (PL. 250, 251). The change in direction was partly due to Morris's withdrawal from this side of the firm's activities; he was now overwhelmingly involved with his book-printing experiments. Owing to this preoccupation Morris also allowed J. H. Dearle, who had arrived with the firm as a young assistant in 1878, to take over the responsibility for much of the stained glass, carpet and tapestry design (PL. 265). The designs were often derivative, since Dearle lacked the genius for pattern making of his employer and was constrained by the necessity to work in the Morris idiom. Jack was supported in the furniture department by Benson with occasional contributions from Mervyn Macartney, which were more or less re-creations of eighteenth-century furniture.

PL. 259 Long drawing room
at Kelmscott House in
Hammersmith, the Morris
home from 1878.

PL. 260 Philip Webb: oak table with heavy mouldings, turned legs and supports and arched stretcher; *c*.1870. The design of the table was ascribed to George Jack, Webb's assistant and successor, who took over responsibility for the furniture after Webb's retirement in 1890. However, the mouldings relate to Webb's sideboard (PL. 166) dating from the mid-sixties. A version of the table formed part of the furnishings of the long drawing room on the first floor at Kelmscott House, where Morris lived from 1878 (PL. 259). A line drawing of a simplified version features in the Morris & Co. catalogue, suggesting that it was still possible to order this table in the twentieth century. The fact that few of the versions of Webb's designs are identical suggest that they were usually made to order from the designs always kept available at the Morris premises. The cabinet-making workshops were at Great Ormond Yard and in Manchester, and from 1890 included the Pimlico workshops of Holland & Co.

PL. 261 William Morris:
'Bird', woven woollen
fabric; designed 1878.
'Bird' was Morris's
favourite pattern and was
used for wall hangings in
the long drawing room at
Kelmscott House. As well
as the table (PL. 260), the
furnishings consisted of
'Sussex' chairs in the
round-seated version
designed by Ford Madox
Brown, an oak bookshelf
for large leather-bound
antiquarian books, with a
sloped top to display
those with the finest
bindings, two ornamental
coffers and, hanging from
the beam dividing the
room, a curtain of
'Peacock and Dragon',
another 1878 design by
Morris to which he was
particularly attached.

PL. 262 William De Morgan: 'Pelican' charger in 'Persian' colours; Fulham period.

PL. 263 William Morris: 'Hammersmith' hand-woven rug, with a central motif of a vase of flowers, and the hammer and 'M' device used to distinguish the carpets of the Hammersmith coach-house workshop set up in 1878; once in the possession of George Howard (Lord Carlisle). Morris had long been fascinated by Persian carpet design. He was a knowledgeable collector, often consulted by the staff at the South Kensington Museum on purchases. His first experiments with hand weaving, undertaken after a thorough examination of an antique Persian rug, took place at Queen Square. With the move to Kelmscott House in Hammersmith he had the space to expand the operation on a commercial scale; and there six young women, instructed by an experienced Glasgow carpet knotter, were expected to accomplish 2 inches (5 cm) a day on the 12 foot (3.7 m) wide frames.

Left PL. 264 William Morris: 'Acanthus' panel of sixty-six tiles painted in enamel colours; made by William De Morgan for Membland House, Devon, *c.*1878. The panel featured in the Morris firm's stock list until the early years of the twentieth century. The acanthus features in many variations across the whole spectrum of Morris's flat pattern: in wallpaper, velveteen, printed and woven textiles, tapestry, and the tile panel.

Above PL. 265 J. H. Dearle (after William Morris): 'Acanthus' woven tapestry panel; made for the seat of a mahogany-framed sofa designed by George Jack. The pattern is a version of Morris's 1870s 'Acanthus' with the background simplified by the omission of the background detail of small flowers and leaves.

PL. 266 William De Morgan: 'Snake', ruby lustre on a tile. A pencil drawing for the snake is in the collection at the Victoria and Albert Museum.

Above PL. 268 Bowl painted in ruby lustre with a galleon; made by the Cantagalli Pottery, Florence, *c.*1880. A close copy of a Hispano-Moresque bowl acquired by the South Kensington Museum in 1864. The shield on the sail bears the arms of Portugal. William De Morgan was in contact with Cantagalli during the winters he spent in Florence from 1892 onwards for the sake of his health.

Left PL. 267 William De Morgan: charger painted in ruby lustre with a galleon. Probably inspired by the same Hispano-Moresque dish in the South Kensington Museum.

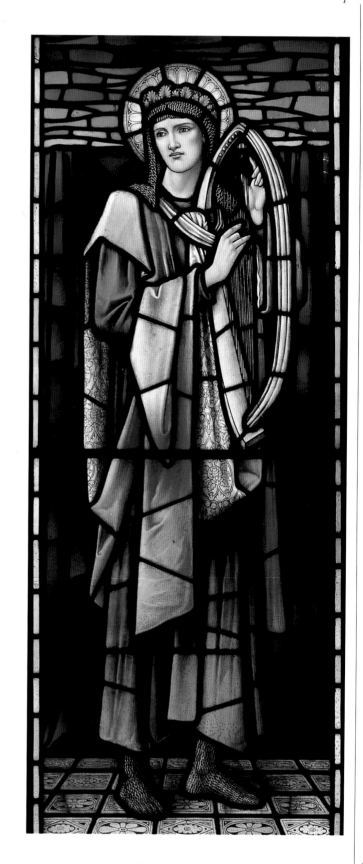

Above PL. 269 George Jack: occasional table, carved mahogany; designed *c.*1888. Shown at the Arts and Crafts Exhibition Society, 1889. The table was also made in a plain version with straight radiating stretchers. The table features in the Morris & Co. catalogue, and one is visible in the photograph of 449 Oxford Street.

Right PL. 270 Edward Burne-Jones: 'King David', stained glass panel, 1895. A typical late example of Burne-Jones's figural glass panels, this panel can be seen in a photograph taken in the twentieth century, in the upper window of the Morris & Co. premises at 449 Oxford Street.

PL. 271 W. A. S. Benson: two-branched table lamp, copper and brass, pleated silk shades. A notable feature of Benson's lamp designs is the decorative use of the electric flex.

PL. 272 W. A. S. Benson: hanging electrolier, copper and brass.

Arthur Lasenby Liberty and Art Nouveau in Britain

Liberty had been in the thick of the Art Movement since his first employment in the Oriental Warehouse attached to Farmer & Rogers' Great Shawl and Cloak Emporium, when he was nineteen years old. At the close of the International Exhibition in 1862 Farmer & Rogers had acquired a good proportion of the Japanese exhibit, and this formed the basis of their stock. In 1864 the twenty-one-year-old Liberty was made manager, but his ambitions centred on a shop of his own. In 1874, when his request to be taken into partnership was refused, and encouraged by the many artist friends he had made in the course of selling blue-and-white porcelain and Oriental silks, he set up in Regent Street.

Initially Liberty concentrated on what he knew best: the shop was an Oriental Warehouse like Farmer & Rogers. The stock expanded quickly from coloured silks imported from the East to encompass an extensive range of goods from the Near and Far East, described in advertisements as 'Ancient and Modern Eastern Art Manufactures from Persia, India, China, and Japan'.

Gradually in the 1880s Liberty began to draw together strands from the fashionable Art Movement and the nascent Arts and Crafts Movement to weave a successful commercial enterprise. There was some resentment, C. R. Ashbee in particular seeing Liberty as responsible for the failure of the Guild of Handicraft, but this did not prevent Liberty from attracting an impressive group of design and manufacturing talent. Echoes of Morris & Co. can be detected, not only in the range of fabrics, wallpapers, embroidery patterns, ornamental ceramics, glass and furniture, but also in the suppliers, for example Powell of Whitefriars and Thomas Wardle. Liberty quickly stifled Wardle's 'Art Drapers, Embroiderers and Decorative Furnishers' venture (1883–8) on the grounds of conflict of interest, Liberty having been one of Wardle's major customers since 1878. He also made enterprising pre-emptive bids, in 1884 speedily patenting the 'Thebes' stool designs from the range of Dresser's defunct Art Furnishers' Alliance in which he had been a partner. Dresser was to be one of Liberty's earliest designers, supplying textiles, metalwork and 'Clutha' glass (PL. 248) from 1882.

The two versions of the 'Thebes' stool (PL. 277) were among the first products of Liberty's Furnishing and Decoration Studio, set up under the direction of Leonard Wyburd in 1883. Wyburd's own preference was for the Moorish style and his early designs incorporated panels of imported *mushrabiyeh* latticework. His later designs for oak furniture of vaguely sixteenth-century inspiration are much heavier, characterized by plank-like elements and doors with leaded glass panels. Godwin's influence is apparent in the elegant mahogany furniture of the 1880s, a thread that carries through the chairs and cabinets designed by George Walton. The most avant-garde of the furniture designs was the chair by Richard Riemerschmid (PL. 276) imported from Germany, used to furnish the shop and also available in modified form from the workshops.

Textiles have remained an important part of Liberty's merchandise and were the earliest to have designs specially commissioned from leading artists; as well as Dresser, Walter Crane, Voysey, Baillie Scott, Lewis F. Day, Arthur Silver and the Silver Studio artists, and Archibald Knox were involved. Liberty Art Fabrics featured in many periodicals internationally and sold through adventurous retailers, such as Bing in Paris, and it was the fame of the bold Art Nouveau patterns that led to the adoption in Italy of the term 'Stile Liberty' to describe the turn-of-the-century look.

After an award of a silver medal at the Rational Dress Exhibition in 1883 for the Liberty Art Fabrics intended for dress, in 1884 Godwin was brought in to supervise the dress department. Dress reform was an important aspect of the Art Movement, and Liberty's costume department provided an alternative to home experiments or the services of a dressmaker working from rough sketches. The costumes suggested by Godwin were described as 'Greek' or 'Medieval', flowing robes to be worn without a tight-laced corset, made up in the subtly coloured Liberty silks and velvets and often finished with bands of embroidery in Liberty silks. They were promoted in *Aglaia*, the journal of the Healthy and Artistic Dress Union, and by Mrs Oscar Wilde in *The Lady's World*.

Along with the Oriental silks, porcelains and metalwork, the stock in the early days included Japanese embossed papers made to simulate leather. Later leather papers and wallpapers were commissioned from the Silver Studio and it seems probable that C. F. A. Voysey's wallpapers, like his textiles, were sold by Liberty's. The carpet stock followed the same pattern, a progression from Oriental rugs to commissioned designs, the hand-knotted Donegal rugs and carpets being made under the supervision of Alexander Morton in Ireland. Voysey (PL. 278) and Archibald Knox provided designs, as did Mrs G. F. Watts, second wife of the artist.

The expansion of the ceramics and glass departments followed the now familiar route from Oriental wares to British and Continental art pottery, starting with Japanese-influenced pieces from C. H. Brannam of Barnstaple, who later provided a stock of green-glazed or blue-glazed 'Barum' wares made specially for Liberty. Liberty stocked Aller Vale, Bretby and a special range of Doulton wares as well as Moorcroft's 'Florian Ware'. Other small firms made ranges for Liberty and stock was held from a number of Continental potteries, including Max Lauger of Karlsruhe and the Hungarian firm of Zsolnay. Terracotta garden ornaments to designs by Archibald Knox (PL. 284) were made at the Compton Pottery set up by the redoubtable Mrs Watts.

The textile designs from the Silver Studio and Liberty's ceramic range were the most visible manifestation of the Continental Art Nouveau style before the turn of the century. Together with the development from 1899 of the 'Cymric' metalwork venture, they added an important dimension to Liberty's pioneering design policy. There was also a jewellery department, started in 1883 and at first stocked mainly with Eastern curiosities. The designers for the 'Cymric' range of silverware and jewellery were Oliver Baker, Archibald Knox (PL. 282, 283, 285), Jessie M. King and Arthur Silver's son and heir Reginald (Rex), and they immediately established a distinctive look inspired by the Celtic revival. The 'Tudric' range of pewter was added in 1903, providing Liberty with an alternative under his own control to the pewterwares from J. Kayser Sohn of Krefeld, which had attracted his attention in Paris in 1900. In Archibald Knox Liberty had found a distinguished artist who provided outstandingly original designs for silver and pewter from 1898 to 1912.

Arthur Liberty died in 1917, and with him died the pioneering initiatives in design. He did not live to see the success of his consolidation of the store's finances triumphantly vindicated when they emerged from the First World War unscathed. The store changed direction in the 1920s, adopting a traditionalist role, but retaining some of the most successful of the earlier designs.

PL. 273 Mahogany cabinet with inlays of stained wood; Liberty & Co., from the 'Rowena' drawing-room suite, *c.*1905.

Above PL. 274 George Walton: 'Holland' cabinet; designed for J. S. Henry, *c.* 1900. Walton was associated with Charles Rennie Mackintosh in one of the earliest Cranston Tea Rooms. He created furniture designs for Liberty which were made at High Wycombe by William Birch, as well as for J. S. Henry.

Right PL. 275 Mahogany cabinet with inlays; made by J. S. Henry.

Opposite PL. 278 C. F. A. Voysey:
'Stag and Swan' carpet; woven by
Alexander Morton & Co., to a
design made for Liberty, *c.*1896.
Also produced as a frieze, a
wallpaper and a woollen textile.

Above PL. 276 Richard
Riemerschmid: oak chair; *c.*1900.
Variants of this chair were
imported from Germany to
furnish Liberty's shop in 1899, as
well as being made at Liberty's
workshops for sale from about
1900.

Right PL. 277 'Thebes' stool,
ebony inlaid with ivory. This
pattern was advertised by the Art
Furnishers' Alliance, set up in
1880. The painter Sir Lawrence
Alma-Tadema had an ebony and
ivory stool of this type in his studio
before 1882, possibly purchased
through the company. When the
company failed in 1883 the design
was taken over and patented by
Arthur Liberty and became a
popular model, remaining part of
Liberty's stock well into the
twentieth century.

PL. 279 Archibald Knox: tea set,
silver set with green and pale
brown cabochons; designed for
Liberty, *c*.1900.

PL. 280 W. A. S. Benson:
iridescent vase, mounted in gilt
metal; by Powell & Sons of
Whitefriars. Shown at the
Glasgow International Exhibition,
1901. Benson designed a pavilion
for the exhibition.

PL. 281 Harry Powell: silver-
mounted glass centrepiece, the
glass body decorated with green
glass feathered banding in wavy
trails; designed for James Powell &
Sons as part of a service
commissioned by the wealthy
Italian diplomat Count Minorbi
in 1906. The enamelled shields
on the handles bear the Minorbi
arms. The drawings for the
Minorbi commission form part
of Powell's archive now in the
Museum of London.

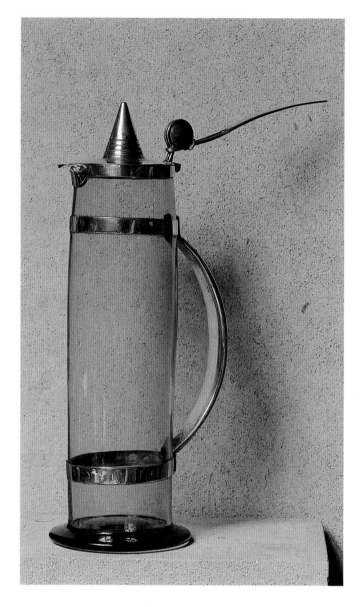

PL. 282 Archibald Knox: cup and
cover in enamelled silver; designed
for Liberty & Co., *c*.1900. The
drawing for the cup is in the
Victoria and Albert Museum in a
collection of Knox's designs given
by his pupil Denise Wren.

PL. 283 Archibald Knox:
claret jug of green glass
mounted in silver, with
lapis lazuli set in the
thumbpiece; Birmingham, 1902.

Right PL. 285 Archibald Knox: tall silver lidded claret jug with raised entrelac decoration; made for Liberty & Co., Birmingham, 1900.

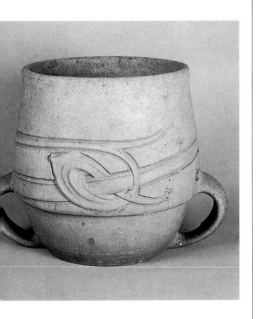

Above PL. 284 Archibald Knox: terracotta jardinière; made at the Compton Pottery, *c.*1905. Catalogues of garden pottery were issued in 1905 and 1907.

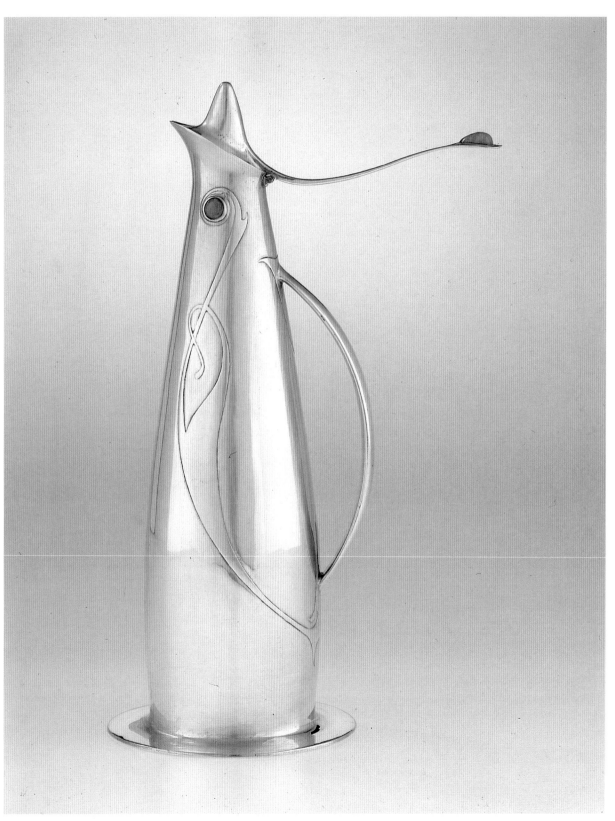

The Art Workers' Guild

Five of the founding members of the Art Workers' Guild came from Norman Shaw's office, W. R. Lethaby, Mervyn Macartney, Gerald Horsley, Ernest Newton and Edward Prior had established the St George's Art Society as a private amusement in 1883. Now they engaged in the more serious purpose of bringing architects, painters, sculptors and craftsmen into one organization. They were joined by another group, known as 'The Fifteen' and led by Lewis F. Day and Walter Crane. There were sixty-five architect members in the early years, including J. D. Sedding, Mackmurdo, George Walton, Voysey and C. R. Ashbee. From Sedding's office came Henry Wilson, Ernest Gimson and Sidney Barnsley. The Guild is still an active force in crafts today. Since its founding everyone seriously involved in the craft tradition has been a member.

The Arts and Crafts Exhibition Society was an extension of the Guild's activities, set up in 1888 by members who felt that exhibiting was an essential part of the Guild programme. T. Cobden Sanderson, printer and founder of the Dove's Press, is credited with coining the term 'Arts and Crafts'. The first of the Society's exhibitions was held in 1888, and was followed in quick succession by two more, in 1889 and 1890. The quality of the exhibits had noticeably declined by the third and it was decided to limit the events to every three years in the future. These exhibitions provided the designers and craftsmen – often these were one and the same – of the Arts and Crafts Movement with an invaluable showcase.

The influence of the Movement was far greater than accounts of the individual enterprises would suggest. Crafts came to occupy a disproportionate amount of time for the architects and artists who had been drawn into Guild and workshop ventures. Wilson's architectural career was to be overshadowed by his metalworking and jewellery; Ashbee became completely absorbed in the running of the Guild of Handicraft; Gimson is now chiefly remembered as a furniture designer; and many others sacrificed an artistic vocation to the tyranny of the workshop. Apart from the Arts and Crafts exhibitions, ways of reaching the public included corporate showings at international exhibitions, and more importantly through exposure in *The Studio* magazine (PL. 299).

The basis of the Arts and Crafts Movement was a deliberate attempt to evolve a classless style of architecture. This was only practicable because of the development of vernacular solutions to suit many levels of demand.

There was still an insurmountable problem of scale. Lethaby encountered this at Avon Tyrell, where he was required to disguise a substantial mansion as a modest manor or farmhouse. The essence of architectural scale is to make the compact seem spacious, and the use of the vernacular for substantial country houses completely reversed this precept. Voysey and Baillie Scott, whose influence has proved the greatest in the long term, both concentrated almost exclusively on smaller houses.

The goal of classlessness in buildings, as in furniture and decoration, continued to be dogged by the cost of fine materials and workmanship, a problem that is no nearer to solution in the present day. As Ruskin had foreseen, mechanical production must result in products that are devoid of character. Simplicity is impossible to achieve cheaply, except at the expense of the craftsmen. This was the experience that soured the Guild movement, and ensured the demise of most of its ideological and philanthropic ventures in the early years of the twentieth century. The provision of craft-style decorative art fell into the hands of one or two commercial operators – dominated by Liberty's – and mechanical techniques were used to simulate hand work at a price no craftsman could possibly match. It was inescapably demonstrated that the expectations of a prosperous and much more equal society had to be met with a show of quality rather than its substance.

Hampered, unlike their Continental contemporaries, by the lack of a living peasant culture, Arts and Crafts designers turned to country crafts. The vernacular theme that runs through Arts and Crafts architecture and design dictated a return to indigenous materials. Much of the furniture is of oak, with beech, holly and other native varieties for fine detail and inlays. For a didactic and experimental initiative, the Arts and Crafts style enjoyed an unusually far-reaching influence in the domestic market, with a successful commercial side in Ambrose Heal's store. The Cotswold tradition, started in the workshops of Ernest Gimson and Sidney and Ernest Barnsley, was carried on in the present century by Gordon Russell. By the 1920s and 1930s his had become an almost lone voice against machine production.

During the Second World War the severely plain but good-quality 'Utility' range was the only furniture sanctioned by the government. 'Standard Emergency Furniture' had to be made from the minimum of raw materials and with the least possible use of manpower – both, by 1941, in chronically short supply. The

currently fashionable Tudor-style furniture with lathe-turned frames and applied carving gave way to severely plain pieces of solid oak and oak-veneered plywood. Russell was one of the designers involved with the 'Utility' range. He was delighted: 'Austerity and utility have useful astringent qualities,' he remarked.

The turn of the century was to see the dissipation of British influence in the field of design reform. European decorative art was dominated by a movement popularly identified by the name of a Parisian dealer's establishment, Siegfried Bing's Maison de L'Art Nouveau; but the roots of this movement can be traced to Englishmen, to Ruskin, Pugin and Morris, and the Aesthetic Movement architects and designers such as E. W. Godwin and Christopher Dresser.

PL. 286 Henry Wilson: chalice of silver, partly gilt with chased and applied ornament, a central knop in the form of grotesque monsters enamelled in blue and green, the stem and part of the cup mounted in carved ivory; made *c.*1898, the year in which it was presented to St Bartholomew's Church, Brighton. Wilson was articled to J. D. Sedding and took over his architectural practice in 1891 when Sedding died of influenza. He set up his metalwork venture in about 1895. His metalwork, like his architecture, was of Renaissance splendour in colour and workmanship.

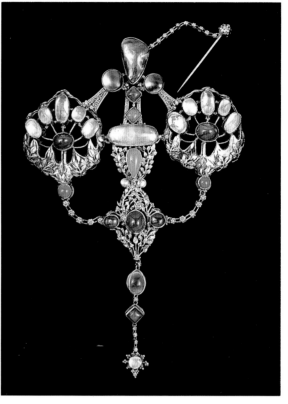

Above PL. 288 John Paul Cooper: double stomacher brooch, gold set with black abalone shell, moonstones, chrysophrases, rubies and amethysts; 1908. Cooper's architectural career was short-lived and his working life was devoted to craft work, principally jewellery and metalwork.

Left PL. 287 Nelson and Edith Dawson: group of enamelled jewellery. Nelson Dawson studied enamelling with Alexander Fisher and he imparted his skills to his wife. The Dawsons set up a metalwork and jewellery workshop in 1891. After a brief involvement with the Artificers' Guild from 1901 to 1903, they continued independently producing jewellery, usually with enamelled decoration, until the workshop was given up in 1914.

PL. 289 C. R. Ashbee and the Guild of Handicraft: group of gold, silver and enamel-set jewellery; showing the range of the Guild's jewellery designs up to its dissolution in 1908. The octagonal silver brooch decorated with fruiting vines bears the Guild mark; the peacock on the right bears London hallmarks for 1907. A design for a variant of the cloak clasp (bottom) is among Ashbee's drawings from the Magpie and Stump, now the property of the Royal Borough of Kensington and Chelsea.

PL. 290 Vase, salt-glazed stoneware with incised decoration; Martin Brothers of Southall, *c.*1885.

PL. 291 Walter Crane: vase, earthenware, painted in 'Lancastrian Lustre'; made at the Pilkington Tile & Pottery Co., *c.*1906.

PL. 292 Lidded vase or bottle, turquoise-blue glaze with impressed decoration; Della Robbia Pottery.
Robbia Pottery, *c.*1900.

PL. 293 Selwyn Image: pair of stained glass panels from a set of the Seasons, illustrated in *The Studio* in 1898. Stained glass by Image was a feature of the Century Guild stand at the Inventions Exhibition in 1885.

PL. 294 Granville Fell: stained glass panel, a dancing figure with flowing hair; *c.*1898. The absence of decorative detail and the heavy leading of the glass are used to emphasize the sinuous Art Nouveau character of the design.

PL. 295 Robert Anning Bell: decorative panel of a mermaid, coloured gesso relief; a version of one of the overdoor panels made for Le Bois des Moustiers, Varengeville, Normandy, designed by Edwin Lutyens for Guillaume Mallet.

PL. 296 Wickham Jarvis: teak chair with a rushed seat; *c.*1900. The chair is comparable with examples by his architect contemporaries like Voysey and Cave, but Jarvis's design combines curving elements of the Queen Anne style with the simplicity and severity of Arts and Crafts.

PL. 297 Walter Cave: walnut chair, *c.*1900. Muthesius described Cave in these terms: 'Another member of the inner circle of the Art Workers' Guild [he] uses forms of expression that are close to those of Voysey.' Cave's forms are less uncompromising than Voysey's, with echoes of eighteenth-century curves where Voysey's lines would be straight.

PL. 298 Painted chest of drawers;
Ambrose Heal & Son, *c.*1900. The
influence of Ford Madox Brown's
stained joiner furniture in simple
shapes, designed for Morris and
featured at the Manchester
Jubilee Exhibition in 1887, is
apparent.

Charles Francis Annesley Voysey

In 1874, at the age of seventeen, Charles Voysey was articled to J. P. Seddon. His youth was marked by the singular experience of his father's expulsion from the Church of England for denying the doctrines of the divinity of Christ, of everlasting hell and the inspiration of the Bible. He himself was not without eccentricities, but his architecture and design are notably sane and rational. From Seddon's office he went, after a brief spell with Saxon Snell, in 1880 as an architectural clerk to join the practice of George Devey, a friend of his father who was a successful country house architect. Devey worked in a refined Queen Anne or vernacular idiom, in which he had anticipated Philip Webb, Richard Norman Shaw and W. E. Nesfield. He was obsessional about detail and his houses are finished with precious touches, as in Lord Kenmare's house at Killarney, where the doorhandles were made from antique gold watch cases. He was caught up in the fashionable world of make-believe rustic simplicity processed for artistic businessmen whose tastes had been formed by a generation of watercolourists of the rural school.

In 1882 Voysey set up in practice as an architect on his own, but commissions were not immediately forthcoming. Through his friendship with Mackmurdo, he was taken up as a designer of wallpapers by Jeffrey & Co. The first papers show Morris's influence transmuted into Art Nouveau, a style that he was later to repudiate as misleading 'good men . . . into thinking that art is a debauch of sensuous feeling'. From the late 1880s onwards he put his pattern-making ability to use for the design of wallpapers, woven and printed textiles and carpets. In 1884 he joined the newly founded Art Workers' Guild. He showed wallpapers and fabrics at the first exhibition in 1888 of the Arts and Crafts Exhibition Society. Soon he was designing wallpapers for Essex & Co., chief rivals to Jeffrey & Co. Both firms pursued a policy of employing as designers promising artists and architects; however, from 1893 the Essex firm was inextricably associated with Voysey, when they undertook to produce the majority of his designs.

Voysey was a thorough professional. If his own taste is summed up in the following remark, he did not let this get in the way of his successful career as a pattern designer. Of *The English Home* he wrote:

'Try the effect of a well-proportioned room, with white-washed walls, plain carpet and simple oak furniture and nothing in it but necessary articles of use, and one pure ornament in the form of a simple vase of flowers.' (Quoted in D. Gebhard, *Charles F. A. Voysey, Architect*, 1975, p. 77) He recognized that the revival of cottage architecture with which the Arts and Crafts Movement was concerned necessitated a change of direction for wallpaper and textile design. The dense, richly coloured patterns by Morris and Walter Crane did not show to advantage in conjunction with severely plain furniture and whitewashed rooms, or under the harsh glare of electric light. Voysey toned down the colours for his designs, using a bright, light palette in contrast to the deep colours of Aesthetic taste, and devised a fresh simple approach to pattern, well exemplified in 'Squire's Garden' (1898) and 'Fool's Parsley' of 1907. His personal motifs of bird and heart were deployed for wallpapers and textiles, as well as in furniture and metalwork.

Voysey built his first house in 1888, and thereafter, until he gave up his architectural practice in 1920, he had a steady progression of commissions. He was productive if not prolific, and his houses are so marked by his distinctive architectural personality that they seem to stand for a greater volume of work than was actually the case. Fortunate in his patrons, he was able to decorate and furnish a number of his houses. The quintessence of his domestic style was achieved in his own house, The Orchard at Chorleywood (1899). The scheme is noticeably simple and free of the eccentricities admired by his best patron W. Ward Higgs.

The miniaturist's hand is sometimes apparent in Voysey's detailing: little pierced grilles and heart-shaped cutouts run through his work like signatures. But the simple massive scale of his 1895 clock design – the painted version is exquisite, though from the point of view of pure design this is seen at its best in plain aluminium (PL. 302) – shows a sculptor's understanding of form. The same feeling for form is apparent in his furniture designs, the plainness being offset by the most fastidious choice of materials. His domestic metalwork and tablewares are smooth-surfaced, in flowing shapes and without any superfluous ornament. Voysey saw himself as Pugin's heir, adhering to the tradition of Gothic initiated half a century earlier. He repudiated attempts to associate his style with early Modernism, insisting 'I make no claim to anything new.' Muthesius admired Voysey's houses, while deploring his indifference to vernacular tradition and local building materials: 'Voysey's total abandonment of historical tradition does rob his houses of that firmly established conviction that we admire so much in the houses of the Norman Shaw group.' (*Das englische Haus*, 1904, English edn. 1979, p. 42.)

In spite of his membership of the Art Workers' Guild Voysey was remarkably detached from the communal ideals of the Arts and Crafts Movement. An individualist, he pursued his vision with remarkable consistency. He was not tempted into any co-operative venture, nor into the founding of a guild or craft workshop. His career was that of a professional designer and architect, and his work displays the clear-thinking, proto-Modernist character that also distinguished Dresser's designs.

PL. 299 C. F. A. Voysey: cover for bound volumes of *The Studio* magazine; vol. I, 1893.

PL. 300 C. F. A. Voysey: street
elevation of a house in St
Dunstan's Road, Hammersmith;
for W. E. F. Britten, 1891.

PL. 301 C. F. A. Voysey: writing desk, the upper panel with ornamental brass cutout, decorative brass strap hinges; designed for W. Ward Higgs, 1895.

PL. 302 C. F. A. Voysey: aluminium clock with copper hands and letters spelling 'TEMPUS FUGIT' in place of the numerals; designed *c*.1895.

Left PL. 303 C. F. A. Voysey: cast iron fire grate; made by the Falkirk Iron Co.

Above PL. 304 C. F. A. Voysey: armchair in oak with a rushed seat, 1902.

PL. 305 C. F. A. Voysey: 'Hunter
and Deer', design for a woollen
hanging, textile or wallpaper;
*c.*1900.

PL. 306 C. F. A. Voysey:
watercolour design for a textile
hanging.

PL. 307 C. F. A. Voysey: woven
textile with birds and leaves;
*c.*1900.

Above PL. 309 C. F. A. Voysey: gilded oak circular mirror with a convex glass; *c.* 1900.

Left PL. 308 C. F. A. Voysey: tile panel; made by Pilkington's, *c.* 1900.

Ernest Gimson and the Barnsleys

Ernest Gimson and Sidney Barnsley came from similar backgrounds, being sons of successful self-made men, a Leicester ironfounder and a Birmingham builder respectively. As younger sons in large families there was no pressure on them to enter the family businesses. All three decided on careers in architecture, Gimson in particular having been inspired by hearing Morris lecture in Leicester. After three years with a local man, Isaac Barradale, Gimson arrived in 1886 in London and through the intervention of Morris joined the office of J. D. Sedding, where he met Ernest Barnsley. Sidney Barnsley was working in Richard Norman Shaw's office. All three were, therefore, in the direct line of influence from G. E. Street.

Apart from the financial independence granted by the profitable family enterprises, which was to free all three men from the necessity of earning their livings, both ironfounding and building provided a background of appropriately practical experience to an architectural career. The Barnsley family firm, in fact, had a close relationship with the Birmingham Gothic Revival architect J. H. Chamberlain. As the obituary of Thomas Barnsley pointed out, 'the architect and the builders may be said to have combined to introduce the application of Gothic architecture both in the streets and suburbs of this city' (*Birmingham Daily Post*, 21 June 1909). Chamberlain was a founder member and the local secretary of Ruskin's Guild of St George. His style of Ruskinian Gothic ornament was carried out in fine cabinetwork in a variety of wood inlays and carved detail (PL. 175). The anteroom of The Grove, Harborne, Birmingham, dating from 1877, is preserved in the Victoria and Albert Museum.

Sedding and Norman Shaw were intimately involved with developments that heralded the Arts and Crafts Movement, and were active participants in the Society for the Protection of Ancient Buildings – Morris's 'anti-scrape' society, founded in 1877 and still strongly interventionist today – and the Art Workers' Guild. From the earliest opportunity Gimson exhibited with the Arts and Crafts Exhibition Society. In 1888 Ernest Barnsley returned to Birmingham, a married man and soon a father, and set up as an architect. Sidney Barnsley and Ernest Gimson both travelled for a period after their training came to an end, and Barnsley embarked in a modest way on his architectural career, whereas Gimson turned to craft work in the form of chair making and plasterwork.

In 1890 Gimson and Sidney Barnsley became partners in the firm of Kenton & Company, a co-operative formed to produce furniture designed by architects. The other partners were W. R. Lethaby, Mervyn Macartney and Reginald Blomfield. Each put in £100, and Colonel Mallet, described by Lethaby as 'a friend of Macartney's who had taste and knew people', was brought in as a 'sleeping partner' and put up £200. Unlike Morris, Marshall, Faulkner & Co., but like Mackmurdo's Century Guild, the furniture was to be made by professional cabinet-makers. The resemblance went deeper, since both ventures made use of the design skills of architects and artists. An exhibition was staged at Barnard's Inn in 1891. A small group of furniture survives from the brief period of the firm's activity, showing the decorative ambitions of the designers and a high standard of finish. The firm enjoyed a modest critical and financial success from the exhibition. It was under-capitalized but could have developed if further funds had been sought. However, the five men knew that they were faced with a turning point where they had to chose between architecture or a craft and design career. It was agreed to wind up the firm and go their separate ways. Kenton & Co. had survived for only eighteen months; but it had established a distinctive style and also, perhaps more importantly, conditioned the subsequent careers of both Gimson and Barnsley.

Lethaby summed up succinctly:

> 'We enjoyed ourselves greatly for about two years making many pieces of furniture, selling some at a little over cost price – nothing being included for design or for the time expended for the proprietor – and finally we divided up the remainder at the end by drawing lots for the first choice. To my share fell what we still call "the Gimson Cabinet" of walnut, "left clean" and unpolished, but now mellow and glossy from use; another cabinet which we call "Blomfield", "Barnsley's table", "my Oak Chair" and a little revolving bookcase designed by Macartney. After all, these five pieces with all the fun and some experience gained were not a bad return for £100 down.'
> (W. R. Lethaby, *Ernest Gimson, His Life and Work*, 1924, p. 6.)

There was a little more to the operation than he suggests in that Lethaby's Kenton furniture found its way into work in progress, at Buller's Wood for example, and into a church, St John the Baptist in Hertfordshire. As usual with these ventures the individual items were too expensive to produce, Blomfield's settee earning criticism for its price of £50 from *The Builder*, a sum that allowed a profit of only 15 per cent.

Perhaps the participants had been encouraged to believe in the potential of the firm by the exposure given by *The Studio* to the Arts and Crafts Exhibition Society. Gimson had shown work, including the plasterwork that was his overriding interest at this stage, at the Society's exhibitions in the New Gallery in 1889 and 1890.

The closure of Kenton & Co. freed Gimson and Sidney Barnsley to give serious consideration to their idea of living and working at architecture and crafts in the country. Since 1889 Gimson had cherished the idea of establishing an ideal community; it remained a preoccupation throughout his life and, although he was never able to achieve it, he was nearer his goal when living in the country. The Cotswolds were chosen after a considerable search, although the location should have been pre-ordained, with Morris established at Kelmscott Manor, near Lechlade, since 1871, and the beautiful countryside still unspoilt in spite of convenient access to Birmingham. Ernest Barnsley abandoned his Birmingham office to join them.

Once they were installed at Pinbury Park on Lord Bathurst's estate, the dream of a workshop became a practical possibility. Alhough there was no existing tradition of furniture making in the locality, Gimson and the Barnsleys had come to a true country area where old ways still dominated the daily life of the inhabitants. It was an easy matter to find a blacksmith for ironwork or a carpenter for woodwork. One of the most respected figures in the nearby village of Sapperton was the wheelwright Richard Harrison, who was to become a close collaborator with the new settlers. The fruits of their work as designer-craftsmen were shown at the 1896 Arts and Crafts Exhibition in London. The type of product was set early on, and the chests, chairs, coffers, tables and settles changed little in the following years, a distinctive woody look having developed from the outset of the experiment. The design of the metalwork was influenced by seventeenth-century work; handsome firedogs by Gimson were based on an example drawn at Haddon Hall in 1889. The candle sconces (PL. 316, 317) come out of the same revivalist tradition.

Architectural ambitions were fulfilled mainly by building for family and close friends. When Lord Bathurst reclaimed Pinbury as a country base for his family, he released land so that cottages could be built at his expense for the three partners. The traditional cottages are a highly intellectualized essay in vernacular, the intention being to achieve an organic relationship between the land and the building. The interiors show a sculptural concern for form, texture and articulation of spaces. There was little concern for comfort and convenience, and Alfred Powell, a friend of Gimson's since his time in Sedding's office, designed two uniquely uncomfortable cottages that were uninhabitable because of draughts.

The commission for Rodmarton Manor was on an entirely different scale. This was designed by Ernest Barnsley, and building work went on from 1909 until 1929. The original idea was for 'a cottage in the country' for the banker The Hon. Claud Biddulph. The first wing, comprising the Kitchen Court, was relatively modest in conception, but ultimately the many-bayed façade reached the dimensions of a large country house. The Manor was furnished to designs by Ernest and Sidney Barnsley by local carpenters and joiners who had been recruited for the building work; true to Arts and Crafts principles but rare in practice, Rodmarton was built without a contractor. Rodmarton far transcended its original conception, eventually becoming a centre for the study and preservation of traditional crafts and practices.

The move to Daneway House, leased by Gimson from Lord Bathurst for use as showrooms in 1902, marked the beginning of a serious professional involvement with the design and manufacture of furniture. Cabinet-makers were employed to execute a gratifying press of orders, and the employment from this date of a Dutchman, Peter van der Waals, set the seal on the commercial viability of the workshop. Gimson and Ernest Barnsley were the two partners in this enterprise, as Sidney Barnsley had decided to maintain his independence and continued designing and making his own furniture in a workshop converted from an outbuilding attached to his cottage at Sapperton. After Gimson's untimely death in 1919 many of the Daneway craftsmen followed Waals to his new premises, where he continued to supply Gimson's former clients. Some of the pieces were actual reproductions of Gimson's designs, but Waals had also devised a distinctive style of his own, with a heavier and more structural approach.

Waals maintained his own workshops in Chalford until 1938, but commercial exploitation of the Cotswold style devolved on Ambrose Heal for his store in the Tottenham Court Road. Gordon Russell, who had not worked with Gimson but was much influenced by him, formed his company, Gordon Russell Ltd., in 1926 with the intention of carrying on the principles developed by Gimson of plain, honest craftmanship. His work up to the 1930s still showed the influence of design ideas first developed by Gimson in the 1890s.

PL. 310 Ernest Gimson: cabinet on a stand, ebony and holly with geometric marquetry on the doors and sides, silver handles with hallmarks for 1891; made by Kenton & Co. Exhibited at Barnard's Inn, 1891.

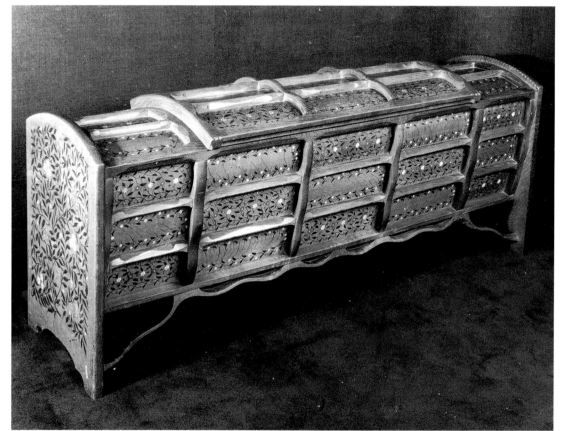

Above PL. 311 W. R. Lethaby: walnut stationery cabinet with snakewood inlays, ivory handles; made by Kenton & Co., *c.*1890.

Left PL. 312 Sidney Barnsley: oak coffer of 'wagon' construction, the panels painted with trailing leaves and flowers by Alfred and Louise Powell; *c.*1905.

Above PL. 313 Ernest Gimson:
table cabinet, with chequered
veneer panels separated by
stringing and inlays of mother-
of-pearl, *c.*1900.

Right PL. 314 Ernest Gimson:
cabinet on a stand, with inset
gessoed and gilded panels;
*c.*1900.

PL. 315 Ernest Gimson: cabinet in walnut and ebony, the drawers with their alternating panels forming a geometric pattern, *c.*1905. This cabinet was illustrated by Walter Shaw Sparrow in *The Modern Home* (p. 128), a showcase for Arts and Crafts furniture.

Above PL. 316 Ernest Gimson: candle sconce in pierced brass and steel; probably made by Alfred Bucknell, *c.*1907.

Below PL. 317 Ernest Gimson: double candle sconce in pierced and engraved brass; probably made by Alfred Bucknell, *c.*1907.

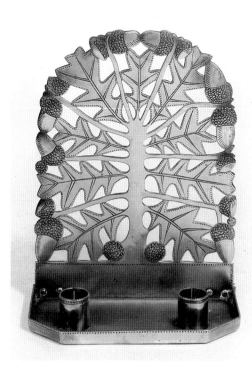

Charles Robert Ashbee and his Influence

Charles Robert Ashbee was inspired by the poet-socialist Edward Carpenter when he went up to Cambridge in 1883, the moment when romantic Carpenterism was in fashion with the young men. This led him, during his time in the office of G. F. Bodley, to live and study at Toynbee Hall, the philanthropic settlement in the East End of London, then an area of extreme poverty and lawlessness. A Ruskin reading class established there led in due course to the founding of the Guild and School of Handicraft in 1888. The workshops and classes were to be interdependent, the craftsmen teaching in the school and the pupils being prepared for eventual graduation to the workshops. Mackmurdo was encouraging: 'This', he wrote, 'is worth all our wordy theories.' Morris was not so enthusiastic, but he lectured to the Guild on 'Gothic Architecture'.

Within a year Ashbee decided that the Guild should operate independently of Toynbee Hall, and after a period in premises in Commercial Street he settled on Essex House, a dilapidated but handsome eighteenth-century brick building with a pretty garden in the Mile End Road. There the Guild remained for twelve years. The early productions of the Guildsmen, including furniture, interior decoration, silver, metalwork and jewellery, were achieved by trial and error – and some of the results were indeed amateurish and rough – but against all probability the experiment was a success.

After the separation of his parents in the early 1890s Ashbee built a house, the Magpie and Stump in Cheyne Walk on the Chelsea Embankment, for his mother and unmarried sisters. He went to live there with them and ran his architectural practice from the house. Commissions were not lacking: he had a number of artistic patrons as well as Earl Beauchamp and Lady Lovelace. Ashbee was an energetic and successful publicist, not reticent about the work in which he believed so strongly, and the Guild activities were widely reported in many Continental art magazines. This was to bring important commissions.

In 1898 M. H. Baillie Scott, still in the early stages of his career, was commissioned to decorate and furnish two rooms in the Grand

Ducal Palace at Darmstadt. He had commenced his independent architectural practice on the Isle of Man in 1889; he was an accomplished watercolourist and indefatigable in sending his beautifully presented schemes to appropriate periodicals. His work came to the notice of the cultivated and artistic Ernst Ludwig, Grand Duke of Hesse, who had plans for the architectural development of Darmstadt, and was establishing an ideal artists' community there at Matildenhohe. Baillie Scott was to be responsible for the drawing room and dining room in the existing Grand Ducal Palace. The furniture was made in the workshops of Ashbee's Guild of Handicraft. One curious feature in the drawing room was a chair like those for the knights in Burne-Jones's *San Graal* tapestry, which C. R. Mackintosh also adapted to armchairs in the Willow Tea Rooms in Glasgow in 1905.

The further development of Matildenhohe went not to Baillie Scott, but to Olbrich, who had just completed his sensational Secession exhibition building in Vienna (PL. 19), and a young Munich architect Peter Behrens. The Behrens House at Matildenhohe (1901–2), his first major commission, was in the new *Jugendstil*, Germany's answer to Art Nouveau. German design reform had been inhibited by lingering influence from the nationalistic obsession with *Historismus*. Now the impulse to advance was exploited by Behrens, Herman Obrist, Patriz Huber and Albin Muller.

Taste for 'Old English' brick and tile houses was still in evidence in Germany, for example, the suburban villa by Hermann Muthesius at Nikolassee, Berlin, with a large half-timbered central gable, and the Cecilienhof at Potsdam, inspired by the mock-Tudor Bidston Court built in 1891 for Robert Hudson the soap manufacturer. Bidston had impressed the Crown Prince on a visit in 1911 and he commissioned Cecilienhof from Paul Schultze-Naumberg in 1914, a moment when British influence would not have been expected to be in the ascendent. However, these essays in picturesque ruralism were increasingly marginal in the context of European twentieth-century design. More to the point, in 1907 Muthesius had initiated an important step towards the establishment of an International Modern Movement with the founding in Munich of the Deutsche Werkbund.

Meanwhile in 1898 Ashbee had acquired, at the death of William Morris, the printing presses and most of the staff of the Kelmscott Press; and the Essex House Press, as he now named it, was established. Increasingly Ashbee was being drawn towards simple country living, at a time when the back-to-the-land movement was at the height of its popularity with progressive thinkers. In 1901 he took the bold step of moving the Guild of Handicraft to the Cotswolds, where Gimson and the Barnsleys had already established

themselves. The decision to move to Chipping Campden had been taken democratically in the best tradition of the Guild idea, though some of the East Enders had misgivings. Although the dream seemed practicable initially, with the beautiful, neglected village buildings coming back to life again and a stream of distinguished visitors to admire this craft experiment in action, in fact Ashbee was fatally over-extended financially.

Rural isolation brought its own problems, not least the need for costly retail premises in London. Ashbee was not willing to compromise standards of craftsmanship, particularly in respect of the furniture. The 'trite' (to quote a critic in *The Studio* in 1896) simplicity of the early pieces was developed on more ornamental lines, possibly under the influence of executing Baillie Scott's designs. The impressive painted and inlaid pieces show a debt to the decorated 'state furniture' made by Morris and his collaborators more than thirty years earlier. This type of furniture required patrons with means and space; although made in the best craft traditions, the pieces look for inspiration not to rural vernacular forms but to the aristocratic furniture of seventeenth-century Spain.

Competition in the craftwork market was increasingly fierce, and there was the shadow of such successful entrepreneurial ventures as Liberty's specially commissioned art manufactures, some of which were too close to Guild designs for comfort. The Guild is best remembered for its metalwork, the activity most praised at the time. This branch had the largest workshop and was the most seriously threatened by Liberty, who shamelessly poached design ideas from the Guild. Ashbee himself was particularly bitter about Liberty's 'Cymric' silverwork and jewellery, blaming the much larger financial investment lavished on this commercial venture for the failure of the Guild.

In 1908 the Guild, which had been a limited company since 1898, went into voluntary liquidation and the remaining stock was sold off. Some of the men remained in Chipping Campden, working at the crafts they had mastered under Ashbee's leadership, vindicating the aims of the Guild that the craftsmen should develop into independent designers able to work on their own. George Hart (1878–1973) adopted the Guild's 'G of H' silver mark and carried on using designs that derived directly from those in use in the Guild's heyday. Ashbee found himself without a cause and seemed to lose direction; in Britain neither his architectural career nor his designing activities survived the breakup of the Guild. His later years were spent in work for the new state of Israel.

Left PL. 318 C. R. Ashbee: 38 and 39 Cheyne Walk, Chelsea. The two remaining houses in a group of three designed by Ashbee, 1894–8. The railings form an integral element of the composition; the unusually narrow windows probably inspired Muthesius to remark of the houses that they 'have a certain distinctive quality though they are not always free of affectation'. The third house, no. 37, known as the Magpie and Stump after an inn that had once stood on the site, was Ashbee's own residence and studio where he lived until 1917; it was demolished in 1968.

Right PL. 319 C. R. Ashbee: watercolour showing the dining room in the Magpie and Stump; made for *Kunst und Kunsthandwerke*, 1901, vol. 4, p. 464. Possibly drawn by Fleetwood Varley.

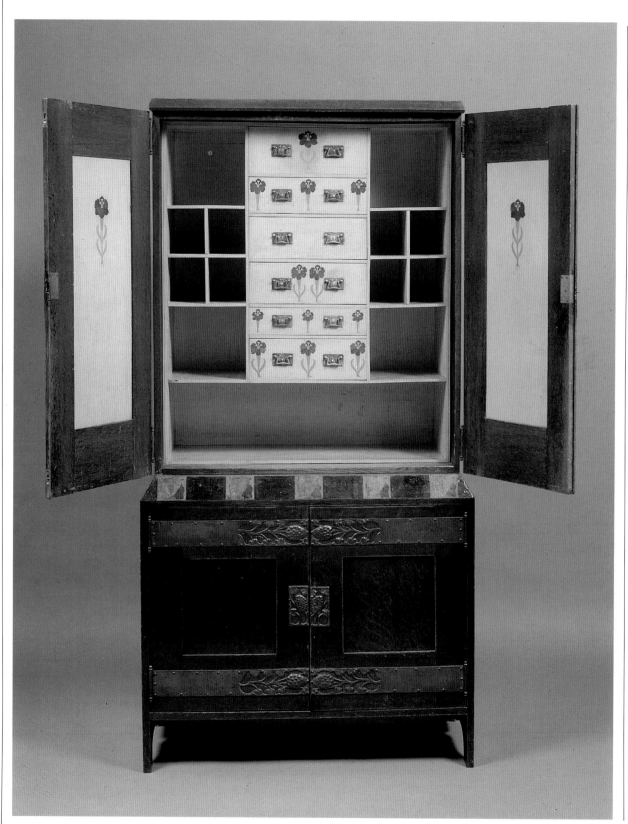

PL. 320, 321 C. R. Ashbee: writing cabinet on stand, painted and inlaid decoration, pierced iron strap hinges; made at the Guild of Handicraft, *c.*1899. A variant of the writing cabinet designed by M. H. Baillie Scott for the Grand Duke of Hesse's palace at Darmstadt, which was made at the Guild of Handicraft in 1897.

Opposite PL. 322 C. R. Ashbee: writing cabinet on stand, mahogany with coloured inlays, pierced iron strap hinges and handle plates; made at the Guild of Handicraft, *c.*1898. The cabinet was shown at the Vienna Secession Exhibition in 1900 and acquired by a Viennese family.

Right PL. 323 C. R. Ashbee: coffee pot and milk jug, hammered and chased silver set with agates, ivory handles; made at the Guild of Handicraft, 1905.

Below PL. 324 C. R. Ashbee: hammered silver pen tray with butterfly cutouts; made at the Guild of Handicraft, *c.*1900.

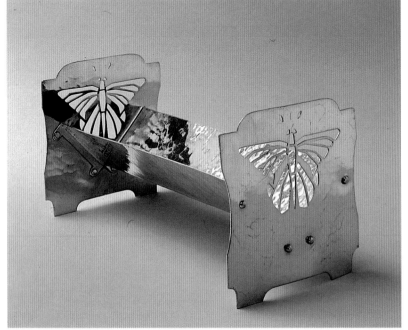

Right PL. 326 C. R. Ashbee: silver-mounted green glass decanter; marked for the Guild of Handicraft and London assay and date marked 1901.

Opposite, below right PL. 325 C. R. Ashbee: loop-handled bowl, silver set with chrysophrases; made at the Guild of Handicraft, *c.* 1900.

PL. 327 M. H. Baillie Scott: detail of fireplace surround and panelled dado; designed for Glencrutchy, Douglas, Isle of Man, 1897–8. A variant of this inglenook composition was used by Baillie Scott in the following year at Blackwell, Bowness-on-Windermere, for Sir Edward Holt, one of his best known houses and still largely unaltered.

Above PL. 328 M. H. Baillie Scott:
circular embroidery and appliqué
of coloured silks on linen, birds
and leafy branches. The design
repeats decorative motifs from
furniture, notably the 'Manxman'
piano (PL. 331). The same birds
and branches were taken up by
Olbrich for the inlaid ornament
on the cabinet, PL. 329.

Left PL. 330 M. H. Baillie Scott: piano, the case of ebonized wood, inlaid with pewter, ivory and various woods, designed for John Broadwood & Sons, 1902. The piano was exhibited by Broadwood in Budapest in 1902.

Opposite PL. 332 M. H. Baillie Scott: panel of carved relief from the piano, PL. 330.

Left PL. 331 M. H. Baillie Scott: piano case for John Broadwood & Sons, with panels of inlay and ornamental hinges; *c.*1902.

PL. 329 J. M. Olbrich: cabinet with mother-of-pearl inlays, *c.*1905. Olbrich was responsible for the flamboyant Art Nouveau 'Viennese Room' at the Paris Centennial Exhibition in 1900.

PL. 333 Peter Behrens: oak chair with chequer-pattern rushed seat. In 1901 Behrens built his own house at Matildenhohe, the artists' colony established by the Grand Duke of Hesse at Darmstadt. From 1906 he was engaged on giving a corporate identity to AEG, the vast German electrical company, with a unified style for the architecture, graphics and products. In 1907 he was a founder of the Deutsche Werkbund, a logical twentieth-century development of the Arts and Crafts Movement in Britain.

PL. 334 Josef Hoffmann: bentwood chair for the Puckersdorf Sanitorium; manufactured by J. & J. Kohn, *c.*1906. In 1903, with the backing of Fritz Warndorfer, Hoffmann and Kolomann Moser set up the Wiener Werkstätte in emulation of Ashbee's Guild of Handicraft. Mackintosh was to be influential in setting the style of the Werkstätte designs. Like the Werkbund and many other Continental craft and workshop initiatives, the Wiener Werkstätte took the Arts and Crafts aesthetic back into the realm of manufactures and the competitive marketplace.

PL. 335 Frank Lloyd Wright: high-backed oak chair; 1902. Wright's early attachments were to the art of Japan and the Arts and Crafts Movement, and he helped to found the Chicago Arts and Crafts Society in 1897. His work was admired by Ashbee who visited him in 1900. From the 'Prairie' style, which was fully developed by 1900, he moved to a highly personal modern idiom based on geometric and stylized form.

Opposite PL. 336 Frank Lloyd Wright: large copper plant urn; made by the architectural metalworkers James A. Miller, *c*.1898–9. Only about eight of the pots were made, one of which was shown at the Chicago Architectural Club in 1902.

Right PL. 337 Frank Lloyd Wright: drawing for an interior, showing his stylized furniture designs.

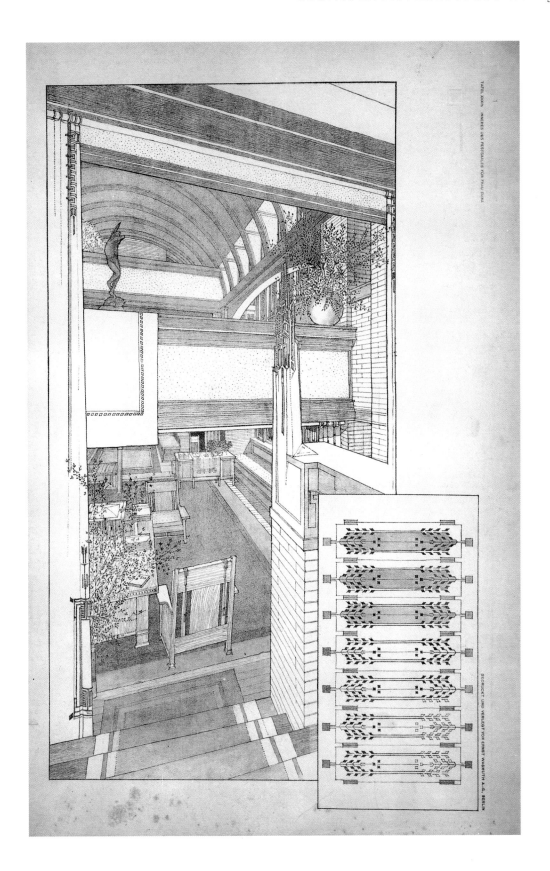

Charles Rennie Mackintosh and the International Modern Movement

'**M**odern architecture to be real must not be an envelope without contents.' This remark was made by Charles Rennie Mackintosh, leader of the Glasgow Group of architects and designer of the Glasgow School of Art, one of the most celebrated late nineteenth-century buildings in Britain. The idea was hardly new, but successive historical revivals had stimulated interest in antiques and collecting and had undermined the concept. With his close contemporary Frank Lloyd Wright, Mackintosh recovered the ideal of complete stylistic integration between the architectural envelope and its contents.

Mackinstosh was leader of the so-called 'Glasgow Four', consisting of himself and Herbert McNair and their respective wives, the Macdonald sisters, Margaret and Frances. He was one of the most accomplished architect-designers to emerge in the late nineteenth century. His most highly evolved scheme was the celebrated 'Music Room' in the 'House for an Art Lover', which gained a prize in the 1901 international competition organized by Alexander Koch, publisher of an influential design magazine. The freedom to make such a striking design statement is not common in a commercial architectural practice.

In 1889 Mackintosh had joined the Glasgow architectural firm of Honeyman & Keppie, where he met McNair. His career gained momentum in 1896 when he won the School of Art competition and was approached by Miss Catherine Cranston over the decoration for the first of her tearooms in Buchanan Street. From this date Mackintosh was fortunate in finding patrons such as Miss Cranston, W. R. Davidson (Windyhill, 1899) and Walter Blackie (Hill House, 1903), who were prepared to suppress preconceived ideas of comfort and convenience in pursuit of an architectural masterpiece.

The Hill House at Helensburgh was one of Mackintosh's most successful projects. An immensely austere scheme, composed of stark linear elements of alternating black and white, it exemplified an aspect of Mackintosh's work that had little popular appeal. Even before he gave up the practice of architecture in the 1920s Mackintosh had despaired of receiving wide acclaim in his native country; his considerable reputation abroad came through extensive coverage in Continental periodicals.

Mackintosh's first designs for furniture show a diversity of influences; vernacular, simple shapes like those of Morris & Co. joiner furniture alternate with attenuated supports like those of Mackmurdo's Liverpool Exhibition furniture of 1886. The commission in 1896 to decorate the Buchanan Street Tea Rooms provided him with an opportunity to express his own artistic personality. The stencilled patterns form a background to the elegant eighteenth-century style furniture designed by George Walton. When in 1897 Mackintosh assumed responsibility for the furniture at the tea rooms in Argyle Street a very much more uncompromising style was adopted (PL. 346). The delicate elegance of Walton's chairs gave way to square, heavy forms. The high-backed chair with pierced oval backrail used in the Luncheon Room at Argyle Street is one of the best known of Mackintosh's designs. It also features in his drawing room at 120 Mains Street in Glasgow.

The furniture for Windyhill, Kilmacolm, designed for William Davidson Jr of Gladsmuir, is marked with the same strongly individual personality. At the International Exhibition of Modern Decorative Art held at Turin in 1902, the ideas used at the Mains Street flat and at Windyhill were refined, making frequent use of the decorative talents of Margaret Mackintosh (they had married in 1900). Mackintosh was responsible for the overall design and the individual room settings in the Scottish section. The first two bays, known as the 'Rose Boudoir' and the 'Writing Room' were furnished by, respectively, the Mackintoshes and Herbert and Frances McNair (married 1899). In the following year the Willow Tea Rooms, most celebrated of the commissions for Miss Cranston, were furnished in another burst of creative energy.

Through such exposure as the *Innen-Dekoration* competition in 1901, at the Turin Exhibition in 1902, and participation in the Secession Exhibitions in Vienna, where Mackintosh and the other members of the Glasgow Four made a considerable impact on the avant-garde Viennese Koloman Moser, Josef Hoffmann and Joseph Maria Olbrich, his work reached an international audience. Mackintosh's work was more directly influential on his contemporaries in Germany and Austria, who admired the uncompromising austerity of his all-white schemes, than on his British contemporaries.

The first Vienna Secession exhibition was held in 1898 in the Horticultural Society building; by the end of the year a striking building by Olbrich was ready to house the second. Part of the brief for the Secession movement was to bring art in Vienna into contact with the principal artists and designers of the European avant-garde, and foreign artists did indeed participate in nearly all the exhibitions. The Glasgow group – and, incidentally, Ashbee – were given particularly valuable exposure by the exhibition in 1900.

There is a parallel with Mackintosh's 'House for an Art Lover' schemes in that of his fellow competitor, M. H. Baillie Scott. Superficially it resembles Mackintosh's in the use of repeating linear elements to define and divide the internal space, but it is based on a more conventional structure.

Art Nouveau in its various aspects had a unifying effect on decoration and design. The insular Arts and Crafts Movement had little impact on the Continent, and it was left to the Americans to exploit its possibilities for the Modern Movement.

Chicago was forging ahead fast, largely due to the genius of Louis Sullivan (1856–1924). Chicago architecture has the pioneering qualities appropriate to an outpost to the vast, still unexploited prairie; indeed it was the Chicago architect William Le Baron Jenney who developed the skyscraper with his iron-framed Home Insurance Building (1884–5). His pupil Sullivan's intricately sculptural architectural ornament, of which the frieze above the entrance and mezzanine on the Carson, Pirie, Scott Building is a brilliant example, remains one of the finest expressions of American *fin-de-siècle* design. In this Frank Furness, for whom Sullivan had also worked, was his inspiration, and there is also visual evidence – if such were needed – of Sullivan's awareness of Dresser's ideas; Sullivan was Frank Lloyd Wright's master, and thus the line from Owen Jones's pioneering eclecticism can be traced from *The Grammar of Ornament* in the 1850s to the Modern Movement in the early twentieth century.

Frank Lloyd Wright spent five years (1888–93) as a draughtsman in Sullivan's office. He had started to train as an engineer before taking up architecture. He was grounded in the nineteenth-century classics, the *Grammar* of course, and Viollet-le-Duc. He progressed quickly from an early flirtation with the organic forms which he developed under the influence of Eduard Colonna's *Essay on Broom Corn* (1887) to the spare linear compositions of his mature style. Although superficially in tune with the American Arts and Crafts Movement – he was a founding member in 1897 of the Chicago Arts and Crafts Society, but he saw little relation between Stickley's simplicities and his own sophisticated Japanesque abstraction. His house in Oak Park, Illinois (1889) was well publicized, and this gave him considerable influence on his Midwestern contemporaries, the

architects and designers of the 'Prairie' school. In the twentieth century he quickly carved out an international reputation for himself, and his name is now identified with modern design rather than with the nineteenth-century tradition in which he was formed.

The American Arts and Crafts Movement shared many architects and designers with the Aesthetic movement and the East Coast Renaissance. Through the acknowledged influence of Ruskin and William Morris, artists such as John La Farge and L. C. Tiffany had a place in the Movement. La Farge's involvement with H. H. Richardson put him in the heart of the American Queen Anne Revival. Richardson's development lay in a direct line from the Reformed Gothic of Isaac E. Scott through their common patron, John J. Glessner of Chicago. Glessner's wife Frances made silver in simple, hammered shapes, closely related to English Arts and Crafts work of around 1900. The Glessners were patrons of Herter Brothers, and had fabrics and a rug from Morris & Co. in their house. This strand of American Arts and Crafts was linked with the world of *Artistic Houses* and the International Art Nouveau Movement. Christian Herter died in 1884 and H. H. Richardson in 1886, aged respectively forty-three and forty-eight. It was left to Frank Lloyd Wright and the brothers Charles Sumner and Henry Mather Greene to develop the ideas they had initiated.

Frank Lloyd Wright is inseparable from the Arts and Crafts Movement, in spite of his reservations about the ideology of its heroes – he despaired of Morris's refusal to understand mechanization and industrial technology – because of his obvious debt to the formal ideas already worked out by Richardson and developed by Gustav Stickley, Charles Rohlfs and the Greenes. Stickley's magazine, *The Craftsman*, spread the ideals and influence of the Movement.

Like Morris, Wright made an excursion into hand printing. At the behest of his patron William Herman Winslow, whose house he had designed in 1893, he devised *The House Beautiful* (1897), which has been described as a 'quintessential expression of Arts and Crafts philosophy'. (See Robert Judson Clark, ed., *The Arts and Crafts Movement in America, 1876–1916*, Princeton University, 1972, p. 101.) The illustrations, however, have none of the idyllic rural message of Morris's *News from Nowhere* and the Cotswold communities in Britain. Wright transcended the limitations of Arts and Crafts.

The essence of California Arts and Crafts is contained in the four houses complete with furniture designed by Greene and Greene – Charles Sumner Greene (b. 1868) and Henry Mather Greene (b. 1870) – between 1907 and 1909. The first, the Robert R. Blacker House in Pasadena, was commissioned because Blacker had noticed

Charles Sumner Greene's own house (begun in 1901) and the Greenes' wooden neighbourhood houses in the quarter that was named 'Little Switzerland' from their resemblance to Alpine chalets. The Swiss connection is superficial, the Greenes' real architectural philosophy deriving, like Wright's, from the formal structure of Japanese buildings.

Friends of the Blackers, Mr and Mrs David B. Gamble, were the next patrons of consequence. Then came the house for Charles R. Pratt, and finally, completing this network of personal recommendation, the Thorsen House. Mrs Thorsen, sister of Mrs Robert Blacker, had roomed with Pratt's future wife when they were both students at Vassar.

The polished wood furniture for these houses was distinctive, with a soft, silky finish, sensuously rounded corners and, in the tradition of British design reform, visible peg joints. The emphatic timber skeleton and fruitwood inlays in the walnut surfaces recall the earlier Japonisme of Godwin and Herter. There were slight practical disadvantages, not uncommon in the artistic interior, chief of which were the dim quality of the light shed from the wood-framed leaded glass fittings, and the impossibility of accommodating a single inappropriate object in the carefully contrived ensemble.

C. R. Ashbee saw the Gamble House in 1909, at the time when his own venture, the Guild of Handicraft, had failed, and it was this homogeneity that he found impressive. He wrote in his journal:

'Here things were really alive and the 'Arts and Crafts' that all the others are screaming and hustling about, are actually being produced by a young architect, this quiet dreamy nervous tenacious little man fighting single handed until recently against enormous odds.' (Quoted in Clive Aslet, 'The Gamble House, Pasadena', *Country Life*, 4 April 1985, p. 882.)

Since the 1880s British designers had seen the initiative slip through their fingers. Economically American development, and with it architecture and design, forged ahead; emergent nationalism and rediscovery of the indigenous peasant culture in Scandinavia, Austro-Hungary and Russia gave novelty to the tired ideologies of the English Arts and Crafts Movement. By the end of the First World War the initiative had moved decisively to architects and manufacturers able and willing to work with functional Modernism. The art of design retreated from the marketplace back into the realms of the rich patron. The career designer became the instrument of technology and mass production. As an individual he was, temporarily at least, in eclipse.

PL. 338 George Walton: armchair, with upholstered seat and back, one of a number of variants of the chair with similarly curving arms designed for the Billiard Room of Miss Cranston's Buchanan Street Tea Room in 1896.

PL. 339 George Walton: Strand showroom of the Kodak photographic company in London; designed *c.*1898. Walton received the commission to decorate the Kodak premises in London, Glasgow, Brussels, Milan and Vienna through his friendship with the head of Kodak's European sales organization, George Davison.

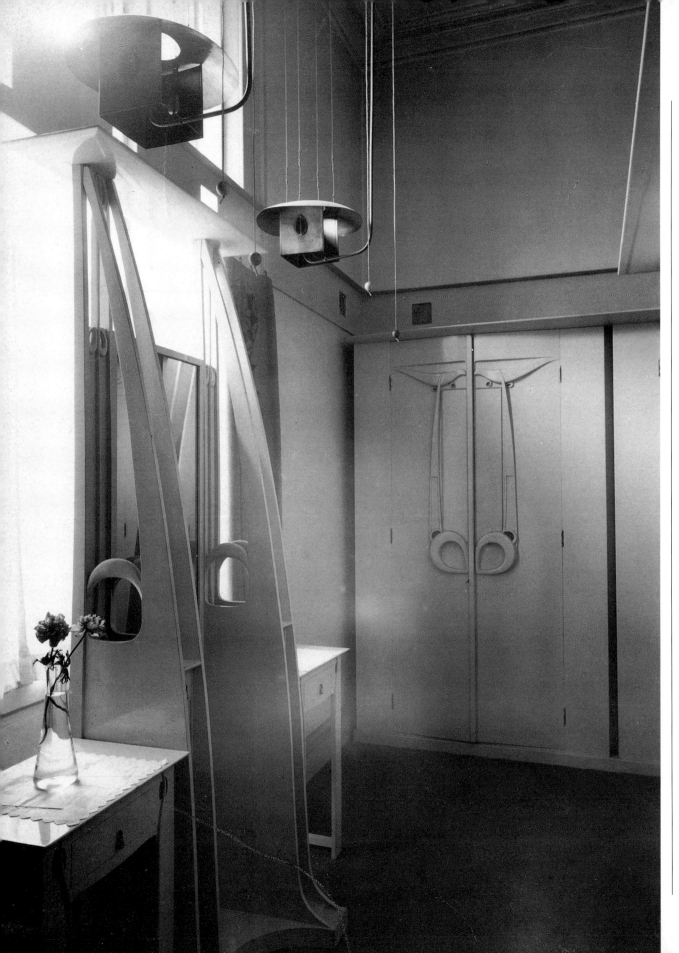

Left PL. 340 C. R. Mackintosh: interior view of 120 Mains Street, Glasgow, the bedroom; designed 1900. Mackintosh's own flat set the style for exhibits on the Continent in the early years of the century, notably at Vienna in 1900 and Turin in 1902. The flat was photographed by the contemporary Glasgow photographer Craig Annan.

Opposite PL. 341 C. R. Mackintosh: ironwork details from the exterior of the Glasgow School of Art. The first phase was completed by 1899 but the work continued for more than ten years, the interiors in the West Wing dating from 1909. Mackintosh was working to a tight brief and budget, and the decorative elements benefit from the bold simplicity that this dictated.

Opposite PL. 342 C. R. Mackintosh: cabinet, oak, painted white, with inlaid glass panels on a silvered ground inside the doors; one of a pair designed for 14 Kingsborough Gardens, Glasgow, 1902. Mackintosh had variants of the cabinet, with four hinges instead of two, in his Mains Street flat; these were shown in an Exhibition Room in Moscow in 1903, and illustrated in the periodical *Mir Isskustva*.

Right PL. 343 C. R. Mackintosh: oval table painted white and inlaid with panels of leaded glass; a variant of the table for the Warndorfer Music Salon in Vienna, 1902. The Viennese businessman Fritz Warndorfer was a backer in the early days of the Wiener Werkstätte and an important patron of the Secession Group; he commissioned a dining room from Josef Hoffmann as well as the music room from Mackintosh. This example of the Warndorfer table is probably the one shown in the Exhibition Room in Moscow in 1903, along with the cabinet like the one in PL. 342.

PL. 344, 345 Margaret Macdonald Mackintosh: 'The Opera of the Wind' and 'The Opera of the Sea', gesso panels originally set into the front of an upright piano made for the Warndorfer Music Salon in Vienna; signed with a monogram and dated 1903. The box-like piano was one of the largest pieces of furniture that Mackintosh designed. It still exists in an incomplete form in Chicago.

Left PL. 346 C. R. Mackintosh:
'Argyle' high-backed oak dining
chair; designed for Miss
Cranston's Argyle Street Tea
Rooms in Glasgow, 1897. The
chair was included in the display
at the Eighth Vienna Secession
Exhibition in 1900.

Opposite PL. 347 C. R.
Mackintosh: writing table, stained
oak with panels of coloured glass
and inset of leaded glass and
metal; made for the Blue Bedroom
at Hous'hill, 1904.

Left PL. 348 C. R. Mackintosh: pen box, ebonized wood inlaid with mother-of-pearl and walnut; made for the White Bedroom at Hous'hill, 1904. The design shows the influence of contemporary Viennese developments by, for example, Hoffmann and Koloman Moser.

Below PL. 350 C. R. Mackintosh: square stained oak table; made for the Blue Bedroom at Hous'hill, 1904. The legs are set at a diagonal to the table top, but otherwise the design is severely simple in keeping with the whole concept at Hous'hill.

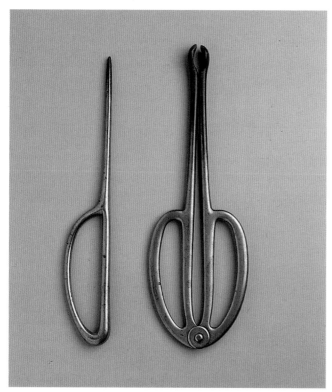

Above PL. 349 C. R. Mackintosh: steel fire irons from Hous'hill, 1904. Another set for the drawing room at The Hill House, Helensburgh, 1903, hang on a mosaic and glass inlay fireplace panel, and complete the abstract composition.

PL. 351 C. R. Mackintosh: ebonized wood chair with inlaid glass decoration; for the Blue Bedroom at Hous'hill, 1904.

Notes in short form at the ends of entries refer to publications in the Select Bibliography, p. 299.

MAURICE BINGHAM ADAMS, 1849–1933
Trained as an architect in Brighton, Adams moved to London in 1870 and joined the staff of *Building News*, of which he eventually became editor. Regarded as the best architectural perspectivist of his time, he exhibited at the Royal Academy from 1876. He worked with R. Norman Shaw and illustrated Shaw's *Sketches for Cottages* (1878). He collaborated with Godwin on *Artistic Conservatories* (1880), and published a study of *Artists' Homes* (1883). He was involved in the Georgian revival and designed for a number of firms, including: Holland & Sons; William Watt (neo-Chippendale furniture during the 1880s); Robertson & Son of Alnwick; Gillow's; Wilcock & Co. (architectural faience, 1880, exhibited in 1881 at Howell, James & Co., and published the following year in a catalogue); Messenger & Co. and the Coalbrookdale Company (both metalwork). Wilcock & Co. established the Burmantofts Pottery.

GEORGE AITCHISON, 1825–1910
The son of an architect-engineer, Aitchison was his father's pupil and then his partner from 1859. He had travelled in Italy with Burges 1853 to 1855 and his style reflected his Continental experiences – the house and studio for the Academician Lord Leighton is a mixture of Germanic classicism and Moorish style. He was appointed architect and surveyor to the St Katharine's Dock Company in succession to his father; but he was a consummate decorator, his masterpiece being the Berkeley Square house of F. Lehmann, MP, in collaboration with Albert Moore (1873). His drawings for decoration were exhibited at the RIBA in 1898, when he was awarded the Institute's Royal Gold Medal.
Margaret Richardson, *George Aitchison: Lord Leighton's Architect*, exhibition catalogue, RIBA, London, n.d.

SIR LAWRENCE ALMA-TADEMA, 1836–1912
This celebrated Dutch-born academic painter and friend of Aitchison designed the architectural restructuring and furniture for his own houses, as well as a suite of ivory-inlaid music room furniture for the American millionaire collector Henry G. Marquand. The Marquand commission was a collaboration with Lord Leighton, the furniture being made by the London firm of Johnstone, Norman & Co. Probably through Marquand's example, Alma-Tadema commissioned one of the 'Wind-Blown Peonies' stained glass panels from John La Farge for his house, which was also furnished by Johnstone, Norman & Co. with versions of the Marquand ivory-inlaid chairs and couches.

AMERICAN ENCAUSTIC TILING COMPANY, 1875–c.1945
Benedict Fisher, founder of the firm, was one of the first to cater for the interest in decorative tiles created by the 1876 Philadelphia Exhibition. Initially the production was in the encaustic method pioneered in Britain by Herbert Minton; from 1880 glazed tiles were added, and in 1881 relief tiles. In 1891 a collaboration with the publisher Edmund Evans resulted in pictorial tiles using the original plates of illustrations by Walter Crane. William Morris patterns were also reproduced on tiles.
Metropolitan Museum, 1986.

JOSEPH-FRANÇOIS-LÉON ARNOUX, 1816–1902
Arnoux trained at Sèvres. He came to England in the mid-1840s after the failure of the pottery that he ran with his father. In 1849 Herbert Minton appointed him art director of Minton's. He successfully revived Renaissance techniques and styles, for example majolica and 'Henri Deux' inlaid slipware. He was responsible for the employment at Minton's of his fellow countrymen Pierre-Emile Jeannest, Hugues Protat and Albert-Ernest Carrier-Belleuse. He retired in 1902 but continued as advisor until his death.

ART FURNISHERS' ALLIANCE CO., 1880–1883
An association of 'Art manufacturers' founded by Christopher Dresser to supply 'whatever is necessary to the complete artistic furnishing of a house'. Dresser was employed as art director and George Hayter Chubb, proprietor of the locksmiths, chaired the directors, John Harrison, Edward Cope and Sir Edward Lee. Chubb & Sons provided the premises for the manufacture of artistic furniture and metalwork, and warehouse space for the suppliers, including Arthur Liberty; Frederick Walton (linoleum and wallpapers); James Dixon (silver); John Brinton (carpets); Benham & Froud (metalware); Hukin & Heath (silver); Jeffrey, Lightbown & Aspinal, Scott Cuthbertson and Arthur Sanderson (all wallpaper manufacturers), Dresser & Holmes (Oriental objects), Sowerby (press-moulded glass); and Cope (lace curtains). A number of the suppliers, including Liberty and Dixon, were also shareholders. Showrooms in New Bond Street were inaugurated in 1881, but the firm went into liquidation in May 1883.
Halen, 1990; Durant, 1993.

ART FURNITURE COMPANY, 1867–1868
An architectural design partnership at 25 Garrick Street, Covent Garden. It was advertised in November 1867 as being 'prepared to supply at ordinary trade prices, domestic furniture of an artistic and picturesque character, designs by C. Eastlake, A. W. Blomfield and W. Godwin and other architects'. By June 1868 it was reported as having failed, although *Building News* illustrated a design for it by Godwin in 1871. Godwin's early domestic furniture was made by the company, and it is likely that Eastlake's designs from the first edition of *Hints on Household Taste* (1868) were also made by them. Clement Heaton was involved with the decoration of Eastlake's furniture and, along with A. W. Blomfield, designed portières and curtains for the Art Furniture Co. Heaton, Butler & Bayne, also of Garrick Street, exhibited at the 1867 Paris Exhibition.
Aslin, 1986.

CHARLES ROBERT ASHBEE, 1863–1942
Son of a rich businessman and owner of a celebrated collection of pornography, Ashbee went to Cambridge, where he came under the influence of Edward Carpenter. He then went to Toynbee Hall, a philanthropic mission in the East End of London, where he set up the School and Guild of Handicraft in 1888. The Guild

made woodwork, leatherwork, metalwork and jewellery, showing at the Arts and Crafts Exhibition Society from 1889. In 1898 the Guild executed the furniture for Baillie Scott's schemes for the Darmstadt Palace of the Grand Duke of Hesse. The Guild's work was shown at the 1900 Vienna Secession Exhibition. In 1901 Ashbee moved to Chipping Campden in Gloucestershire, taking some 150 people – Guildsmen and their families – with him. The Guild's finances were overstretched and the venture failed in 1907. Ashbee had made contact with Frank Lloyd Wright when he visited America in 1896, and kept up with him later. He also admired the architecture of the brothers Charles Sumner and Henry Mather Greene.
MacCarthy, 1981; Crawford, 1985.

ASSOCIATED ARTISTS, 1879–1884
Founded by Louis Comfort Tiffany, with Samuel Colman, a Hudson River painter and specialist in colour, Lockwood de Forest for carved and ornamental woodwork and Candace Wheeler as textile specialist. During its four-year existence Associated Artists executed a number of grand commissions, including the redecoration of four rooms in The White House and various clubs and residences. In 1884 the partnership was dissolved, but Candace Wheeler remained in business until 1907.
Metropolitan Museum, 1986.

GEORGE ASHDOWN AUDSLEY, 1838–1925
Audsley trained as an architect in Elgin and practised in Liverpool from 1856, where he also made an important contribution to the Art Movement as a publisher of chromolithographic books with his brother, William James Audsley. The first, *The Sermon on the Mount* (1861), contains a plate by Owen Jones. *The Guide to the Art of Illumination* (1861) was extremely popular, reaching twelve editions in seven years. Their manuals of ornamental pattern included *Outlines of Ornament* (1878) and *Polychromatic Decoration as Applied to Buildings in the Medieval Styles* (London and Paris 1882; and Stuttgart 1883). He published a number of books on Japanese art in the 1870s, and on ornament, including *Keramic Art of Japan* (1875), and *The Practical Decorator and Ornamentist* (1892).

MACKAY HUGH BAILLIE SCOTT, 1865–1945
After serving his articles in Bath, Baillie Scott began his career in Douglas, Isle of Man. There he came into contact with Archibald Knox and collaborated with him on the design of stained glass and ironwork. He exhibited furniture, metalwork and wallpaper at the 1896 Arts and Crafts Exhibition, the year in which he designed the 'Manxman' piano case. The commission from the Grand Duke of Hesse to decorate rooms in the palace at Darmstadt came in 1898. In 1901 he gained the highest award for his entry in the *Innen-Dekoration* competition for the 'House for an Art Lover'. He had moved to Bedford in 1901, and from there he conducted a successful practice in suburban homes, which gained greatly from his partnership with A. Edgar Beresford.
Baillie Scott, 1906; Kornwolf, 1972.

BARNARD, BISHOP & BARNARD, 1826–1955
The founder of the Norwich firm, Charles Barnard, entered into a partnership with John Bishop in 1846; the name was changed to the final form in 1859 with the arrival of two Barnard sons. The early prosperity of the firm was based on the manufacture of household and garden equipment. The production of ornamental ironwork was commenced in 1851, and celebrated with a prize-winning hinge and a doorknocker at the Great Exhibition. Decorative fire surrounds were a speciality, providing an outlet for the early tile production of the Morris firm. One of William De Morgan's most characteristic tile designs, a large cornflower, is known as the B. B. B. from its use in the firm's fireplaces. The partnership between the firm's chief craftsman and the Norwich architect Thomas Jeckyll resulted in a spectacular contribution to ornamental ironwork, starting with the Norwich Gates, acclaimed at the 1862 Exhibition, and culminating in the two-storey Japanese pavilion at the 1876 Philadelphia Exhibition. Jeckyll designed andirons and a number of Japanese-style grates for Barnards. In the twentieth century the firm returned to utilitarian products.

SIDNEY BARNSLEY, 1865–1926
Barnsley was born in Birmingham, the son of the

head of a prosperous building firm and principal contractor of the Birmingham architect J. H. Chamberlain. He studied at the Birmingham School of Art before departing for London and the Royal Academy Schools department of architecture in 1885 with his brother Ernest (1863–1926). In 1886 Sidney entered Norman Shaw's office while Ernest went to J. D. Sedding's office, and it was thus through Ernest that Sidney met Gimson with whom he made a lifelong friendship. In 1890 he joined Gimson, W. R. Lethaby, Reginald Blomfield and Mervyn Macartney in founding Kenton & Co. After the disbanding of the firm Sidney went with Gimson to the Cotswolds, where he established a modest furniture workshop for carrying out his own designs. After Gimson's untimely death he was fully occupied in completing architectural projects, notably the library at Bedales School.
Comino, 1980.

HENRY W. BATLEY, *fl.* before 1872–after 1910
A pupil of Talbert, Batley designed furniture for Collinson & Lock, including a chair shown in Philadelphia in 1876 and an elaborate drawing room illustrated in *Decoration* in 1884. He designed the interiors for Doulton's terracotta house at the Paris Exhibition of 1878 which were carried out by Shoolbred & Co. (an intricately decorated piano for Shoolbred is now in the Victoria and Albert Museum) and a cabinet for Henry Ogden & Son of Manchester. He was awarded the cross of the Légion d'Honneur, probably for his contribution to the Paris Exhibition. Batley's *Series of Studies for Domestic Furniture, Decoration Etc.* (1883), while showing the influence of Talbert, also betrays a reliance on Godwin and Jeckyll. He designed wallpapers for Jeffrey & Co., as well as textiles and carpets. In 1873 Arthur Silver became his apprentice. Batley founded the Guild of Decorators Syndicate Ltd. in 1908 with the stated aim of working in close association with commercial manufacturers, unlike the utopian Arts and Crafts guilds.

ROBERT ANNING BELL, 1863–1933
Having chosen initially to study architecture, Bell changed to painting, training at the Royal Academy Schools. He made his reputation as an illustrator, and designed reliefs for the Della

Robbia pottery, mosaics for Harrison Townsend's Horniman Museum building and for J. F. Bentley's Westminster Cathedral, as well as stained glass. He was Master of the Art Workers' Guild in 1921.

BENHAM & FROUD, fl. before 1855–after 1893

Copper and brass manufacturers, successors to Kepp & Co., copper and platinasmiths, at 40–42 Chandos Street, Charing Cross. They exhibited at the Paris 1855 and London 1862 exhibitions; a catalogue of 1874 gives their specialities as 'art metal and wood work'. Dresser designed for the firm from 1873 to 1893, and it was a supplier to the Art Furnishers' Alliance. C. L. Eastlake, S. J. Nicholl and O. W. Davis also made designs for the company. The relationship with Benham and Sons of Wigmore Street, whose chief designer, R. Norman Shaw, had been the architect of their works and produced medal-winning designs for the 1862 Exhibition is unclear.

WILLIAM ARTHUR SMITH BENSON, 1854–1924

Educated at Winchester and Oxford, Benson served his articles in the office of Basil Champneys and remained with the practice until 1880. He had met Morris through his friendship with Edward Burne-Jones, and was inspired to set up a metalworking workshop in that year. He expanded into a well equipped factory in Hammersmith and from 1887 had a retail shop in Bond Street. In 1896 he became chairman of Morris & Co., for which he designed furniture. He also worked for J. S. Henry and the Coalbrookdale and Falkirk iron foundries. Benson's simple, well designed and utilitarian copper and brass tablewares, jugs and lighting equipment were praised by H. Muthesius. Bing chose his work for exhibition and sale at his Paris gallery, Maison de L'Art Nouveau. Benson was an active founder member of the Art Workers' Guild and in 1914 founder of the Design and Industries Association. He retired and the firm was bought by Allen-Liversedge Ltd, a lighting company, in 1920.
Collins, 1981; P. Rose, 'W. A. S. Benson: a pioneer designer of light fittings', *Journal of the Decorative Arts Society*, 9, 1985.

CHARLES BEVAN, fl. before 1865–1883

Bevan was listed as a 'pattern drawer' in 1869. The earliest record of his activities is the illustration in the *Building News* in 1865 of an inlaid Gothic-style davenport. In the same year he advertised his 'New Registered Reclining Chair', made by Marsh & Jones (later Marsh, Jones & Cribb). His style derives from Seddon, and it seems likely that he was Seddon's pupil and then assistant before setting up on his own account. His association with Marsh & Jones of Leeds may have begun when Seddon & Co. collaborated on designs with Kendall & Co. of Leeds, the firm which was absorbed by Marsh & Jones in 1864. He appears to have ended the association by 1867. He designed for James Lamb of Manchester (a bookcase was shown at the 1867 Paris Exhibition), Holland & Sons, Gillow & Co., and Gregory & Co. In 1872, in partnership with his son George Alfred he set up as 'C. Bevan & Son, Designers, Woodcarvers and Manufacturers of Art Furniture'. Furniture designed by Bevan was shown at the London International Exhibitions of 1871, 1872 & 1873, and ceramics in 1871. He also designed encaustic tiles, gasoliers, stained glass and brass pole cornices.
Simon Jervis, 'Charles, Bevan and Talbert', in *The Decorative Arts in the Victorian Period*, ed. Susan M. Wright, Society of Antiquaries, London 1989.

FORD MADOX BROWN, 1821–1893

Brown met Rossetti and Holman Hunt in 1848 and became closely associated with the Pre-Raphaelites. In the 1850s he became interested in the education of working men and in 1856 he met Morris, a meeting that led to his becoming a founder member of the Morris firm in 1861. Before this he had been experimenting with furniture and stained glass design, and it was in this latter capacity that he continued to work for Morris until about 1874. As well as his involvement in the decoration of Seddon's 'King René' cabinet, his other exhibit at the 1862 London International Exhibition was a bookcase illustrating scenes from the life of an English family from 1810 to 1860. The drawings for it are in the Ashmolean Museum. From 1878 until his death he was engaged on the decorations for Manchester Town Hall. Benson took up the simple joiner

furniture that Madox Brown had designed in the early days of the firm, and versions of the bedroom furniture featured in the firm's catalogue in the twentieth century.
Newman & Watkinson, 1991.

WILLIAM BURGES, 1827–1881

After completing his articles with Edward Blore, Burges assisted Matthew Digby Wyatt in the preparation of his illustrated volumes, *Metal Work and its Artistic Design* (1852) and *The Industrial Arts of the Nineteenth Century* (1851–3). The experience gave him a thorough grounding in decorative design. He began to design furniture in 1858 with the first of a series of pieces for the Yatman family. Although Burges acknowledged a debt to Viollet-le-Duc, especially the *Dictionnaire raisonné de l'architecture* (1858–68) and the *Dictionnaire du mobilier français* (1858–71), he had himself made drawings on his Continental travels in 1853, including the thirteenth-century Noyon cupboard on which one of the Yatman cabinets is based. His contributions to Gilbert Scott's *Gleanings from Westminster Abbey* (1860) reveal the source of many of his ideas. His Cantor Lectures given at the Royal Society of Arts in 1864 were published as *Art Applied to Industry* (1865). In 1864 he took over the supervision of church plate for the Ecclesiological Society from G. E. Street. He designed furniture for his patron the Marquess of Bute, for whom he worked from 1869 until his death, and wallpapers for Jeffrey & Co., but his own comfortable financial circumstances and the patronage of Lord Bute protected him from any real need to pander to the whims of manufacturers with an eye to public demand.
Crook, 1981 (book and exhibition catalogue).

SIR EDWARD BURNE-JONES, 1833–1898

Burne-Jones met William Morris at Oxford and became his lifelong friend and longest collaborator. They set up house together in Red Lion Square and one of the earliest pieces of painted furniture, Morris's most conspicuous contribution to the early production of his firm, was a wardrobe designed by Philip Webb and painted by Burne-Jones with an episode from Chaucer's 'Prioress's Tale'. In 1857 Burne-Jones began designing stained glass for Powell's of Whitefriars, he worked also for Lavers & Barraud; from the founding of the Morris firm in 1861 he was continually occupied with stained glass designs, tiles, gesso-work, embroideries and tapestries for them, which he consistently complained of as ill remunerated. One of the last tasks for Morris was the fifty-seven illustrations for the Kelmscott *Chaucer* (1895), completed when Morris was already mortally ill.

G. Burne-Jones, *Memorials of Edward Burne-Jones*, 1904.

WILLIAM BUTTERFIELD, 1814–1900

Butterfield was working in London from 1840; in 1843, on his own suggestion, the Cambridge Camden Society retained him as arbiter in the design of church fittings. His designs were published in *Instrumenta Ecclesiastica* (1844–7). He supervised the production of his church plate by John Keith & Son, who won a medal at the Great Exhibition in 1851, and metalwork by Potter. In the 1870s many of his silver plate designs were made by Hart, Son & Peard. Butterfield was responsible for some of the most intricate polychromatic buildings of his time but, beyond the highly original church art – his fonts are outstandingly memorable – he was not much involved with decorative design.

Thompson, 1971.

COLIN MINTON CAMPBELL, 1827–1885.

Herbert Minton's nephew and successor, Colin Minton Campbell joined Minton & Co. in 1845 and was jointly responsible for running the company with Michael Daintry Hollins from 1858 to 1868. A dispute over tiles broke up the firm in 1868 and Hollins set up Minton, Hollins & Co. making decorative tiles. Campbell was responsible for the 'Art' initiatives set up by the firm of Minton & Co. Dresser was designing for the firm from 1866; the cloisonné wares were produced soon after; the Art Pottery Studio at Kensington Gore was set up in 1871. These experiments, though in the case of the Kensington Gore Studio unprofitable and short-lived, paved the way for the Art Pottery movement in Britain and America. In 1875 he established the Campbell Brick & Tile Co. to produce decorative Gothic tiles, exhibiting in Philadelphia in 1876 and Paris in 1878.

Atterbury & Batkin, 1990.

CAMPBELL, SMITH & CO., founded 1873

Decorating firm founded by Charles Campbell in partnership with Frederick George Smith. The firm was retained to paint and gild furniture designed by William Burges, and this led to extensive decorative work at Cardiff Castle and Castell Coch for the Marquess of Bute under Burges's direction. Much of the painted furniture and decoration at Burges's Tower House in Melbury Road was carried out by the firm. A succession of church and theatre decorating commissions followed.

WALTER FREDERICK CAVE, 1863–1939

Cave was educated at Eton before studying art at the Royal Academy Schools and then architecture under Arthur W. Blomfield. In 1889 he set up a practice in London and joined the Art Workers' Guild. Maple & Co. exhibited a piano designed by Cave for Bechstein at the Arts & Crafts Exhibition Society, of which Cave was later president, in 1893, and in subsequent exhibitions he showed chairs, metalwork and textiles, often executed by his wife. He took over one of Voysey's commissions and other Voysey-esque houses followed, but his later style was closer to the French Renaissance manner of Reginald Blomfield, nephew of his former master.

Stamp, 1986.

JOHN HENRY CHAMBERLAIN, 1831–1883

Chamberlain was articled to an architect named Goddard in his native Leicester, and after an abortive attempt to set up his own practice there he established himself in Birmingham, where he had well-to-do relatives. His Birmingham career was inaugurated with commissions from his family; a shop in Union Street for his uncle's firm of Eld & Chamberlain, and a house in Edgbaston for Mr Eld. He wrote essays on Ruskinian subjects, adopting and expanding his mentor's ideas. He remained an unswerving Ruskinian throughout his career and became trustee of Ruskin's Guild of St George. His furniture exemplified the relationship of Gothic and nature, the surfaces being richly inlaid with leaves and flowers.

Brooks, 1989.

COALBROOKDALE COMPANY

Founded in the early eighteenth century, the pioneering ironworks of the Industrial Revolution at Ironbridge, Shropshire, had by the early nineteenth century reached a low ebb in its fortunes; in 1830 Abraham Darby IV and his brother Alfred took control and reversed the downward trend. Among the new ventures was the manufacture of artistic and ornamental castings, initiated in 1834 and continued until World War I. Prominent Victorian designers worked for the company, including John Bell, whose work was acclaimed at the Great Exhibition in 1851; Christopher Dresser, who provided designs from 1867 to 1887; M. B. Adams; W. R. Lethaby; B. J. Talbert; A. Stevens; A.-E. Carrier-Belleuse; George Walton and A. H. Mackmurdo. The company exhibited at many of the major exhibitions, including London in 1851, 1862, 1871; Paris in 1855; and the 1890 Arts and Crafts Exhibition Society. Although absorbed by Glynwed International in the late twentieth century, decorative cast iron is no longer produced under the Coalbrookdale Co. name.

THOMAS EDWARD COLLCUTT, 1840–1924

Collcutt was born in Oxford, and after articles with R. E. Armstrong and work in the firm of Miles & Murgatroyd he became an assistant to G. E. Street. His contemporaries in Street's office, R. Norman Shaw and W. E. Nesfield, were pioneers of the Queen Anne movement; his fellow designer for the firm of Collinson & Lock, for whom he began working in 1870 – commencing with luxurious new premises – was E. W. Godwin. The 1871 catalogue published by Collinson & Lock, *Sketches for Artistic Furniture*, consisted chiefly of his designs, although J. Moyr Smith drew the plates and may have contributed some of the designs. Collcutt's ebonized 'Art' furniture shown in Philadelphia in 1876 contributed to the fashion for the style in the United States, and at the Paris 1878 Exhibition he designed a house and contents on the 'Street of Nations'. Collcutt also designed for Gillow's and Jackson & Graham, and a number of his designs were published in *Building News*. His architectural career was successful, encompassing notably the Renaissance-style Imperial Institute in South Kensington (now demolished except for the tower).

COLLINSON & LOCK, 1870–1897

'Art Furnishers', founded with the partnership of F. G. Collinson and G. J. Lock, former employees of Jackson & Graham. Designers employed by the firm included T. E. Collcutt, the architect of their premises; E. W. Godwin, who was paid a retainer to produce exclusive designs for the company from 1872 to 1874, H. W. Batley and Stephen Webb. They made furniture for the new Law Courts to designs by G. E. Street, along with Gillow's and Holland & Sons, and began decoration of the Savoy Theatre in 1881. Jackson & Graham was taken over in 1885, at the time when the firm had moved to Oxford Street and begun to focus on expensive commissions for grandiose London houses. The change of direction was not a success, and the firm was taken over by Gillow's in 1897.
Kinchin, Juliet, 'Collinson and Lock', *Connoisseur*, vol. 201, May 1979, pp. 46–53.

DANIEL COTTIER, 1838–1891

Cottier was born in Glasgow and apprenticed to a local stained glass manufacturer. After a spell in London in 1860, where he attended lectures by Ruskin and Ford Madox Brown, he returned to Scotland to work with stained glass manufacturers in Edinburgh. There he established his own studio in 1864. By 1867 he was back in Glasgow and had added decoration to his stained glass work. Two years later he returned to London to set up Cottier & Company, Art Furniture Makers, Glass and Tile Painters. B. J. Talbert was briefly a partner in the firm, alongside J. M. Brydon and W. Wallace. In 1873 he established a branch in New York, where he spent a good deal of his time. In the same year he expanded still further with a branch in Melbourne, Australia, which was largely run by his partner John Lamb Lyon. Cottier's work is featured in Clarence Cook's *The House Beautiful* (1878). Godwin-style designs were manufactured by Cottier's firm in the United States. The New York firm survived the founder's death by nearly quarter of a century, only closing in 1915.
Metropolitan Museum, 1986.

COX & SON, 1837–1881

Ecclesiastical warehouse at 28–9 Southampton Street, off the Strand. By 1872 the firm was listing Gothic and monumental metalworks in Lambeth and stained glass works in Covent Garden, and described itself as an artistic furniture manufacturer, japanner and cabinet carver. The catalogue stated that the firm had acquired much of the stock of furniture and designs by E. W. Pugin for the Granville Hotel and working drawings from the Society of Decorative Art, of Great Marlborough Street. Cox & Son commissioned furniture, metalwork, stained glass and ceramic designs from a number of leading designers including B. J. Talbert, S. J. Nicholls, G. Goldie, J. Moyr Smith, O. W. Davis, C. Rossiter and E. W. Godwin. From 1870 to 1874 the silversmith John James Keith worked under the firm's name, producing prize-winning designs principally by Talbert. Cox & Son were represented at international exhibitions in London in 1862, 1871, 1872, 1873; Paris in 1867; and Philadephia in 1876; as well as later at the Arts & Crafts Exhibition Society. Dresser used Cox's stained glass at Bushloe House. In 1881 the firm merged with Buckley & Co. and continued as Cox, Son, Buckley & Co. into the twentieth century, concentrating again on church furnishings. Between 1896 and 1903 James Keith, successor of John James Keith, was a partner in the company.

JOHN GREGORY CRACE, 1809–1889

Crace entered the family decorating firm (established in about 1768 by his great-grandfather Edward, a coach decorator) in 1826, soon after his grandfather and father had completed extensive works on royal commissions, at Carlton House and the Brighton Pavilion respectively. He himself was to be closely associated with A. W. N. Pugin from 1843, when he commenced work on the interiors of the New Palace of Westminster, also supplying furniture for the Grange from 1844. He supervised the decoration of the Medieval Court at the Great Exhibition in 1851 and was responsible for the interior of the 1862 Exhibition building, and the Manchester Art Treasures Exhibition in 1857. He also showed at Paris in 1855. After Pugin's death he continued to work in a Puginesque Gothic,

completing elaborate furniture and decoration at Abney Hall in Cheshire, and made furniture to E. W. Pugin's designs for Scarisbrick in the 1870s. In 1854 he was joined by his son John Diblee Crace, who rose to prominence as an exponent of the revived Renaissance style. The firm closed in 1899.
Aldrich, 1990.

WALTER CRANE, 1845–1915

Crane was a prolific designer of wallpaper, textiles, embroideries and ceramics, but his most important influence was through his highly original book illustrations. His earliest ceramic designs were for Wedgwood, in 1867; he designed tiles for Maw & Co., from 1874 and for Pilkington's; wallpapers for Jeffrey & Co., from 1874; and embroideries for the Royal School of Art Needlework from the same date. His designs for damask tablecloths were made by John Wilson & Sons, London. He designed the mosaic frieze for Aitchison's Arab Hall in Lord Leighton's Kensington house and studio in 1877. He was a founder member of the Art Workers' Guild. He visited America in 1891–2, where his work made a considerable impact. He was given a special award for his contribution to the English Section at Turin in 1902.
Smith & Hyde, 1989.

LEWIS FOREMAN DAY, 1845–1910

In 1864 Day started work at the stained glass manufacturers Lavers & Barraud; he subsequently spent time with Clayton & Bell and Heaton, Butler & Bayne, where he was involved with the decoration of Eaton Hall, reconstructed in the High Victorian style for the Duke of Westminster. In 1870 he established his own design business providing wallpapers for W. B. Simpson and Jeffrey & Co., tiles for Maw, Pilkington and Craven Dunnill; textiles for John Wilson, Turnbull & Stockdale and others; and furniture and silver for a number of different manufacturers. At the 1878 Paris Exhibition Aesthetic clocks by Day were shown by Howell, James & Co., and a cabinet with his panels by H. J. Cooper. He was a founder member and later secretary of the Art Workers' Guild; a member of the Arts & Crafts Exhibition Society; a prolific journalist, contributing to the *Art*

Journal, *Magazine of Art* and *The Architect*; and an influential theorist of design and decoration.

JOSEPH-THÉODORE DECK, 1823–1891

Born in Alsace, the son of a silk worker, Deck studied sculpture and chemistry in preparation for his career as a potter. He first settled in Paris in 1847; after an absence following the 1848 revolution he established his own atelier in 1856, and in 1858 opened 'Faience d'Art Th. Deck', with his brother Xavier. Deck was attracted to the design and techniques of Islamic wares, which he had become aware of through the example of Adalbert de Beaumont, author of the *Encyclopédie des arts décoratifs de l'Orient* (1859). Deck showed these at the London 1862 Exhibition (see J. B. Waring, *Masterpieces of Industrial Art*, 1862, III, pl. 297). As well as the admired Isnik wares and distinctive 'bleu Deck' colouring, Japonisme was an important aspect of his work from 1870. He won many medals at international exhibitions, showing at London in 1871; Vienna in 1873; Paris in 1867, 1878 and 1889; and Philadelphia in 1876, where Deck's faience was shown on the Collinson & Lock stand. Deck collaborated with many artist friends in producing painted chargers, including Félix Bracquemond, Françoise Gluck, Eléonore Escallier, Albert Anker and Joseph Ranvier. In 1887 he was appointed Director of the National Porcelain Manufactory at Sèvres. After Deck's death in 1891 the factory continued under Xavier and Deck's nephew Richard until 1905.

Deck, 1887; Catalogue of the Musée Florival, Guebwiller, 1991.

WILLIAM FREND DE MORGAN, 1839–1917

From 1861 De Morgan was involved with stained glass design; in 1863 he began to concentrate on ceramics, designing tiles for William Morris, alongside Simeon Solomon and Albert Moore, his contemporaries at the Academy Schools. His Orange House pottery at Cheyne Row in Chelsea started production in 1873; in 1882 he moved with Morris to Merton Abbey. He worked at the Sands End Pottery in Fulham from 1888–98 in partnership with the architect Halsey Ricardo. He continued the Sands End Pottery until 1907 when he turned to writing novels; his partners from 1898, Charles and Fred Passenger and Frank Iles, kept the pottery in production until 1911. De Morgan made a significant contribution to the Art Pottery movement with the revival of lustre techniques; among his contemporaries in this field he most admired the work of the Frenchman Clément Massier and the Cantagalli factory in Florence. Although De Morgan's wife claimed that there had been no commercial collaboration between Cantagalli and De Morgan, they did make pieces to each other's designs.

Greenwood, 1989; Catleugh, Jon, *William De Morgan Tiles*, London 1983.

JAMES DIXON & SONS, founded *c*.1806

Sheffield plateworkers and silversmiths. Initially the firm manufactured Britannia metal; silverware and electroplate were added later. A London showroom in Ludgate Hill was opened in 1873. Dixon's costing book of 1879 includes designs by Christopher Dresser, registered from 1880, and these were produced until at least 1885, according to the trade catalogue issued in that year. The company exhibited under its own name and also supplied goods to Elkington & Co. and Howell, James & Co., and electroplate to Tiffany & Co.

DOULTON & CO., Lambeth Pottery, 1853–1956

Successor to Doulton & Watts, makers of salt-glazed stoneware for domestic and manufacturing purposes and chemical works from 1815. When Watts retired Henry Doulton merged his drainpipe company with his brother's share of Doulton & Watts to form Doulton & Co. He was persuaded by John Sparkes to take on George Tinworth, an unemployed ex-student from the Lambeth School of Art, to produce decorative wares, and to set up an experimental art pottery studio for other ex-students of the school in the 1860s. The firm had shown successfully at the exhibitions in 1851, 1862 and 1867. The new range of art pottery was so successful at the London exhibition of 1871 that he extended his support, and by the 1880s the Lambeth Pottery was employing over 200 artists and designers, many of whom were women. Dresser described it as the first example of the artist controlling the manufacturer. The art wares were also shown at London in 1872, Philadelphia in 1876, Paris in 1878 and Chicago in 1893. The list of artists and designers is endless, but includes Hannah Barlow who had worked at Minton's Art Pottery Studio, George Tinworth, Mark V. Marshall, who had worked as a decorator for the Martin Brothers, and Frank Butler. The Lambeth pottery closed down in 1956. Royal Doulton has become the largest manufacturer of ceramics in the UK, having merged with other producers including Minton, making decorative architectural and sanitary wares. The company was absorbed into Betashire Ltd in the twentieth century.

Paul Atterbury, and Louise Irvine, *The Doulton Story*, exhibition catalogue, Victoria and Albert Museum, London 1979. Louise Irvine, 'Doulton and the Victorian exhibition', in *The Decorative Arts in the Victorian Period*, ed. Susan M. Wright, Society of Antiquaries, London 1989.

CHRISTOPHER DRESSER, 1834–1904

Dresser was born in Glasgow, and from 1847 to 1854 studied at the Government School of Design, Somerset House, where he was awarded a prize for a fabric design which was put into production by Liddiard & Co. He lectured on botany at the School before going on as a lecturer to the Department of Science and Art at South Kensington, specializing in botany. In 1856 he supplied a plate depicting 'the geometrical arrangement of flowers' for Owen Jones's *Grammar of Ornament*. The *Art Journal* published a series of his lectures on 'Botany as adapted to art and art manufactures' in 1857 and 1858, and in 1859–60 he wrote several books on botany and plant morphology, gaining a doctorate from the University of Jena in 1860. By 1862 he had established a studio of pupils at Chiswick and supplied a number of designs at the London International Exhibition. Dresser made drawings and purchases of objects from Sir Rutherford Alcock's collection of Japanese art, shown at the exhibition. In the same year his first design book was published: *The Art of Decorative Design*. Ceramics for Minton and Wedgwood, and carpets for Brinton's, were shown at Paris in 1867, metalwork for Coalbrookdale at London in 1871, and designs for eleven wallpaper companies exhibited at Paris in 1878. In 1876 Dresser visited the Philadelphia Exhibition, en

route to Japan at the invitation of the Japanese Government, to report on their art industries. He brought with him many gifts from the South Kensington Museum for the Emperor, and acted as a buying agent for Londos & Co. and Tiffany & Co. In 1879 he established Dresser & Holme, with the later editor of *The Studio*, importing Oriental goods; and Linthorpe Pottery, for which he made radical new designs. His designs for metalwork for Hukin & Heath, first shown in 1879, James Dixon & Sons, and Elkington (for whom he had worked since the 1860s) reflected his Japanese experience in their simplicity. He established the Art Furnishers' Alliance in 1880; worked as art editor at the *Furniture Gazette* from January to December 1881; and in 1882 published *Japan, Its Architecture, Art and Art Manufactures*. After the collapse of the Alliance in 1883 Dresser moved to Sutton, Surrey, before returning to Barnes in 1889. He supplied designs to at least fifty companies, both in Britain and overseas. An anonymous article in *The Studio* (1899) described him as 'perhaps the greatest of commercial designers'.
Halen, 1990; Durant, 1993.

CHARLES LOCKE EASTLAKE, 1836–1906

Born in Plymouth, Eastlake was virtually adopted by his uncle Charles Lock Eastlake, painter and a director of the National Gallery in London. He studied architecture under Philip Hardwick, but his career was spent mainly in journalism and as secretary to the Institute of British Architects. His seminal *Hints on Household Taste* (1868), was originally conceived as magazine articles. Included in the book are designs by Eastlake himself for furniture and wallpapers; the frontispiece shows his design for a cabinet which was exhibited by Heaton, Butler & Bayne in Paris in 1867, and was probably made by the Art Furniture Co., for whom he supplied designs in the 1860s. In later editions he shows furniture to his designs made by Jackson & Graham, and metalwork by Benham & Froud. He also designed fabrics for Cowlishaw, Nicol & Co. and wallpapers for Jeffrey & Co. Jewellery by Eastlake was shown by Howell, James & Co. at the London exhibitions of 1871 and 1872. His most ambitious work was the *History of the Gothic Revival in England* (1872).

ROBERT WILLIAM EDIS, 1839–1927

Edis began his career as an architect in 1861; his preferred style was 'Queen Anne' and he built up a wide and successful practice. His Cantor lectures delivered at the Society of Arts became a manual not unlike Eastlake's *Hints*; they were entitled *Decoration and Furniture of Town Houses* (1881), and illustrated by M. B. Adams. He was one of Burges's circle of close friends, and lists him among the pioneers in design reform, with G. E. Street, R. Norman Shaw, Alfred Waterhouse, Philip Webb and E. W. Godwin, with whom he collaborated. He designed furniture for Maple & Co., wallpapers, and tiles for Minton, Hollins & Co. He was concerned with health in the domestic environment and wrote *Healthy Furniture and Decoration* for the London Health Exhibition in 1884, where furniture to his designs was exhibited by Jackson & Graham.

ELKINGTON & Co., 1824–1968

Metalworking firm founded by George Richard Elkington. Its fortunes were immensely enhanced by foresight of the founder and Henry Elkington in taking out the earliest patents for the electrodeposition process in 1836. The electrotyping reproductive technique was also profitably pioneered by the company. As well as the profitable electroplate, the firm made elaborate prize-winning silverware designed by the Frenchmen Emile Jeannest and Leonard Morel-Ladeuil. Albert (Auguste Adolphe) Willms also supplied designs to the company and was head of the firm's design studio from 1859 until his death in 1899. Dresser's connection with Elkington lasted from 1865 to 1890. During this period a number of experiments were made with Japanese techniques of cloisonné enamels – the first piece was registered in 1866 – *komai* engraved and chased decoration, and mixed-metal techniques. The firm later abandoned manufacturing cloisonné in favour of importing cheaper Japanese wares. Elkington exhibited at the international exhibitions in 1851, 1855, 1862, 1867, 1871, 1873, 1876 and 1878.

GILLOW, 1729–1900

Decorators, cabinet-makers and upholsterers, founded by Robert Gillow of Lancaster. London premises were opened in Oxford Street in 1769.

After Robert Gillow's death in 1772 his son Richard ran the Lancaster branch, and his son Robert (junior) the London branch. The firm was celebrated in the early nineteenth century for innovative furniture, for example the davenport, introduced *c*.1816. The firm's stamp was used from the 1780s and very full records exist of its activities throughout the nineteenth century until the amalgamation with Waring in 1900. Although the Gillow family connection came to an end in 1830 the firm continued and flourished, with many prize-winning pieces at international exhibitions. Furniture was made for the New Palace of Westminster to Pugin's designs, for the New Law Courts to Street's designs, for the Midland Grand Hotel and St Pancras railway station to designs by T. G. Jackson and G. Gilbert Scott, and for the Marquess of Bute, to Burges's designs. Architect-designers employed by the firm include B. J. Talbert and E. W. Godwin as well as a number of inhouse and professional designers: C. J. Henry, J. W. Hay, H. Noble, E. Tarver, C. Bevan and possibly J. P. Seddon. Gillow's exhibited at Paris in 1855, 1867 and 1878; London in 1851, 1862, 1871 and 1873; and Vienna in 1873. The firm absorbed Collinson & Lock in 1897.

ERNEST GIMSON, 1864–1919

Born in Leicester, Gimson was inspired by a meeting with William Morris to take up architecture. He was in Sedding's office, where he met Ernest Barnsley and through him his brother Sidney. After the brief experiment with the Kenton & Co. architectural partnership, making furniture of good workmanship and design, Gimson went with the Barnsleys to live and work in the Cotswolds. His architectural work took second place to furniture and metalwork design in revived vernacular technique and style. At his death Sidney Barnsley completed his unfinished architectural commissions and his assistant Peter Waals continued the furniture workshop, which survived at Chalford until 1938.
Comino, 1980.

EDWARD WILLIAM GODWIN, 1833–1886

Born in Bristol, Godwin intended training as a civil engineer and was articled to William Armstrong, a local architect-cum-engineer and

friend of Isambard Kingdom Brunel. He set up his own office in 1854 and travelled to Ireland to assist his brother, also a civil engineer, with a design for a railway bridge. He met Burges in 1858 and they became good friends, visiting Ireland together in the 1860s when Godwin began Dromore and Glenbeigh Towers. His first major commission, Northampton Town Hall (1861), was based on Ruskin's *Stones of Venice*. His designs for furniture and interior decoration were carried out by Green & King, London, and stained glass was supplied by Heaton, Butler & Bayne. Godwin was among the group who made purchases of Japanese objects after the 1862 exhibition, and he became very influenced by Japanese culture. His designs for applied art included furniture for the Art Furniture Co. and later William Watt, W. Smee, Cox & Son, Gillow's, Waugh & Co., C. Greaves, James Peddle, and Collinson & Lock, by whom he was paid a retainer from 1872 to 1874; wallpapers for Jeffrey & Co.; fabrics for Warner & Ramm; ceramics and tiles for Brownfield, Minton, Hollins & Co. and Wilcock & Co.; and metalwork for Messenger & Co. and Jones & Willis. During his affair with the actress Ellen Terry, Godwin wrote a series of articles on theatrical scenery and costume, became increasingly interested in dress design, working at Liberty's dress department from 1884. Godwin also wrote articles on Japanese art, Celtic and Saxon architecture, and contemporary issues for the *British Architect*, *The Architect* and *Building News*. In 1875 Godwin left Ellen and their two children, and soon after married Beatrice Philip, who became a pupil of his friend Whistler, with whom he collaborated on the furniture for Watt at the 1878 exhibition. After Godwin's death Beatrice married Whistler. He built Whistler's controversial White House in Tite Street, Chelsea, and helped Oscar Wilde decorate his house in the same street in 1884. William Burges, J. P. Seddon, Peter Paul Pugin, H. Crisp (his partner from 1864 to 1871), R. W. Edis, M. B. Adams and J. M. Brydon were also among his circle of friends and partners.
Aslin, 1986; D. Harbron, *The Conscious Stone*, London 1949.

JOHN HARDMAN & CO., founded 1838

Metalworking and decorating firm founded by John Hardman the Younger (1811–67), partner in the Birmingham button-making firm of Hardman & Illiffe. John Hardman, John Hardman junior and Jeremiah Illiffe were in partnership with G. R. Elkington from 1837 to 1843 to find ways of exploiting Elkington's patents for gilding base metals. In 1837 he met A. W. N. Pugin, who persuaded him to initiate the 'Medieval Metalworkers' venture with which his name was to be associated from the 1840s. The business partnership commenced in the following year, setting up a textile department in 1842 and producing stained glass from 1845, and by the late 1840s they were large-scale interior decorators. As well as Pugin's association with the firm as designer, Hardman's were involved in executing Pugin's designs for the New Palace of Westminster and the 1851 Medieval Court at the Great Exhibition, for which they made the stove covered with Minton majolica tiles designed by Pugin. The company also exhibited in London in 1862; Paris in 1867 and 1878; and Philadelphia in 1876. Hardman's chief draughtsman from 1848 to 1850, F. W. Oliphant, had previously been at Wailes of Newcastle, Pugin's sole stained glass supplier from 1842 to 1845. The firm also made a silver cameo stand for Lord Bute, probably designed by Burges, in 1869. Pugin's pupil John Hardman Powell succeeded him as chief designer to the firm in 1852. The firm continued to make stained glass as John Hardman Studios into the twentieth century.

HARLAND & FISHER, *fl.* 1859–after 1870

Ecclesiastical decorators, situated at 33 Southampton Street, off the Strand, next door to Cox & Sons. They made the 'Wines & Spirits' cabinet designed by William Burges in 1859 and showed it in the 1862 Medieval Court. They also supplied one of a series of mosaics for the South Kensington Museum.

HART, SON, PEARD & CO., *c.*1842–after 1920

Metalworkers in Wych St, off the Strand, and in Birmingham. Founded by Joseph Hart, an ironmonger, they became artistic metalworkers specializing in ecclesiastical manufactures after

merging with Peard & Jackson in 1866–7. They were represented at all the major international exhibitions: London in 1851 and 1862; Paris in 1855, 1867 and 1878, Dublin in 1855 and 1865, and Philadelphia in 1876, winning many medals. They made designs by J. P. Seddon and B. J. Talbert, and at least one example of silver for William Burges. William Butterfield used them to make his silver plate designs in the early 1870s and Alfred Waterhouse contracted them to supply ironwork for almost all his architectural commissions. The company had an agent, Henri Collet, in Paris.

HEAL & SON, 1810 to present

Furnishers in Tottenham Court Road, London. Established as a bedroom specialist, the firm was revitalized by Ambrose Heal (1872–1959), who joined the company in 1893 after studying furniture design at the Slade and an apprenticeship with Messrs Plucknett of Warwick, and was responsible for furniture designs from 1896 until his retirement. Although the firm had exhibited earlier, at London in 1851 and 1862 and at Vienna in 1873, it was through Ambrose Heal's involvement with the Arts and Crafts Movement it developed its distinctive simple, vernacular style, which was seen in their first furniture catalogue (1898), and praised by Gleeson White, editor of *The Studio*. Heal's also began to advertise 'artistic textiles'. It exhibited at the Arts & Crafts Exhibition Society from 1899 and was one of the few British firms to show at the 1900 Centennial Exhibition in Paris.
Susanna Gooden, *At the Sign of the Fourposter: A History of Heals*, London 1984.

HEATON, BUTLER & BAYNE, founded 1855

Stained glass manufacturers and decorators in Garrick Street, Covent Garden. Founded by Clement Heaton (1824–82) and J. Butler (1830–1913) in 1855 and joined by R. T. Bayne in 1862, who became the principal glass painter. Heaton collaborated with C. L. Eastlake, painting a cabinet illustrated in *Hints on Household Taste* (1868), which was exhibited in Paris 1867, and probably made by the Art Furniture Co., also in Garrick Street. He provided designs for portières for the Art Furniture Co., and probably decorated other furniture made by them.

The firm supplied stained glass windows for E. W. Godwin's Northampton Town Hall, and employed Lewis F. Day to help decorate Alfred Waterhouse's Eaton Hall in the 1870s. The company produced catalogues from 1862. At the London International Exhibition in 1871 it showed art tiles designed by Henry Holiday, and it was also represented at Philadelphia in 1876. Heaton's son Clement John succeeded his father in 1882, but left in 1885 after a dispute. He was involved with Mackmurdo's Century Guild before moving to Switzerland, where he set up a stained glass and enamels studio, moving later to America. In the twentieth century the firm was controlled principally by the Bayne family; the company archives were sold off in the 1970s.

J. S. HENRY, founded c.1880

Wholesale manufacturers in Old Street, London, of light, ornamental furniture from about 1880, and Art Nouveau pieces of mahogany and satinwood with decorative inlays in the 1890s. Their pieces were retailed through a Paris agent at the 1900 Centennial Exhibition, where they won two silver medals. At the Arts & Crafts Exhibition Society in 1903 the company showed designs by George Walton and W. A. S. Benson. G. M. Ellwood (1875–c.1960) was their most prolific designer, and although they used designs by C. F. A. Voysey, E. G. Punnett and W. J. Neatby, few designers were named.

HERTER BROTHERS, c.1851–1906

Luxury decorators and cabinet-makers founded in New York by Gustave Herter (1830–98), a native of Stuttgart in Germany. Gustave worked for Tiffany for three years after arriving in the USA, and participated in the 1853 New York International Exhibition. His half-brother Christian (1840–83) joined Gustave in 1865, at which time the name Herter Brothers was adopted. From 1870 until his early death in 1883 from tuberculosis, Christian, who had had a Beaux-Arts training, was the artistic driving force behind the firm. He had visited England, travelling to Birmingham, Manchester and London in the early 1870s, and had absorbed the ideas of E. W. Godwin, B. J. Talbert and other members of the design reform movement; he had probably also visited major manufac-turers. As well as the Japonisme inspired by these English encounters and a brief spell with Tiffany in the early 1860s, the Herter firm specialized in impressive Renaissance and classical revival schemes for millionaire patrons. They employed several designers, among whom were A. Sandier, who went on to Sèvres, and W. Kimbel. They did not exhibit at Philadelphia in 1876, owing to reorganization of the firm. Nor did they have their own stand in Paris in 1878; but they did design and supply the stand for Tiffany's new wares, which caused a sensation. Metropolitan Museum, 1986.

JOSEF HOFFMANN, 1870–1956

Hoffmann studied architecture in Munich and Vienna, where he was briefly a pupil of Otto Wagner. In 1897 he joined the Vienna Secession, and designed the Ver Sacrum room at the first Secession exhibition in 1898. The elongated rectilinear quality of Hoffmann's designs owed much to Mackintosh. Hoffmann visited England in the company of Koloman Moser in 1903 and, inspired by Ashbee's Guild of Handicraft and with the backing of Fritz Warndorfer, they started the Wiener Werkstätte. Hoffmann designed silver and jewellery, bentwood furniture and glass for the Lobmeyer firm. He was professor of architecture at the Vienna School of Applied Arts until 1941, and his work was widely illustrated. He was associated with, among others, J. M. Olbrich, K. Moser, G. Klimt, O. Prutscher and D. Peche. P. Noever and O. Oberhuber, *Josef Hoffman*, Vienna 1987.

HOLLAND & SONS, c.1815–1968

Furnishers in Mount Street, Mayfair. Established as Taprell & Holland, makers of high-quality furniture, the firm was employed at Osborne, Balmoral, Sandringham and Windsor. It supplied furniture for the New Palace of Westminster to Pugin's designs, along with John Webb and Gillow's. The firm showed at international exhibitions in Paris in 1855, London in 1862, Paris in 1867, Vienna in 1873, and Paris in 1878, winning many medals. B. J. Talbert was a designer from 1866, and the firm also made furniture to designs by C. Barry, G. E. Street, G. Semper, J. K. Collings, M. B. Adams and J. Bell.

With the recession in the 1890s the firm had to retrench and the Pimlico cabinet-making workshops were disposed of to Morris & Co.

HOWELL, JAMES & CO., 1819–1911

Jewellers and silversmiths of Regent Street, London. Founded as silk mercers and retail jewellers, they rapidly expanded, employing over 100 staff by 1865. Noted for their variety and quality of stock, including items by designers and students of the South Kensington School, they exhibited in London in 1851 and 1862; in Paris in 1867; and at London in 1871 and 1872 when they showed jewellery by C. L. Eastlake, M. D. Wyatt, F. Leighton, and L. F. Day. From 1876, Howell, James & Co. held a series of popular exhibitions of ceramics painted by amateurs. The company's 1878 Paris Exhibition stand was designed by L. F. Day, who also contributed designs for Aesthetic Movement clocks along with the architect Thomas Harris. The firm stocked silver goods by J. Dixon & Co., Dresser's Linthorpe Pottery and Brannam Pottery from 1880 to 1889, when their employee, J. Llewellyn, moved to Liberty & Co. taking exclusive selling rights with him. The premises were reconstructed in 1881, incorporating art pottery galleries, where they held an exhibition of architectural faience made by Burmantofts to M. B. Adams designs.

HUKIN & HEATH, 1855–1953

Manufacturing silversmiths and electroplaters of Birmingham, established by Jonathan Wilson Hukin and John Thomas Heath, who registered London marks in 1879. When Hukin retired in 1881 the partnership continued with Heath and J. H. Middleton. The firm's association with Christopher Dresser began in 1877; the first registered design dates from 1878, and others were entered up to 1881. Dresser's designs were launched at the opening of the firm's showrooms in Charterhouse Street in August 1879. They also stocked Persian and Kashmiri works of art which had been plated with gold and silver, Japanese metalwork and imitations by the firm, and Linthorpe, Doulton and Oriental pottery that they had mounted in metal. Some of Dresser's designs were manufactured until after 1900.

JACKSON & GRAHAM, c.1840–1885
Cabinet-makers in Oxford Street, London, probably the most important High Victorian cabinet-making firm. Strong French connections in the 1850s led to the employment of French designers and craftsmen and to the manufacture of elaborate and expensive pieces in an opulent interpretation of French eighteenth-century royal taste. The firm expanded rapidly, with a team of 250 employees in 1855, which grew to 600 by 1875. It was responsible for supplying furniture and decoration to Owen Jones's designs for Alfred Morrison in the early 1860s; Jones also designed a range of carpets, curtains, wallpapers (printed by Jeffrey & Co.) and other furnishings, which were manufactured exclusively for the firm. Jackson & Graham had won many prizes at international exhibitions, and the change to British reformed design was a radical departure. Jones and B. J. Talbert provided the most striking of the firm's exhibits for the Paris exhibitions in 1867 and 1878 respectively and Jones for the 1873 Exhibition in Vienna. Resident designers included Peter Graham, Alfred Lorimer and Eugène Prinot, but they also made designs by R. W. Edis and C. L. Eastlake as well as Talbert. After a financially troubled period the firm was absorbed by Collinson & Lock in 1885. Graham went on to establish a decorating company, Graham & Banks, in Oxford Street.

THOMAS JECKYLL, 1827–1881
The son of a Norwich clergyman, Jeckyll began his career in his native city. He moved to London, but in 1859 began an eighteen-year association with the Norwich ironfounders Barnard, Bishop and Barnard. He designed ceremonial gates for the firm's exhibits at a series of international exhibitions, beginning with London in 1862, and fire grates in the Japanese taste. His greatest feat for Barnard's was the Japanese pavilion first shown at the 1876 Philadelphia Exhibition, and two years later at Paris. Among his patrons were Alexander Ionides, for whose Holland Park house he designed a Japanesque addition and furniture in 1870. His last commission was the restoration of F. R. Leyland's house in Prince's Gate. His disastrous experience with James Whistler over the decoration of Leyland's dining room (the notorious 'Peacock' room) precipitated a mental collapse, and he spent the last years of his life in a Norwich asylum.
Metropolitan Museum, 1986.

JEFFREY & CO., c.1836–1930
Wallpaper manufacturers in Islington, founded as Jeffrey, Wise and Co. By 1840 the firm had introduced roller printing of paper on the principle previously employed for the printing of calico. In 1864 the firm was engaged by William Morris to print the Morris firm's first wallpapers. In 1866 Metford Warner (1843–1930) joined as a junior partner, and it was due to his adventurous design policy that C. L. Eastlake, William Burges, E. W. Godwin, L. F. Day, B. J. Talbert and C. F. A. Voysey were associated with the firm, which also printed designs by Owen Jones for Jackson & Graham and by A. H. Mackmurdo for the Century Guild. In 1871 Warner became the sole proprietor of the company. The much publicized 'combination papers', with integrated designs for dado, filling and frieze were devised for the company by the Ipswich architect Brightwen Binyon. Other designs by H. W. Batley, Heywood Sumner, Henry Wilson, G. A. Audsley, W. J. Neatby and George Walton were also printed. A series of tripartite papers by Walter Crane gained two gold medals at the 1876 Philadelphia Exhibition. Many more prizes followed, among others at Paris in 1878, 1889 and 1900, and at Chicago in 1893. Metford Warner continued to direct the company with his sons until the 1920s; in 1930 Jeffrey & Co. was absorbed by Arthur Sanderson.
Metropolitan Museum, 1986.

OWEN JONES, 1809–1874
Jones trained as an architect under Lewis Vulliamy, but in 1830 he began the extensive travels that were to result in his most important contribution to the advancement of nineteenth-century design, the great series of colour-illustrated publications that commenced with *Plans, Elevations, Sections and Details of the Alhambra* (1836–45) and included the seminal *Grammar of Ornament* (1856). His Moresque colour scheme for the interior of the 1851 Crystal Palace transformed Paxton's severely utilitarian structure. He was responsible for the Alhambra Court in the transported Crystal Palace whose re-decoration he supervised with Sir Matthew Digby Wyatt at Sydenham (1854), and for the Indian, Chinese and Japanese Courts in the newly erected South Kensington Museum (1863–4). His talents as a decorator exemplified the greatest refinement that the Victorian grand manner could attain; the rooms for Alfred Morrison, shown in Paris in 1867 and Vienna in 1873, gained gold medals for Jackson & Graham, who had provided the consummate craftsmanship demanded by Jones's intricate schemes. Jones designed wallpapers and silks, and carpets which were manufactured exclusively for Jackson & Graham. His silk designs were made by Warner & Ramm; wallpapers by Jeffrey & Co., John Trumble and Townsend & Parker; and mosaic floors by Wyatt & Parker and J. M. Blashfield. Jones also designed tiles for Maw & Co. and biscuit packaging for Huntley & Palmer, as well as book covers and playing cards.
Darby, 1983.

JONES & WILLIS, fl.1851–after 1906
Church furnishers of Birmingham; originally Newton, Jones & Willis. They produced eighty illustrated catalogues supplying everything needed for the church, as well as interior decoration and medieval-style metalwork. They showed at the international exhibitions in London in 1851 and 1862, Vienna in 1873 and Paris in 1878. G. E. Street's embroideries and Burges's lectern for St Fin Barre's Cathedral, Cork, were made by the company, and in 1876 E. W. Godwin sent them designs. In the early twentieth century they took over the Birmingham Guild of Handicraft.

KEITH & CO., c.1824–1929
Silversmiths in Britannia Terrace, City Road, London. Founded by John James Keith in about 1824, the company operated for more than a century, interrupted between 1868 and 1874 when his son John Keith and his employees were working at Cox & Sons, based in the same street as his London agent Franck Smith & Co. From 1843 Keith & Co. made silver for the Ecclesiological Society under William Butterfield's

and, from 1856, G. E. Street's supervision, to designs by them and other architects. From 1867 pressure from the Society – particularly from William Burges, who complained about Keith's quality – to use another maker forced bankruptcy. Keith & Co. were represented at the London exhibitions in 1851 and 1862, and John Keith under Cox & Sons were awarded medals in 1871 for silver designed by Talbert. By the 1870s they were also supplying non-precious metals and church furniture. John James Keith, the son of John Keith, was later a partner of Cox, Son & Buckley.

KENTON & CO., 1891–1892

A short-lived architect-furniture design co-partnership in Bloomsbury founded by Ernest Gimson, Sidney Barnsley, W. R. Lethaby, Reginald Blomfield and Mervyn Macartney and one non-executive investor, Colonel Mallet, with the object of supplying 'good design and good workmanship'. Stephen Webb was also briefly a member. Insufficiently businesslike, the partners decided to wind the venture up after only a year, during which they had staged a well received exhibition. They also sold plaster friezes, leadwork and needlework. Their furniture was exhibited at the Arts and Crafts Exhibition Society until 1896.
Comino, 1980.

ARCHIBALD KNOX, 1864–1933

Born on the Isle of Man, Knox studied at the Douglas School of Art where he subsequently taught. He worked with H. M. Baillie Scott before coming to London in 1897, where he designed for the Silver Studio; in the following year he started his long association with Liberty's. Knox was principally responsible for the singularly original character of Liberty's two metalworking ventures, the 'Cymric' silver and jewellery and the 'Tudric' pewter wares, but he also designed carpets and textiles for them. The association lasted until 1912, but Knox's designs had already been sold to James Connell & Co. in 1909. From 1912 he designed carpets for Bromley & Co. of Philadelphia. After the First World War he painted and taught.
Tilbrook, 1976.

JAMES LAMB, 1840–1899

A firm of Manchester cabinet-makers, upholsterers and decorators. The firm was noted for its dedication to artistic design and construction, using the best materials and workmanship. It exhibited elaborate furniture in the French taste by Hugues Protat (who had worked with Minton and with Jackson & Graham at Paris in 1855) and W. J. Estall at the London Exhibition of 1862. A change of direction took place with the employment of Charles Bevan to make designs for inlaid Gothic-style pieces in the late 1860s. Lamb made furniture to Alfred Waterhouse's designs for the Manchester Assize Courts, shown at Paris in 1867 and 1878, and exhibited 'Quaint' furniture at the 1887 Manchester Jubilee Exhibition; the firm was absorbed into Goodall, Lamb & Heighway in 1899.

WILLIAM RICHARD LETHABY, 1857–1931

Lethaby was born in Devon, where he commenced his architectural career. In 1879 he joined Richard Norman Shaw's office as chief clerk. He was a founder member of the Art Workers' Guild in 1884 and its Master in 1911, and was active in the foundation of the Arts and Crafts Exhibition Society in 1887. He was involved with the Morris firm in the decorations of Stanmore Hall, and he joined Gimson and Barnsley in Kenton & Co. in 1890. His architectural career was overshadowed by his design work (for Coalbrookdale, Farmer & Brindley, Longden & Co., Portland Metalworks and Marsh, Jones & Cribb), writing, and teaching at the newly set-up Central School of Arts and Crafts. In applying for the post of Art Inspector at the school in 1892 he submitted references from Norman Shaw, William Morris, Sir Edward Burne-Jones, Walter Crane and Philip Webb.

LIBERTY & CO., 1875 to present

Arthur Lasenby Liberty (1843–1917) established his firm as an Oriental Warehouse, and soon built it into a household word for artistic decoration and furnishing. Much of the early furniture stock was imported or locally made 'Anglo-Oriental' bamboo furniture. From 1883 the Furnishing and Decoration studio was run by Leonard Wyburd. After the failure of the Art Furnishers' Alliance, of which he was a shareholder, Liberty took out patents for the two versions of the 'Thebes' stool, which was to become one of the most popular products of the furniture studio. Furniture was supplied by wholesale companies such as William Birch and J. S. Henry, who made designs by George Walton, and the firm also stocked chairs designed by the German Richard Riemerschmid (1868–1957). The dress department was under the direction of E. W. Godwin. From 1898 Liberty's began to import German pewter by J. P. Kayser und Sohn among others, and in the following year they began their own metalworking venture using designers such as Archibald Knox, Oliver Baker and John Pearson, who had worked with C. R. Ashbee, 1888–1892. These along with wallpapers and fabrics by C. F. A. Voysey, Walter Crane, L. F. Day and the Silver Studio put the firm into the mainstream of Art Nouveau. Textiles were supplied by Thomas Wardle, who had made Morris's early prints, and by G. P. & J. Baker and Morton & Co. Liberty's stocked Donegal carpets by Voysey; enamels by C. J. Heaton; art pottery by Brannam, Doulton, Moorcroft, Linthorpe, Compton and other European potteries such as Max Lauger, which made designs especially for Liberty; as well as amateur work by the Home Arts & Industries Association; and Clutha glass by Christopher Dresser and Walton. Many other 'Art manufacturers' were represented and their products are illustrated in the gift and furniture catalogues from the 1890s.
Liberty's, 1875–1975, exhibition catalogue, Victoria and Albert Museum, London 1975.

LINTHORPE ART POTTERY, 1879–1889

Set up in Middlesborough, Yorkshire, by Christopher Dresser with a businessman associate John Harrison. Harrison owned land with a deposit of red brick clay, and it was intended that the art wares produced by the company would be supported, and the local unemployment alleviated, by commercial production. Dresser served as art director for three years until 1882. The company supplied retail outlets such as the Art Furnishers' Alliance, Howell, James & Co. and Liberty & Co. The pottery closed after Harrison's death. Henry Tooth, who

had been recruited to the Linthorpe pottery, left in 1883 to establish the Bretby Art Pottery at Woodville in Derbyshire with William Ault: Ault set up his own pottery at Swadlincote in 1887 in competition with Linthorpe. He was able to acquire the Dresser moulds at auction when Linthorpe closed, and continued to produce Dresser designs at least until Dresser's death in 1904. Many of the staff from Linthorpe went to Burmantofts Pottery after 1889, which may explain the similarities in their products.
Rudoe, 1991.

FRANCES MACDONALD, 1874–1921

The younger of the Macdonald sisters, Frances studied at the Glasgow School of Art from about 1890. There she met Herbert MacNair, whom she married in 1899, and they moved to Liverpool where Herbert had been appointed to teach at the University. They participated in the Vienna Exhibition of 1900 and the Turin one of 1902 with Charles Rennie Mackintosh and his wife, her sister Margaret. From 1907 Frances taught enamelling, metalwork and jewellery at the Glasgow School of Art.

MARGARET MACDONALD, 1865–1933

Elder sister of Frances, Margaret also studied at Glasgow School of Art: there she met Charles Rennie Mackintosh, whom she married in 1900. She collaborated in Mackintosh's decorative work, providing distinctive textiles and low-relief gesso panels for wall decoration and furniture, notably for the Turin Exhibition of 1902 and the Warndorfer Music Room.

CHARLES RENNIE MACKINTOSH, 1868–1928

Born in Glasgow, Mackintosh was apprenticed in 1884 to a local architect, John Hutchinson. He entered the office of Honeyman & Keppie in 1889, and there became friendly with a fellow draughtsman, J. Herbert MacNair. From about 1896 Mackintosh was designing furniture for Messrs Guthrie & Wells of Glasgow. In 1897 he won the competition to design the new Glasgow School of Art. In the same year Mackintosh received the first of the Cranston Tea Room commissions, working on the decoration of the Buchanan Street premises in collaboration with George Walton, who made some of his early

furniture. In 1900 he participated by invitation in the Vienna Secession Exhibition, and he was responsible for the Scottish section at Turin in 1902. He married Margaret Macdonald in 1900. Important individual projects included Windyhill for Walter Blackie (1899), the Warndorfer Music Room (1902), Hill House (1903) and the second stage of the Glasgow School of Art (1906), as well as a number of commissions from the Misses Cranston. Mackintosh left Glasgow in 1914. Apart from one or two architectural projects, including work for W. J. Bassett-Lowke, he concentrated mainly on watercolour painting and textile designs for Foxton's and Sefton's. His designs were well illustrated in European periodicals.
Billcliffe, 1986; Rudoe, 1991.

ARTHUR HEYGATE MACKMURDO, 1851–1942

Mackmurdo began studying architecture in 1869, and in 1873 entered the office of James Brooks. He attended Ruskin's drawing classes in Oxford and in 1874 accompanied Ruskin to Italy as companion and assistant. He came into contact with William Morris through his membership of the Society for the Protection of Ancient Buildings, and designed a settle for Morris & Co. In 1882 he founded the Century Guild with Selwyn Image, Herbert Horne and Clement J. Heaton, 'to bring about complete unity in architecture, decoration and furniture'. In 1883 Mackmurdo published *Wren's City Churches*, with the distinctive title page that was to ensure his place in the mainstream of the Art Nouveau movement. The *Hobby Horse*, journal of the Guild, first appeared in 1884; contributors included D. G. Rossetti, William Bell Scott and Ford Madox Brown. In the same year Mackmurdo exhibited a Music Room at the International Health Exhibition in London. He showed at the Liverpool 1886 Exhibition and the Manchester Jubilee Exhibition in the following year. The Guild's furniture was made by Collinson & Lock, Wilkinson and E. Goodall & Co. Textiles were supplied by Simpson & Godlee and A. H. Lee. The Guild also sold De Morgan ceramics and some experimental carpets by Morris & Co. It was disbanded in 1888, although it showed at the Arts & Crafts Exhibition Society that year. The partnership with

Herbert Horne dissolved in 1890, and in the same year Wilkinson & Son showed a writing table designed by Mackmurdo at the Arts and Crafts exhibition. Mackmurdo was active as an architect until about 1906, but in later life his interests were in social reform.

J. HERBERT MACNAIR, 1868–1953

MacNair studied painting in France before joining the Glasgow office of Honeyman & Keppie in about 1888. In the following year C. R. Mackintosh joined the firm, and both studied at the Glasgow School of Art. Encouraged by the head of the Art School, Francis Newberry and his wife Jessie, Mackintosh and MacNair joined forces with the Macdonald sisters to become a group known as the 'Glasgow Four'. MacNair is credited with being the first to explore the sinuous Art Nouveau style which became the hallmark of the group. In 1895 MacNair established himself as an 'architect and designer' in Glasgow; in 1899, having been appointed to the School of Architecture in Liverpool University, he married Frances Macdonald. He participated in the Vienna Secession Exhibition of 1900 and the Turin Exhibition of 1902. He gave up his post at Liverpool in 1906 and pursued his career as an independent designer until his wife's death in 1921.

MARSH, JONES & CRIBB, founded *c*.1850

Cabinet-makers of Leeds and Cavendish Square, London. The firm of Marsh & Jones, 'Medieval Cabinet Makers', of Leeds became Marsh, Jones & Cribb in 1868. They made Charles Bevan's 'New Registered Reclining Chair' under licence and furniture for Titus Salt junior's marital home at Basildon, near Saltaire, in 1865, as well as more commerical designs by Bevan and B. J. Talbert in the 1860s, exhibiting at Paris in 1878. W. R. Lethaby became their chief designer in the late 1880s, exhibiting his designs at the 1890 Arts and Crafts Exhibition Society.

MARTIN BROTHERS POTTERY, 1873–1915

Established in Fulham by Robert Wallace Martin, son of a wholesale stationer's clerk, one of four who ran the pottery. The pottery moved to Southall in 1877 and a showroom in Holborn was opened in 1879. R. W. Martin (1843–1923) was responsible for the grotesque figures and jugs and other sculptural items characteristic of the pottery. Charles Douglas Martin (1846–1910) was the business manager; Walter Fraser Martin (1857–1912) supplied the technical expertise, specializing in coloured glazes; Edwin Bruce Martin (1860–1915), who had worked like his brother Walter at Doulton's of Lambeth, was a thrower and decorator. Incised marks on the wares give the brothers' names and when and where they were made ('London and Southall', referring to the showroom in Holborn and the pottery at Southall in Middlesex). The pottery was in operation until 1915.

Malcolm Haslam, *The Martin Brothers, Potters,* London 1978.

Maw & Co., 1850–1967

Tile manufacturers at the Bethnall Works, Broseley, Shropshire. John Henry Maw bought up the stock of the merged Worcester firms Chamberlain & Co. and Fleming, St John & Barr in 1850, moving to Shropshire in 1852. By 1862 his son George had introduced the manufacture of majolica for architectural use, exhibiting a fire surround designed by M. D. Wyatt at the London exhibition, and publishing a catalogue of his mosaic designs. The firm showed at subsequent international exhibitions, including Dublin in 1865; Paris in 1867, 1878 and 1889; London in 1871; Philadelphia in 1876 and Chicago in 1893, making designs by a number of architects, G. E. Street, G. Goldie, Owen Jones and J. P. Seddon among others. George Maw travelled to Spain and the Middle East in search of new designs. In the 1880s the firm moved to new works at Jackfield and employed Francis Derwent Wood, L. F. Day and Walter Crane to design a range of ruby lustre wares and tiles, shown at the Arts & Crafts Exhibition Society in 1890.

Minton & Co., 1796–1968

Potters. Thomas Minton began to manufacture blue transfer-printed earthenware at Stoke-on-Trent in 1796. His son Herbert Minton initiated great changes when he took over in 1836, with innovative production methods and a greater range of products: parian, porcelain, majolica and encaustic tiles were all shown at the 1851 Great Exhibition. Herbert Minton's friendship with Pugin led to a continued collaboration supplying tiles for commissions such as the New Palace of Westminster, designs for retail using new techniques and to involvement in the Medieval Court at the 1851 Exhibition. Léon Arnoux, art director from 1849, encouraged the introduction of brightly glazed majolica and 'Henri Deux' ware. When Herbert Minton died in 1858, the remaining partners divided the company: Michael Daintry Hollins managing the encaustic floor tile and mosaic production, under the name Minton, Hollins & Co. and Colin Minton Campbell managing the china ware and decorative tile manufacture, under the name Minton & Co. and employing prominent designers including L. M. Solon, J. Moyr Smith, C. Dresser, H. S. Marks and W. Wise. Campbell and Hollins dissolved their partnership in 1868, but continued to run the companies much as before. Campbell was also instrumental in setting up the short-lived Minton Art Pottery Studio, Kensington Gore, in 1871, with W. S. Coleman as director. Many designers and artists as well as South Kensington students worked for the studio. Robert Minton Taylor, a partner in Minton, Hollins & Co. from 1863 to 1868, set up his own encaustic tile factory in 1869, initially called R. Minton Taylor Brick & Tile Co.; its name was changed in 1875, when Campbell became involved, to Campbell Brick & Tile Co. Minton & Co. introduced an Art Nouveau line at the turn of the century. The firm was represented at all the major international exhibitions and it continued in production in the twentieth century until it was absorbed into the Doulton company in 1968.

Atterbury, 1990; Jones, 1993.

William Morris, 1834–1896

Born into a wealthy family in Walthamstow and educated at Marlborough School and Exeter College, Oxford, where he met his life-long friend Edward Burne-Jones, Morris entered G. E. Street's architectural office in 1856 where Philip Webb was senior clerk. He founded the co-operative firm of Morris, Marshall, Faulkner & Co. on the suggestion of Ford Madox Brown in 1861. It remained a partnership until Morris took sole proprietorship in 1875 changing the name to Morris & Co., and introducing an extensive range of textiles and wallpapers many of which he designed. In 1878 he moved his family to Kelmscott House in Hammersmith where he began the manufacture of hand-knotted carpets. In the search for space to improve the quality of the firm's manufactures Morris moved his works from London to Merton Abbey Mills in 1881. Here there was now room to manufacture carpets and tapestries that had previously only been possible on an experimental scale. From 1870 Morris had been interested in illuminating manuscripts and planned publications of his own poems, but it was not until 1891 that he set up the Kelmscott Press for which he designed three typefaces. It produced 53 books before closing in 1898. Morris was a founder member of the Society for the Protection of Ancient Buildings in 1877. During the 1870s Morris became involved with politics and from 1883 with the Socialist movement as a member of the Social Democratic Federation. He was a founder member of the Socialist League and editor and financier of the weekly *Commonweal*. Morris died in Hammersmith after a prolonged illness.

Morris & Co., 1861–1940

Founded as Morris, Marshall, Faulkner & Co., by William Morris in 1861, the firm exhibited for the first time in London in 1862. Commissions followed for the South Kensington Museum and St James's Palace, as well as for stained glass and private decorating work. Morris became the sole director in 1875, when the firm was renamed Morris & Co. Retail premises in Oxford Street were opened in 1877. With the acquisition of Kelmscott House in Hammersmith in 1878 Morris was able to set up carpet looms. In 1881 he expanded into weaving and dyeing workshops at Merton Abbey. Morris's last venture, the Kelmscott Press, was also housed in Hammersmith. At Morris's death in 1896 W. A. S. Benson took over the directorship of the firm. In the 1920s the showrooms were transferred to George Street, and in 1940 the business closed.

Parry, 1983; Harvey and Press, 1991.

HERMANN MUTHESIUS, 1861–1927

Muthesius studied philosophy and architecture in Berlin, and in 1893 became a Prussian government architect. In 1896 he was appointed to the German Embassy in London; his seminal work, *Das englische Haus* (1904–5), was the result of his stay in England. His contemporary, but objective, point of view has been of lasting value. Muthesius was the driving force behind the foundation of the Deutsche Werkbund in 1907. A prolific journalist, he wrote tirelessly on modern design and the need for improvement in industrial art and production.

WILLIAM EDEN NESFIELD, 1835–1888

Son of a landscape gardener, Nesfield was articled to the architect William Burn, admired for his rational and convenient planning, but Nesfield broke his articles after two years and went into the office of his uncle Anthony Salvin (1799–1881). Richard Norman Shaw had been at both Burn's and Salvin's offices at the same times and they became inseparable friends, and devotees of the Gothic Revival. During his european travels from 1856 to 1858 Nesfield spent a short time in Viollet-le-Duc's office. *Specimens of Mediaeval Architecture* (1862) was the result of later trips to France. Nesfield embarked on an independent architectural practice in 1859; he shared offices with Shaw from 1863 to 1876, and was his partner for three years, from 1866 to 1869; but they never collaborated directly. They developed the 'Old English' style through the study of English vernacular architecture, although Nesfield used a number of styles for his country houses, often with a Japanese influence. From the early 1860s, he was a collector of Oriental objects, and a friend of William Burges, James Whistler and Simeon Solomon. He frequently collaborated with artist friends such as Albert Moore, Thomas Armstrong and Randolph Caldecott, and always used the best craftsmen he could. James Forsyth (1827–1910), a renowed stone- and woodcarver who had worked with Salvin and George Gilbert Scott, worked regularly for Nesfield and Shaw. Little of Nesfield's furniture has been identified; most was probably made for commissions rather than retail sale. His best known assistant was J. M. Brydon, a Scot and friend of B. J. Talbert, E. W.

Godwin, Daniel Cottier and J. Moyr Smith. Nesfield retired in 1880.

Andrew Saint, essay in *A Deuce of an Uproar: William Eden Nesfield's Letters to the Rector of Radwinter in Essex*, Radwinter, 1988.

JOSEPH MARIA OLBRICH, 1867–1908

Olbrich was a contemporary of Hoffmann, studying architecture in Vienna before entering the office of Otto Wagner. Founder member of the Vienna Secession, he was the architect of the strikingly original Secession building in Vienna. He went to Darmstadt in 1899 to live and work on the development of the Grand Duke of Hesse's artists' colony at Matildenhohe and, as the only architect, built most of the public buildings. His furniture featured at the Turin Exhibition of 1902 and at the 1904 St Louis Exhibition. He also designed posters, wallpapers, embroideries, cutlery, lighting and ceramics.

Peter Haiko and Bernd Krimmel, *Joseph Maria Olbrich: Architektur*, Vienna, 1988.

JAMES POWELL & SONS, WHITEFRIARS GLASSWORKS, 1834–1980

The original Whitefriars works were established in London in the late seventeenth century. They were acquired in 1834 by a wine merchant, James Powell (1774–1840), to provide employment for his three sons. The firm was managed from 1840 to 1894 by Arthur Powell, an outstandingly able and imaginative manufacturer. Important producers of stained glass, the firm experimented with the revival of medieval techniques under the direction of the glass historian Charles Winston from 1853. D. G. Rossetti, Edward Burne-Jones and Ford Madox Brown were approached to design for the firm. The Waltham Abbey east window made by Powells was commissioned by William Burges and designed by Burne-Jones. With the foundation of the Morris firm the connection with Powell's was continued. In 1859 Morris commissioned Philip Webb to design table glass for the Red House. His simple Venetian-inspired designs were made by Powell and stocked by the Morris firm in 1860; another architect, Thomas Graham Jackson (1835–1924), an assistant of G. Gilbert Scott, also designed table glass for Powell's from

1870 to 1874, which was sold by Morris & Co. Powell's supplied glass liners to Liberty and C. R. Ashbee's Guild. The firm exhibited at Philadelphia in 1876, Paris in 1878 and 1900, and Turin in 1902. The South Kensington Museum bought examples of glass for the collection in 1876. The production of artistic domestic glass was continued by Harry Powell (1853–1922) in the twentieth century.

AUGUSTUS WELBY NORTHMORE PUGIN, 1812–1852

Trained as a draughtsman with his father's pupils, Pugin embarked on a design career as early as fifteen years of age, with Gothic furniture to be made by Morel & Seddon for Windsor Castle and metalwork for the royal goldsmiths, Rundell, Bridge & Co. His numerous publications were highly influential; his Reformed Gothic ecclesiastical and domestic buildings set the pattern of the Gothic Revival in Britain for two decades; his work on the interior decoration of the New Palace of Westminster initiated many patterns and techniques that found their way into the commercial repertory of domestic design. His early stained glass was made by Wailes but from 1845 he used Hardman & Co., who were already making his designs for metalwork, silver and embroideries. Pugin worked very closely with his manufacturers, encouraging the introduction of new products and techniques. His closest allies, Hardman, Crace, Myers and Minton, began to plan their contribution to the 1851 Great Exhibition in March 1850. A number of their exhibits for the resulting Medieval Court were chosen by the purchasing committee for the new South Kensington Museum, on which Pugin sat with Owen Jones, Henry Cole, and Richard Redgrave. His crowded career came to an end with his mental collapse and he died insane aged only forty.

Ferrey, 1861; Stanton, 1971; Wedgwood, 1985.

DANTE GABRIEL ROSSETTI, 1828–1882

A founder member of the Pre-Raphaelite Brotherhood in 1848, Rossetti met William Morris in 1856 through Edward Burne-Jones, and was instrumental in persuading Morris to take up painting. Although the experiment was unsuccessful it led to Rossetti's partnership in the

Morris firm, for which he made a number of his finest stained glass designs. He was involved in many of the decorative painting projects, starting with the interior of Red House and including several pieces of furniture. He had a joint tenancy with Morris of Kelmscott Manor in Oxfordshire in 1871 until his death.

Virginia Surtees, *The Paintings and Drawings of Dante Gabriel Rossetti, 1828–1882. A Catalogue Raisonné*, Oxford, 1971.

ROYAL SCHOOL OF ART NEEDLEWORK, 1872 to present

The School was founded in London under the presidency of HRH Princess Christian of Schleswig-Holstein (Queen Victoria's daughter Helena) and a committee of ladies, with Lady Marion Alford, a noted needlewoman and author of *Needlework as Art* (1884) as Vice-President. Another of Queen Victoria's daughters, HRH Princess Louise (later Duchess of Argyle) was a member of the committee. Princess Christian chose to take an unusually close interest in the affairs of the School, generously meeting day-to-day expenses out of her own purse. The School's Articles of Association for the Charities Commission in 1878 set out the 'Objects of the Foundation . . . the teaching and giving instruction in ornamental needlework and supplying suitable employment for poor gentlewomen'. Walter Crane, Selwyn Image, Henry Holiday and Edward Burne-Jones designed embroideries for the School, Crane's great portière framing the entrance to the display mounted by the School at the Philadelphia Exhibition of 1876. Two associated ventures were initiated soon after the School, neither concerned with teaching, but concentrating on the execution of embroidery commissions. Princess Louise became Patron of the Ladies' Work Society and provided many of their designs; Lady Welby Gregory set up and financed the Decorative Needlework Society. In 1880 *The Magazine of Art* remarked of the latter: 'Lady Welby Gregory . . . had a great desire to find out whether decorative art needlework could be made profitable as a business.' From the outset large-scale works were undertaken, notably the vast curtains in the main room of Waterhouse's Manchester Town Hall, designed by Princess Louise. The same important scale of work is still undertaken today.

Callen, 1979.

JOHN DANDO SEDDING, 1838–1891

Sedding spent time in G. E. Street's office, and with his brother Edmund (d. 1868) in Penzance, before setting up his own practice in London in 1874. An admirer of Pugin and Ruskin, he was a designer of embroideries (executed by the Leek Embroidery Society), wallpapers and church metalwork. His metalwork was made by Barkentin & Krall and Longden & Co., whose London showrooms were in the same building as Sedding's offices. Jeffrey & Co. showed wallpapers by Sedding, among others, at the Architectural Association in 1883. He was a member of the Art Workers' Guild and its Master in 1886 and 1887. He showed his 'Westminster' and 'Jacobean' wallpapers at the first Arts and Crafts Exhibition Society show in 1888. His pupils included Ernest Gimson, Alfred Powell, and Henry Wilson, who took over the architectural practice on Sedding's death from influenza.

Henry Wilson, *A Memorial of the Late J. D. Sedding*, London 1892.

JOHN POLLARD SEDDON, 1827–1906

Born in London into a family of long established cabinet-makers who supplied the furniture for Windsor Castle and Buckingham Palace, and brother of the Pre-Raphaelite artist Thomas Seddon, he studied architecture under T. L. Donaldson. During his partnership with John Prichard, who had worked on the plates for Pugin's *Gothic Architecture*, in Llandaff from 1852 to 1862, he published a book of Gothic ornament (1852) and became a member of the Medieval Society in 1857. His furniture was featured on the Medieval Court at the 1862 London Exhibition, and examples found their way into Myles Birket Foster's house, The Hill at Witley in Surrey, an early decorating commission for the Morris firm. Seddon was a prolific designer of furniture, for the Seddon firm and for Gillow's; he designed stoneware for C. J. C. Bailey's Fulham Pottery; tiles for Minton, Godwin of Lugwardine and Maw & Co.; church and domestic metalwork for Hart & Son (from 1858) and G.

Smith & Sons; and stained glass for S. Belham & Co. He had a succession of partners including E. W. Godwin, H. Crisp and Phene Spiers, and was friends with the Pre-Raphaelites, especially Ford Madox Brown and D. G. Rossetti. C. F. A. Voysey was among his pupils.

Darby, 1983.

RICHARD NORMAN SHAW, 1831–1912

Born in Edinburgh, Shaw moved to London in about 1849 and entered the office of William Burn, where he met W. E. Nesfield. His travels in Europe from 1854 to 1856 resulted in *Architectural Sketches from the Continent* (1858). In 1856 he joined W. E. Nesfield in Anthony Salvin's office, and in 1859 he succeeded Philip Webb as G. E. Street's principal assistant. Furniture to his design was shown at the Architectural Exhibitions of 1859 and 1861, and his work was featured in the 1862 Medieval Court. This early furniture was made by James Forsyth, Salvin's carver, whom he and Nesfield frequently used. Shaw set up his own architectural practice in the same year, sharing an office with Nesfield from 1863. Shaw's stained glass was usually supplied by Heaton, Butler & Bayne to his own or Henry Holiday's designs, and his embroidery designs were executed by the Leek Embroidery Society. His busy and successful architectural office consumed most of his time and energy but he continued to design furniture, moving from the Gothic of his early pieces to Queen Anne revival style, such as the pieces made by Lascelles, his builder, and decorated by J. Aldam Heaton, exhibited at the Paris Exhibition of 1878, where Shaw also designed the layout of the Minton display. He designed cast iron fire surrounds for Elsleys and Coalbrookdale, and glass for the Italian firm of Salviati. His pupils and assistants, who included W. R. Lethaby, J. M. Brydon, Sidney Barnsley and Robert Weir Schultz, formed the nucleus of the Art Workers' Guild in the 1880s.

Andrew Saint, *Richard Norman Shaw*, London 1976.

SILVER STUDIO, 1880–1963

Arthur Silver (1853–1896) had been apprenticed to H. W. Batley from 1872. The speciality of his commercial design studio was flat pattern for textiles and wallpapers, and the most talen-

ted contributors were Lindsay Butterfield, John Illingworth Kay and Harry Napper. The studio supplied wallpaper designs to Woollams, Jeffrey & Co. and Charles Knowles & Co. and fabric designs to Warners. Arthur Silver died in 1896 and the studio was managed by his widow. In 1901 it was taken over by his elder son Rex (1879–1965), who continued to run it until 1963. Rex designed silverwork and jewellery for Liberty's 'Cymric' range, probably through the influence of Archibald Knox, who had some connection with the studio in 1898.
A London Design Studio 1880–1963: the Silver Studio Collection, Middlesex Polytechnic, London 1980.

SKIDMORE ART MANUFACTURERS, founded 1845

Church plate manufacturers in Coventry. Established as Francis Skidmore & Son, the firm worked to its own designs as well as those of G. Gilbert Scott. It exhibited plate at the Great Exhibition of 1851. In 1861 the firm expanded under Francis Skidmore junior (1816–1896), a member of the Ecclesiological Society from 1863, to include a large base-metal works and changed its name. Its architectural works included the Oxford Museum; Gilbert Scott's screens for Lichfield and Hereford Cathedrals, exhibited in 1862; and metalwork for the Albert Memorial. They also made metalwork for G. E. Street. B. J. Talbert among others worked with the firm from this time as a draughtsman in the design studio. The firm showed at the Paris Exhibition of 1867. It was taken over by a Birmingham company in the twentieth century.

JOHN MOYR SMITH, fl. 1860–1887

Decorative artist who, like Bruce J. Talbert, trained as an architect in Glasgow and spent time in Manchester in the 1860s. He was established in Christopher Dresser's studio some time before the publication of his *Studies for Pictures* (1868), which was dedicated to Dresser. Many of his designs would have been sent out under the studio's name, so few from this period can be identified. He was friends with fellow Scotsmen Daniel Cottier, William Wallace, Talbert and J. M. Brydon, described by Alexander Thomson (1817–1875) as the 'London brethren' in 1871. In the same year he drew all the plates and contributed designs to Collinson & Lock's *Sketches for Artistic Furniture*, and in 1872 Cox & Son showed furniture designed in collaboration with S. J. Nicholl at the London Exhibition. Smith was a member of the Society of Decorative Art, whose designs were carried out by Cox from about 1872, and which were noted for their close resemblance to those of Christopher Dresser's studio. Smith also designed cards for M. Ward, plaques for W. B. Simpson, decorative schemes for J. G. Crace and a number of series of designs for Minton tiles exhibited at the Paris exhibition of 1878. His designs for metalwork may have been made by Cox. He published a number of books, from 1881 he edited *Decoration: Painting, Sculpture, Arhitecture & Art Manufactures*, and in 1887 wrote a history of interior decoration, *Ornamental Interiors*.

GEORGE EDMUND STREET, 1824–1881

After serving his articles with the architect Owen Carter in Winchester and working in the London office of George Gilbert Scott, Street began his independent career in Oxford. He moved his successful and busy practice to London in 1856. Although primarily a church architect and restorer, he won the important secular commission to build the new Law Courts in London, which occupied him from 1868 until his death. Furniture for the Law Courts was made by Gillow's and other Street furniture by Holland & Sons – Street was related to the Hollands by his second marriage. In the second series of *Instrumenta Ecclesiastica* (1856), some of his metalwork designs were published, and in 1857 he took over from William Butterfield the supervision of the manufacture of church plate by Keith & Co. for the Ecclesiological Society. Street in turn was replaced by William Burges in 1864. His metalwork was also made by Hardman, Skidmore, and Barkentin & Krall. Street's ecclesiastical embroidery designs were executed by Jones & Willis, who exhibited them in the London Exhibitions of 1851 and 1862, and by the Ecclesiological Embroidery Society, founded by his sister in 1854. Stained glass designs were made by Hardman and Clayton & Bell, and the encaustic floor tiles designed by Street for the restoration of Dublin Cathedral were exhibited by Craven Dunnill & Co. at the Paris Exhibition of 1878. He was a deeply committed Gothic revivalist, believing in the inevitable rightness of Ruskin's views on the subject. His travels resulted in two influential studies of Continental Gothic architecture, *Brick and Marble Architecture in North Italy* (1855), and *Some Account of Gothic Architecture in Spain* (1865). Assistants and pupils in his busy studio included Philip Webb, William Morris, Norman Shaw and J. D. Sedding.

LOUIS SULLIVAN, 1856–1924

Sullivan studied architecture at the Massachusetts Institute of Technology before going to Philadelphia, where he worked in the office of Frank Furness (1839–1912). In 1874 he went to Paris, where he spent some time at the Ecole des Beaux-Arts. From 1875 he was in Chicago, where his subsequent career was to be based, forming a partnership with Dankmar Adler in 1881. In his early buildings his grounding in English Reformed Gothic is apparent. He evolved a distinctive ornamental style based on organic forms. Throughout his career Sullivan wrote a number of treatises on contemporary architecture. From 1888 Frank Lloyd Wright worked for Sullivan, imbibing the mixture of French Beaux-Arts and English influence (through Furness) that had formed Sullivan himself. G. G. Elmslie, (1871–1952) a contemporary of Wright's in the Chicago architect J. L. Silsbee's office, joined Sullivan & Adler in 1889 as a draughtsman and designed furniture, stained glass and textiles in a style derived from Sullivan.

BRUCE JAMES TALBERT, 1838–1881

Originally a carver, Talbert later trained as an architect, but his main activity was to be in the field of domestic decoration and design. In 1863 he won the competition to design the masthead for *Building News*. He worked from about 1861 at Skidmore's Art Manufactures Co., Coventry, making detailed drawings and designs for George Gilbert Scott's Albert Memorial and the Hereford Cathedral screen. His *Gothic Forms Applied to Furniture, Metal Work and Decoration for Domestic Purposes* (1868) was dedicated to G. E. Street. A prolific commercial designer, Talbert was employed by Holland & Sons, Gillow's, Marsh, Jones & Cribb of Leeds and Jackson &

Graham. He was a friend of J. M. Smith, J. M. Brydon, and D. Cottier, in whose company he was briefly a partner. He met Norman Shaw and W. E. Nesfield through Brydon and subsequently worked with their (and Scott's) carver, James Forsyth. In 1868 he designed an advertisement for James Lamb of Manchester. Talbert ran a very busy design studio, in which Batley was a pupil, commissioning designs from other draughtsmen, such as George C. Haité (1855–1924), and designing himself: metalwork and furniture for Cox & Co., wallpaper designs for Jeffrey & Co.; textiles for Templetons, Barbour & Miller and Cowlishaw, Nicol & Co.; carpets for Messrs Brinton and Templetons; and cast iron for the Coalbrookdale Company. A sequel to *Gothic Forms* was entitled *Examples of Ancient & Modern Furniture, Metal Work, Tapestries, Decorations &c.* (1876). *Fashionable Furniture* (1881) was published posthumously after his death from chronic alcoholism.

Sally Macdonald, 'Gothic Forms Applied to Furniture: the Early Work of Bruce James Talbert', *Furniture History: the Journal of the Furniture History Society*, vol. XXIII, 1987, pp. 39–66.

TIFFANY & Co., 1837 to present

Metalwork and glass firm founded by Charles Louis Tiffany (1812–1902), selling tableware and jewellery from American manufacturers and imports from Samuel Bing (1838–1905) in Paris. Gustave Herter worked at the company after arriving in America. Edward C. Moore (1827–91) designed silver for the firm from 1851, became chief designer in 1868 and transformed the firm into an important manufacturer, experimenting in the forefront of Japonisme style and techniques. Moore was a pioneer collector of Japanese art, and Tiffany's wares had the authenticity of the true innovator. The firm commissioned Christopher Dresser to collect Japanese curios when he visited the Philadelphia Exhibition in 1876 en route to Japan. For international exhibitions in the United States Tiffany's explored native styles taken from American Indian patterns. Their silver was acclaimed at the Paris exhibitions in 1867 and 1878. Louis Comfort Tiffany (1848–1933) took over as artistic director on his father's death in 1902. He had founded the Society of American Artists in 1877, and Associated Artists in 1879. From 1885 he designed stained glass windows, which were made by the Tiffany Glass Co. In the 1880s he developed his iridescent 'Favrile' glass, which was sold through Bing's Maison de L'Art Nouveau in Europe.

J. Zapata and C. H. Carpenter, *The Silver of Tiffany & Co. 1850–1987*, exhibition catalogue, Museum of Fine Arts, Boston 1987; Rudoe, 1991.

EUGÈNE VIOLLET-LE-DUC, 1814–1879

Viollet spent much of his time on the restoration of Gothic buildings, but it was through his massive works of architectural scholarship that he exercised a wide influence on his contemporaries and successors. The *Dictionnaire raisonné de l'architecture* consisted of ten volumes (1854–68). The *Dictionnaire du mobilier français*, in six volumes (1858–75), provided designers with models for Gothic furniture. *Entretiens sur l'architecture* (1863) contained theories of iron construction which influenced Hector Guimard and others involved with the Art Nouveau movement at the turn of the century. He made designs for stained glass executed at Sèvres in the 1840s, and in 1849 was commissioned to improve the national manufactories of Sèvres, Gobelins and Beauvais.

Michael Barker, 'Viollet-le-Duc and his influence on English Architects', *Journal of the Decorative Art Society*, 1992.

CHARLES FRANCIS ANNESLEY VOYSEY, 1857–1941

Articled to J. P. Seddon, Voysey worked for G. Devey in 1880, but at the outset of his own career turned to decorative design while waiting for his architectural practice to gain momentum. He joined the Art Workers' Guild in 1884 and exhibited with the Arts and Crafts Exhibition Society from 1888. He designed the cover for the first volume of *The Studio* magazine in 1896. Voysey had a great talent for pattern making and designed wallpapers for Jeffrey & Co. and Essex & Co.; textiles for Alexander Morton; tiles for Pilkington's and later Minton's; and carpets sold through Liberty. From the mid-1880s he experimented with furniture, much of which was made by F. C. Nielsen, in a severe, distinctive vernacular-influenced manner using oak. His large table clock, with versions in plain aluminium, painted wood and polished oak, is one of the most original pieces. He also designed tablewares, cutlery, metalwork and lighting made by Thomas Elsley & Co. Although Voysey carried out no public architectural commissions, publication of his designs gave him an international reputation.

C. F. A. Voysey: Architect and Designer 1857–1941, exhibition catalogue, Brighton Pavilion Art Gallery and Museum, 1978.

GEORGE WALTON, 1867–1933

Son of a painter, Walton initially worked as a bank clerk and attended evening art classes. His brother E. A. Walton was one of the 'Glasgow Boys'. George Walton & Co., Ecclesiastical and House Decorators, was established in Glasgow in 1888 as a result of a commission to decorate a new smoking room in one of Miss Cranston's Tea Rooms. Walton showed with the Arts and Crafts Exhibition Society in 1890, and in 1892 designed the frames and interior for his friend J. Craig Annan's second photography exhibition. Annan later bought shares in Walton's company. In 1896 Walton received a further commission from Miss Cranston, to decorate the Buchanan Street premises. His collaborator was C. R. Mackintosh, for whom Walton made some early pieces of furniture. In 1897 Walton moved to London and, as well as retaining his Glasgow showroom, opened a branch in York. Walton's decoration of Annan's home and exhibitions and his subsequent introduction to the Linked Ring – a group of photographers founded to promote photography as art – led to many commissions, including a design for the cover of *Practical Photographer*. Despite having no formal architectural training he built a number of houses including The Leys, Elstree, in 1901 for J. B. B. Wellington, the manager of Kodak at Harrow; and in 1907 the White House and a houseboat, the Log Cabin, for G. Davison, the retired managing director of Kodak Great Britain. He was retained by the Kodak Company to decorate showrooms in London, Glasgow, Brussels, Milan and Vienna, and his designs were illustrated by Hermann Muthesius in *Dekorative Kunst*. Walton designed for James Couper's range of 'Clutha' glass, furniture made by J. S. Henry for Liberty, wallpapers for Jeffrey

& Co., textiles for Alexander Morton, and carpets. The later years of his career were spent as architect to the Liquor Control Board.

Nikolaus Pevsner, *George Walton*, reprinted from *Journal of the RIBA*, 3rd Series, XVLI, 1939, in *Studies in Art, Architecture and Design. Victorian and After*, 1968. Moon, 1993.

THOMAS WARDLE, 1831–1909.

Son of a leading silk dyer of the 1840s and 1850s, Wardle knew of traditional vegetable dyes as well as being experienced with aniline dyes. In 1870 he set up as a silk and calico dyer and printer at Leek, Staffordshire. Thomas was introduced to William Morris through his brother George, who had joined the Morris firm in the 1860s and became general manager after Warrington Taylor's death in 1870. Morris made frequent visits to Leek from 1875 to 1877, and the two corresponded about their experiments with dyes and printing. By 1878 Wardle was printing fourteen of Morris's designs, and dyeing yarns for woven textiles and velvets and silks for embroidery. Morris became dissatisfied with the quality of printing at Leek, and with his firm's move to Merton Abbey in 1881 ceased using Wardle. A founder member of the Silk Association, Wardle was involved with experiments in silk manufacture and dyeing, and he imported Indian silks which were often dyed or overprinted at Leek. He also bought patterns from freelance designers including L. F. Day, Walter Crane, C. F. A. Voysey and Léon Solon. In 1883, encouraged by Morris, Wardle opened a shop in New Bond Street, Wardle & Co., Art Drapers, Embroiderers and Decorative Furnishers; but it closed in 1888 because of difficulties with some of its customers, probably Liberty & Co. although it also supplied Heal's, Story's and Debenham & Freebody. A member of the Arts and Crafts Exhibition Society, Wardle exhibited frequently. His wife Elizabeth set up the Leek Embroidery Society in 1879. They embroidered over Wardle and Morris fabrics and Indian imported silks, using threads dyed by Wardle, and executed ecclesiastical designs for Shaw, J. D. Sedding and Wardle's son, also called Thomas.

C. Woods, *Sir Thomas Wardle*, in D. J. Jeremy, (ed.), *Dictionary of Business Biography*, vol. v, 1986.

WARNER & SONS, 1867 to present

Silk weavers, founded by Benjamin Warner (1828–1908) in partnership as Warner, Sillet & Ramm, becoming Warner & Sons in 1891. The firm moved from Spitalfields to Bethnal Green and then to new weaving works in Braintree, Essex, in 1895, but retained links with other makers such as J. W. & C. Ward of Halifax, who were contracted to make some patterns. Although Warner relied on traditional silk patterns, the firm also engaged freelance designers such as Walter Crane, G. C. Haité, A. H. Mackmurdo and the Silver Studio and continued to make designs by Owen Jones, for Jackson & Graham, and by B. J. Talbert and E. W. Godwin. The firm supplied retail outlets such as Liberty & Co., Collinson & Lock, and Debenham & Freebody, who along with Warner's exhibited at international exhibitions in London, Paris, Vienna and Philadelphia. From the 1920s Warner's produced printed textiles.

Hester Bury, *A Choice of Design 1850–1980. Fabrics by Warner & Sons Ltd*, exhibition catalogue, 1981.

ALFRED WATERHOUSE, 1830–1905

Born in Liverpool and articled to Manchester architect Richard Lane, Waterhouse set up his own practice in 1854. In 1859 he won the Manchester Assize Courts competition, travelling to London to study Pugin's furniture for the Palace of Westminster. His own designs were executed by the Manchester firms of Doveston, Bird & Hull, Goodall's and Lamb's. He moved to London in 1864 and secured important commissions to design the Natural History Museum, South Kensington (built 1870–80), and Manchester Town Hall (built 1868–77). He was a friend of R. Norman Shaw, who had designed a cradle for his son. In the 1870s he rebuilt Eaton Hall for the Duke of Westminster, the interiors of which were executed by Heaton, Butler & Bayne. His furniture for Blackmore was made by J. Capel, and he designed tiles for Craven Dunnill & Co., and offered designs to Wedgwood for their 'Marsden' patent art tiles. J. M. Brydon is among the long list of assistants who worked in Waterhouse's office. Waterhouse retired in 1901, and his son Paul took over his practice after ten years as a partner.

Colin Cunningham and Prudence Waterhouse, *Alfred Waterhouse 1830–1905: Biography of a Practice*, Oxford, 1992.

WILLIAM WATT, ARTISTIC FURNITURE WAREHOUSE, 1857–1887

William Watt (1834–1885) established his upholstery business in 1857, although it only appears in the directories in Grafton Street, Mayfair, in 1860. Watt made much of the small furniture for E. W. Godwin's Dromore Castle, and for Godwin's own use from 1867. His 1877 catalogue illustrates Anglo-Japanese and 'Old English' furniture, wall and ceiling papers and stained glass by Godwin. The popular 'Shakespeare' suite was said to be in every upholsterer's showroom. Watt exhibited at London and Vienna in 1873, and Godwin collaborated with Whistler on his stand for Paris in 1878. After Watt's death in 1885 the firm was carried on for two years by his trustees.

Aslin, 1986.

PHILIP WEBB, 1831–1915

Webb met William Morris in G. E. Street's office in Oxford. His subsequent architectural practice as well as his design career were bound up with the fortunes of the Morris firm. Commissions for both were interdependent, Webb specifying the Morris firm as decorators and Morris recommending Webb as architect. Webb was responsible for the decorative scheme in an important early Morris commission, the 'Green Dining Room' at the South Kensington Museum (still intact and recently restored by the Victoria and Albert Museum) and drew almost all the birds and animals in Morris's fabric, tapestry and wallpaper designs. He was commissioned by Morris to design table glass made by Powell's, and furniture for the Red House in 1859. Webb provided furniture designs for Major Gillum in 1860 and for the Morris firm from 1861 until the responsibility was taken over by his assistant George Jack in the 1880s. Metalwork for gates and fireplaces was executed by Longden, whose London premises were next to Morris & Co.'s showrooms. He used the distinguished carver James Forsyth, who had also worked for R. Norman Shaw, his successor in Street's office, and W. E. Nesfield among others. Webb retired

in 1900, unable to come to terms with what he foresaw of the future of architecture. Shaw described him as 'A very able man indeed, but with a strong liking for the ugly'.
Lethaby, 1935.

JOSIAH WEDGWOOD & SONS, 1759 to present
Pottery at Stoke-on-Trent, one of the most important industrial ceramic manufacturers. Recognizing the significance of the Art Movement in the nineteenth century, the manufactory established a sideline in art pottery. It produced ornamental tiles from 1875 to 1902, under the direction of Thomas Allen, who had studied at South Kensington and worked at Minton's. Allen increased the output and range of studio and art wares at Wedgwood, produced a great number of designs, and introduced many artists to the firm. Outside designers were used, including Christopher Dresser and Walter Crane, both of whom produced a number of designs for the Paris 1867 and London 1871 exhibitions. Wedgwood exhibited at all the major international exhibitions from 1851. Some of William De Morgan's earliest works were fired here, and he bought Wedgwood's blanks to decorate. Many of the artists who worked at the firm were friends of the family, including the Lessores, whose father Emile (1805–1876) had worked at Sèvres and Minton's, and encouraged the manufacture of art pottery and majolica at Wedgwood in the 1860s. The art pottery side was continued in the present century with artist-designed and hand-painted wares, notably by Alfred and Louise Powell.
Maureen Batkin, *Wedgwood Ceramics 1846–1959. A New Appraisal*, London 1982.

JAMES ABBOTT MCNEILL WHISTLER, 1834–1903
Whistler is widely credited with stimulating the early interest in Japonisme in London artistic circles. Born in America, he travelled to Paris, where appreciation of Japanese prints was in advance of Britain, and arrived in London in 1859. His exhibits at the Royal Academy at this date revealed the abstract possibilities of Japonisme in painting. His decorative work included the notorious collaboration with Thomas Jeckyll, which resulted in the 'Peacock' room at F. R. Leyland's London house (now carefully restored in the Freer Gallery in Washington), and his scheme with E. W. Godwin for William Watt's exhibit at the 1878 Paris Exhibition.

HENRY WILSON, 1864–1934
Wilson was in the offices of the architects John Oldrid Scott and John Belcher before becoming chief assistant to J. D. Sedding, where he met E. Gimson and A. H. Powell; he took over the practice at the time of Sedding's death in 1891. His interest in metalwork dates from about 1890, and he taught the subject at the Central School of Arts and Crafts from 1896 under W. R. Lethaby. He had the services of professional jewellers in his studio, preferring this to the more usual Arts and Crafts ideal of trial and error by untrained workmen. John Paul Cooper and Harry G. Murphy both started their metalworking careers in Wilson's studio. Wilson also designed fireplaces for Longden & Co., who had made Sedding's metalwork; furniture, which was made by C. Trask & Co.; and wallpapers for Jeffrey & Co. Wilson was the first editor of the *Architectural Review* and an indefatigable organizer in the Arts and Crafts cause. His was the moving spirit behind the exhibition of British decorative art in Paris in 1914, and the by now anachronistic show at the Royal Academy in 1917. He was Master of the Arts Workers' Guild in 1917. In 1922 he went to live in France.

WORCESTER ROYAL PORCELAIN CO. LTD., 1751 to present
Established as the Worcester Porcelain Co. with fifteen partners, the firm underwent many changes of name and directorship until 1862 when R. W. Binns, collector of Far Eastern ceramics and one-time partner in the Worcester factory of Kerr & Binns, rescued the Worcester Chamberlain factory from looming collapse and formed the present company. Worcester's 'ivory porcelain', launched at the 1862 London Exhibition and adapted to Japanesque wares by the modeller James Hadley, caused a sensation. At Vienna in 1873 the firm won joint first prize with Minton. Worcester was highly praised, particularly for its technical quality, an area where Britain was at pains to rival the French Imperial Manufactory at Sèvres. The firm employed a large number of highly skilled and specialist artists, including one Cantonese enamellist, Po-Hing. It also produced Persian, Indian and Italian Renaissance style vessels, which were very successful. Binns travelled to the Philadelphia exhibition of 1876 and returned with a large number of Japanese curios, which inspired a new experimental porcelain which was shown at Paris in 1878, winning the Gold Medal. In 1889 Binns took over Grainger & Co., though production continued with little change. From 1875 Hadley had worked as an independent designer, although almost exclusively producing designs for Worcester until he set up his own factory in 1896 producing art pottery and faience. On his death in 1905 the company was amalgamated into Royal Worcester.
Henry Sandon, *Royal Worcester Porcelain from 1862 to the Present Day*, London 1973.

FRANK LLOYD WRIGHT, 1869–1959
Wright spent two years at engineering school before a brief period with J. L. Silsbee, the Chicago architect. In 1883 he joined Louis Sullivan's office, becoming chief draughtsman. He established his own practice in 1893. Wright was a collector and dealer of Japanese prints, although he was reluctant to admit their influence. He was a founder member of the Chicago Arts & Crafts Society, modelled on London's Toynbee Hall, with which C. R. Ashbee was involved; but unlike them he believed in the advancement of design through use of machinery. Ashbee had met Wright in Chicago and they became friends. Wright's designs were published in *The House Beautiful*, an architectural magazine which had illustrated work by Morris, Crane, Voysey and Ashbee in its first issue in 1896. His designs for furniture, leaded glass windows and metalwork (much of which was made by J. A. Miller) maintained a consistent abstract structuralism, now seen as an early expression of International Modernism. With Wright the thread of Viollet's and Dresser's architectural theories can be traced through to the concrete buildings of the twentieth century.
Wilk, 1993.

SELECT BIBLIOGRAPHY

GENERAL

Adburgham, Alison, *Liberty's: A Biography of a Shop*, London 1975.

Agius, Pauline, *British Furniture, 1800–1915*, Woodbridge 1978.

Aldrich, Megan (ed.), *The Craces: Royal Decorators 1768–1899*, exhibition catalogue, Brighton Royal Pavilion, Art Gallery and Museums, 1990.

Ames, Francis, *Prince Albert and Victorian Taste*, London 1967.

Anscombe, I. and Gere, C., *Arts and Crafts in Britain and America*, London 1978.

Ashbee, C. R., *Modern English Silverwork*, London 1909.

Aslin, Elizabeth, *Nineteenth-Century English Furniture*, London 1962.

Aslin, Elizabeth, *The Aesthetic Movement: Prelude to Art Nouveau*, London 1969.

Aslin, Elizabeth, *French Exhibition Pieces, 1844–78*, London 1973.

Aslin, Elizabeth, *E. W. Godwin: Furniture and Interior Decoration*, London 1986.

Atterbury, Paul and Batkin, Maureen, *The Dictionary of Minton*, Woodbridge 1990.

Baillie Scott, M. H., *Houses and Gardens*, London 1906.

Banham, J. and Harris, J., *William Morris and the Middle Ages*, exhibition catalogue, Whitworth Art Gallery, Manchester 1984.

Bascou, M., Massé, M. M., Thiebaut, P., *Catalogue sommaire illustré des arts décoratifs, Musée d'Orsay, Paris*, Paris 1988.

Bell, Quentin, *The Schools of Design*, London 1963.

Bennett, Ian, (introduction to) *Ruskin Pottery*, exhibition catalogue, Haslam & Whiteway, London 1981.

Billcliffe, Roger, *Charles Rennie Mackintosh, Furniture and Interiors*, London 1986.

Birmingham City Museum and Art Gallery, *Birmingham Gold and Silver*, exhibition catalogue, Birmingham 1973.

Boe, Alf, *From Gothic Revival to Functional Form*, Oslo 1957.

Bonython, Elizabeth, *King Cole*, London 1982.

Bowman, L. Greene, *American Arts and Crafts: Virtue in Design. A catalogue of the Palevsky/Evans Collection in the Los Angeles County Museum*, Los Angeles 1990.

Brandon-Jones, J. *et al.*, *C. F. A. Voysey, Architect and Designer*, London 1974.

Brooks, Michael W., *John Ruskin and Victorian Architecture*, London 1989.

Bury, Shirley, *Victorian Electroplate*, London 1971.

Callen, Anthea, *The Angel in the Studio: Women in the Arts and Crafts Movement*, London 1979.

Clark, Kenneth, *The Gothic Revival*, London 1929 (new edn 1962).

Clarke, Robert Judson, *The Arts and Crafts Movement in America, 1876–1916*, exhibition catalogue, Princeton 1972.

Cleveland Museum of Art, *Japonisme: Japanese Influence on French Art*, exhibition catalogue, Clevelend 1975.

Collard, Frances, *Regency Furniture*, Woodbridge 1985.

Collins, Michael, *Christopher Dresser, 1834–1904*, exhibition catalogue, Camden Arts Centre, London 1979.

Collins, Michael, (introduction to) *W. A. S. Benson Metalwork*, exhibition catalogue, Haslam & Whiteway, London 1981.

Collins, Michael, *Towards Post-Modernism, Design Since 1851*, London 1987.

Comino, Mary, *Gimson and the Barnsleys*, London 1980.

Conner, Patrick (ed.), *The Inspiration of Egypt*, exhibition catalogue, Brighton Museums and Art Gallery, 1983.

Conway, Moncure, *Travels in South Kensington*, London 1882.

Cook, Clarence, *The House Beautiful*, New York 1878.

Cooper, Jeremy, *Victorian and Edwardian Furniture and Interiors*, London 1987.

Crawford, Alan, *C. R. Ashbee, Architect, Designer and Romantic Socialist*, London 1986.

Crook, J. Mordaunt, *William Burges and the High Victorian Dream*, London 1981.

Crook, J. Mordaunt, *The Strange Genius of William Burges*, exhibition catalogue, National Museum of Wales, Cardiff, 1981.

Culme, John, *Nineteenth-Century Silver*, London 1977.

Culme, John, *The Directory of Gold & Silversmiths, Jewellers and Allied Traders 1838–1914*, Woodbridge 1987.

Curl, J. Stevens, *The Egyptian Revival*, London 1982.

Darby, Michael, *The Islamic Perspective*, exhibition catalogue, Leighton House Art Gallery, London 1983.

Darby, Michael, *John Pollard Seddon*, London 1983.

Darby, Michael and Physick, John, *Marble Halls*, exhibition catalogue, Victoria and Albert Museum, London 1973.

Deck, Théodore, *La Faience*, Paris, 1887.

Dennis, Richard and Jesse, John, *Christopher Dresser, 1834–1904, exhibition catalogue, Fine Art Society, London 1972*.

Dresser, Christopher, *The Art of Decorative Design*, London 1862.

Dresser, Christopher, *Principles of Decorative Design*, London 1873.

Dresser, Christopher, *Studies in Design*, London 1875–6.

Dresser, Christopher, *Japan: Its Architecture, Art and Art-Manufactures*, London 1882.

Dresser, Christopher, *Modern Ornamentation*, London 1886.

Durant, Stuart, *Ornament*, London 1986.

Durant, Stuart, *C. F. A. Voysey: Decorative Designs*, exhibition catalogue, Royal Institute of British Architects, London 1990.

Eastlake, C. L., *Hints on Household Taste*, 1868 (new edn introduced by John Gloag, FSA, New York 1969).

Eastlake, C. L., *A History of the Gothic Revival in England*, 1872 (new edn introduced by J. Mordaunt Crook, Leicester 1970).

Edis, Robert, *Decoration and Furniture of Town Houses*, London 1881.

Ferrey, Benjamin, *The Life of Pugin the Architect*, London 1861.

Fine Art Society and Haslam & Whiteway Ltd., *The Aesthetic Movement and the Cult of Japan*, exhibition catalogue, London 1972.

Fine Art Society and Haslam & Whiteway Ltd., *The Arts and Crafts Movement*, exhibition catalogue, London 1973.

Fine Art Society and Haslam & Whiteway Ltd., *Morris & Company*, exhibition catalogue, London 1979.

Fine Art Society and Haslam & Whiteway Ltd., *Architect-Designers: Pugin to Mackintosh*, exhibition catalogue, London 1981.

Floud, Peter (ed.), *Victorian and Edwardian Decorative Art*, exhibition catalogue, Victoria and Albert Museum, London 1952.

Galéries Nationales du Grand Palais, *Japonisme*, exhibition catalogue, Paris 1988.

Gere, Charlotte and Munn, Geoffrey C., *Artists' Jewellery, Pre-Raphaelite to Arts and Crafts*, London 1989.

Gere, Charlotte, *Nineteenth-Century Decoration: The Art of the Interior*, London 1989.

Germann, George, *Gothic Revival in Europe and Britain*, London 1972.

Giedion, Siegfried, *Mechanisation Takes Command*, London 1948.

Girouard, Mark, *The Victorian Country House*, Oxford 1971 (new edn London 1979).

Girouard, Mark, *Sweetness and Light: The Queen Anne Movement, 1860–1900*, Oxford 1977.

Gradidge, Roderick, *Dream Houses: the Edwardian Ideal*, London 1980.

Greenwood, M., *The Designs of William De Morgan*, Ilminster 1989.

Halen, Widar, *Christopher Dresser*, Oxford 1990.

Hamilton, Jean and Oman, Charles, *Catalogue of Wallpapers: Victoria and Albert Museum*, London 1982.

Harrison, Martin, *Victorian Stained Glass*, London 1980.

Harvey, Charles and Press, Jon, *William Morris: Design and Enterprise in Victorian Britain*, Manchester 1991.

Haslam, Malcolm, *English Art Pottery, 1865–1915*, Woodbridge 1975.

Haslam, Malcolm, *Arts and Crafts Carpets*, London 1990.

Hayward, Helena (ed.), *World Furniture*, London 1965.

Hobhouse, Hermione, *Prince Albert: His Life and Work*, London 1983.

Howarth, Thomas, *Charles Rennie Mackintosh and the Modern Movement*, 2nd edn, London 1977.

Jervis, Simon and Wainwright, Clive, *High Victorian Design*, exhibition catalogue, National Gallery of Canada, Ottawa 1974.

Jervis, Simon, *High Victorian Design*, Woodbridge 1983.

Jervis, Simon, *The Penguin Dictionary of Design and Designers*, London 1984.

Jervis, Simon (ed.), *Art and Design in Europe and America*, London 1987.

Jones, Owen, *The Grammar of Ornament*, London 1856.

Jones, Owen, *The Grammar of Chinese Ornament*, London 1866–7.

Joy, Edward (ed.), *Pictorial Dictionary of British 19th Century Furniture Design*, Woodbridge 1977.

Kornwolf, J. D., *M. H. Baillie Scott and the Arts and Crafts Movement*, London 1972.

Lambourne, Lionel, *Utopian Craftsmen*, London 1980.

Lethaby, W. R., *Philip Webb and his Work*, London 1932.

Lever, Jill, *Architects' Designs for Furniture*, London 1982.

Lever, Jill and Richardson, Margaret, *The Art of the Architect*, exhibition catalogue, Royal Institute of British Architects, London 1984.

Lynn, Catherine, *Wallpaper in America*, New York 1980.

MacCarthy, Fiona, *All Things Bright and Beautiful: Design in Britain 1830 to Today*, London 1972.

MacCarthy, Fiona, *The Simple Life: C. R. Ashbee in the Cotswolds*, London 1981.

Mackail, J. W., *The Life of William Morris*, London 1899.

Macready, Sarah and Thomson, F. H., *Influences in Victorian Art and Architecture*, Society of Antiquaries, London 1985.

Madsen, S. Tschudi, *Sources of Art Nouveau*, Oslo 1956.

Metropolitan Museum of Art, *In Pursuit of Beauty: Americans and the Aesthetic Movement*, exhibition catalogue, New York 1986.

Morris, Barbara, *Victorian Embroidery*, London 1962.

Morris, Barbara, *Victorian Table Glass and Ornaments*, London 1978.

Morris, Barbara, *Inspiration for Design: the Influence of the Victoria and Albert Museum*, London 1986.

Morris, Barbara, *Liberty Design, 1874–1914*, London 1989.

Moyr Smith, J., *Ornamental Interiors*, London 1887.

Muthesius, Hermann, *Das englische Haus*, 3 vols, Berlin 1904–8 (English translation by Janet Seligman, introduced by Denis Sharp, London 1979).

Naylor, Gillian, *The Arts and Crafts Movement*, London 1971.

Newman, Theresa and Watkinson, Ray, *Ford Madox Brown*, London 1991.

Nuttgens, Patrick (ed.), *Mackintosh and His Contemporaries in Europe and America*, London 1988.

Ostergard, Derek E. (ed.), *Bentwood & Metal Furniture*, New York 1987.

Parry, Linda, *William Morris Textiles*, London 1983.

Parry, Linda, *Textiles of the Arts and Crafts Movement*, exhibition catalogue, Victoria and Albert Museum, London 1988.

Pevsner, N., *Pioneers of the Modern Movement from William Morris to Walter Gropius*, London 1936.

Pevsner, N., *The Sources of Modern Architecture and Design*, London 1968.

Pevsner, N., *Studies in Art, Architecture and Design*, London 1968.

Physick, John, *The Victoria and Albert Museum*, London 1982.

Port, M. H. (ed.), *The Houses of Parliament*, London 1976.

Pugin, A. W. N., *Gothic Furniture in the Style of the 15th & 16th Centuries, Designed & Etched by A. W. N. Pugin*, London 1835.

Pugin, A. W. N., *Details of Ancient Timber Houses of the 15th & 16th Centuries*, London 1836.

Pugin, A. W. N., *Designs for Iron and Brass Work in the Style of the XV and XVI Centuries*, London 1836.

Pugin, A. W. N., *Designs for Gold and Silver Smiths*, London 1836.

Pugin, A. W. N., *Contrasts; or a Parallel between the Noble Edifices of the Fourteenth and Fifteenth centuries, and Similar Buildings of the Present Day*, London 1836.

Pugin, A. W. N., *The True Principles of Pointed or Christian Architecture*, London 1841.

Pugin, A. W. N., *An Apology for the Revival of Christian Architecture in England*, London 1843.

Pugin, A. W. N., *The Present State of Ecclesiastical Architecture in England*, London 1843.

Pugin, A. W. N., *Glossary of Ecclesiastical Ornament and Costume*, London 1844.

Pugin, A. W. N., *Floriated Ornament*, London 1849.

Reynolds, Jan, *Birket Foster*, London 1984.

Richardson, Margaret, *Architects of the Arts and Crafts Movement*, London 1983.

Royal Academy of Arts, *Victorian and Edwardian Decorative Art: the Handley Read Collection*, exhibition catalogue, London 1971.

Rubens, Godfrey, *W. R. Lethaby*, London 1986.

Rudoe, Judy, *Decorative Arts, 1850–1950: A Catalogue of the British Museum Collection*, London 1991.

Saint, Andrew, *Richard Norman Shaw*, London 1976.

Sala, G. A., *Notes and Sketches of the Paris Exhibition*, London 1868.

Sala, G. A., *Paris Herself Again in 1878*, 2 vols, London 1880.

Schmutzler, Robert, *Art Nouveau*, New York 1962.

Schaeffer, Herwin, *The Roots of Modern Design*, London 1970.

Sewter, A. C., *The Stained Glass of William Morris and his Circle*, New Haven 1974.

Smith, Greg and Hyde, Sarah, *Walter Crane: Artist, Designer and Socialist*, exhibition catalogue, Whitworth Art Gallery, Manchester 1989.

Snodin, Michael (ed.), *Karl Friedrich Schinkel: A Universal Man*, exhibition catalogue, Victoria and Albert Museum, London 1991.

Sparrow, Walter Shaw, *The British Home of Today*, London 1904.

Stamp, Gavin, *The English House 1860–1914*, London 1986.

Stanton, Phoebe, *Pugin*, London 1971.

Talbert, Bruce, *Gothic Forms Applied to Furniture, Metalwork and Decoration for Domestic Purposes*, Birmingham 1867.

Talbert, Bruce, *Examples of Ancient and Modern Furniture, Metalwork, Tapestries, Decorations, Etc.*, London 1876.

Talbert, Bruce J. *et al.*, *Fashionable Furniture*, London 1881.

Thompson, Paul, *The Work of William Morris*, London 1967.

Thompson, Paul, *William Butterfield*, London 1971.

Tilbrook, Adrian, *The Designs of Archibald Knox for Liberty & Co.*, London 1976.

Vallence, Aymer, *The Art of William Morris*, London 1897.

Victoria and Albert Museum, *Victorian Church Art*, exhibition catalogue, London 1971.

Vergo, Peter (ed.), *Vienna 1900*, exhibition catalogue, Royal Museum of Scotland, Edinburgh, 1983.

Wainwright, Clive, (introduction to) *George Bullock: Cabinet Maker*, exhibition catalogue, H. Blairman & Sons Ltd., London 1988.

Wainwright, Clive, *The Romantic Interior*, London 1989.

Waring, J. B., *Masterpieces of Industrial Art & Sculpture at the International Exhibition 1862*, London 1863.

Watkin, David, *Thomas Hope and the Neo-Classical Ideal*, London 1968.

Wedgwood, Alexandra, *Pugin Family Drawings*, London 1985.

Weisberg, Gabriel, *Art Nouveau Bing: Paris Style 1900*, New York 1986.

Williamson, G. C., *Murray Marks and His Friends*, London 1919.

Yapp, G. W. (ed.), *Art Industry, Furniture, Upholstery & House Decoration*, London n.d.

1993 PUBLICATIONS

Durant, Stuart, *Christopher Dresser*, London 1993

Jones, Joan, *Minton, The First Two Hundred Years of Design & Production*, Shrewsbury 1993

Moon, Karen, *George Walton*, Wendlebury, Oxon, 1993

Wilk, Christopher, *Frank Lloyd Wright: The Kaufman Office*, London 1993

NINETEENTH-CENTURY PERIODICALS

Ackermann's Repository of Arts, London 1809–28.

American Architect and Building News, Boston 1876–1938.

The Architect: a Weekly Illustrated Journal of Art, Civil Engineering and Building, London, first issued 1869. Now a trade journal.

Architectural Review, London, first issued 1896.

The Art Amateur: a Monthly Journal Devoted to Art in the Household, New York 1879–90.

Art et Décoration, Paris, first issued 1897.

The Art Interchange: a Household Journal, New York 1878–1904.

The Artist, Journal of Home Culture, London 1880–1902 (From 1895 *The Artist, Photographer and Decorator*.)

Artistic Japan, London 1888–91. English-language edition of Bing's *Le Japon artistique*.

Art Journal, London 1839–1911. Incorporating supplements, the *Art Journal Illustrated Catalogues*, to accompany international exhibitions.

L'Art pour tous, Paris, 1861–1906.

The Art Workman, London 1873–83.

Brush and Pencil, Chicago 1897–1907.

The Builder, London, first issued 1843. Now a trade journal.

Building News, London 1855–1926. Latterly merged with *The Architect*.

Cabinet Maker and Art Furnisher, London, first issued 1880.

The Craftsman, Eastwood, New York 1901–7.

Decoration: Painting, Sculpture, Architecture and Art Manufactures, London 1881–9.

Dekorative Kunst, Munich 1897–1929.

Deutsche Kunst und Dekoration, Darmstadt 1897–1933.

Decorator and Furnisher, New York 1882–94.

The Furnisher, London, 1899–1901. Incorporated into *The Furniture Record*, 1901–28.

The Furniture Gazette, London 1872–93. Incorporated into *Furniture and Decoration* (1890–98) from 1894.

Gazette des Beaux-Arts, Paris, first issued 1859.

The House Beautiful, Chicago, first issued 1896.

Innen-Dekoration, Darmstadt, 1889–1939.

Journal of Design and Manufactures, London 1849–52.

Journal of the Society of Arts, London, first issued 1852. From 1908 as the *Journal of the Royal Society of Arts*.

Kunst und Gewerbe, Weimar and Nuremberg 1867–98.

Kunst und Handwerk, Munich 1889–1907.

Kunst und Kunsthandwerk, Vienna 1898–1921.

Kunstgewerbeblatt, Leipzig 1885–1917.

The Magazine of Art, London 1878–1904.

The Quest, Birmingham 1894–6.

Revue des Arts décoratifs, Paris 1880–1902.

The Studio, London, first issued 1893.

Ver Sacrum, Vienna 1898–1903.

ACKNOWLEDGEMENTS

The importance of the architectural profession to the progress of design in the nineteenth century has been a preoccupation with historians since Nikolaus Pevsner wrote his seminal *Pioneers of Modern Design* in 1936. In this book our attempt to link the separate movements into a continuous story has been helped immeasurably by discussions with friends and colleagues over more than twenty years; we would like to thank particularly: Stuart Durant, Albert Gallichan, Malcolm Haslam, Andrew M. Patrick, Peter Rose, John Scott, Peyton Skipwith, Clive Wainwright and Pete Waldron.

The book itself could not have been achieved without the help of Peter Barnett, Marc Bascou, Ivor Braka, George Breeze, Frances Collard, Michael Collins, Jeremy Cooper, Peter Cormack, Alan P. Darr, The Fine Art Society, Denis Gallion & Daniel Morris, Norah Gillow, Donald Green, Widar Halen, Martin Harrison, Julian Hartnoll, Mr Hasebee, Toshihiko Hayashi, Simon Jervis, John Jesse, Stuart Johnson, James Joll, Joan Jones, Graham Kirkland, Dan Klein, Kathy Kurland and Lori Zabar, Martin Levy, Jo Mordaunt Crook, Barbara Morris, Geoffrey Munn, Kathy Niles, Seiji Okumiya, Mary Oliphant, Graham Ovenden, Linda Parry, Sylvia Pearson, Paul Reeves, Judy Rudoe, Seibu Department Store, Joan Slack, Michael Snodin, Ciran Stapleton, William S. and Ellen Taubman, Andy Tilbrook, Massimo and Francesca Valsecchi, Toshio Watanabe, Bill Waters, Anne Watson, Alexandra Wedgwood, Christopher Wilk and Mitchell Wolfson.

This list reflects a long period of time and it seems appropriate to remember with gratitude the late Elizabeth Aslin and the late Charles and Lavinia Handley-Read.

Annamarie Dryden has borne the burden of three years of organizing a welter of material and of assisting with the photography, of listening to and contributing to our never-ending discussions and reading the resulting texts. In addition a very large part of the appendix is due to her special interest in the relationships between the designers and the manufacturers. Without her help our task would have been much greater.

At Weidenfeld and Nicolson we have had the support and encouragement of Michael Dover and our patient and long-suffering editor Alice Millington-Drake. Harry Green has tolerated much interference over the design.

Through our preoccupation with the book our partners have had much to put up with; to John Gere and Mariko Whiteway our heartfelt gratitude.

PHOTOGRAPHIC ACKNOWLEDGMENTS

The authors and publisher would like to thank the following for their kind permission to reproduce photographs. Numbers refer to plates except where specified.

Frontispiece	Haslam & Whiteway (Photo Seiji Okumiya)
page 6	Haslam & Whiteway (Photo Michael Whiteway)
page 9	Private Collection (Photo Seiji Okumiya)
page 30	Private Collection (Photo Michael Whiteway)
page 110	Haslam & Whiteway (Photo Michael Whiteway)
page 196	Private Collection (Photo Michael Whiteway)

1 The British Architectural Library, RIBA, London
2 Fine Art Society, London
3 Fine Art Society, London
4 Haslam & Whiteway (Photo Michael Whiteway)
5 Haslam & Whiteway (Photo Michael Whiteway)
6 Haslam & Whiteway (Photo Michael Whiteway)
8 H. Blairman & Sons Ltd, London
9 (Photo Michael Whiteway)
10 H. Blairman & Sons Ltd, London
11 H. Blairman & Sons Ltd, London
12 By courtesy of the Board of Trustees of the Victoria & Albert Museum
13 Private Collection (Photo Michael Whiteway)
14 By courtesy of the Board of Trustees of the Victoria & Albert Museum
15 Private Collection (Photo Michael Whiteway)
16 Haslam & Whiteway (Photo Michael Whiteway)
17 (Photo Michael Whiteway)
18 (Photo Michael Whiteway)
19 (Photo Annamarie Dryden)
20 Haslam & Whiteway (Photo Michael Whiteway)
21 Royal Commission on the Historial Monuments of England
22 (Photo © Christie's)
23 Private Collection (Photo Michael Whiteway)
24 Private Collection (Photo Michael Whiteway)
25 Reproduced by courtesy of the Trustees, The National Gallery, London
26 (Photo Michael Whiteway)
27 Charles B. Wood III Inc.
28 (Photo Michael Whiteway)
29 (Photo Michael Whiteway)
30 (Photo Michael Whiteway)
31 The British Architectural Library, RIBA, London
32 Private Collection (Photo Michael Whiteway)
33 Haslam & Whiteway (Photo Michael Whiteway)
34 Haslam & Whiteway (Photo Michael Whiteway)
35 Private Collection (Photo Michael Whiteway)
36 Private Collection (Photo Haslam & Whiteway/Fine Art Society)
37 By courtesy of the Board of Trustees of the Victoria & Albert Museum
38 Private Collection (Photo Seiji Okumiya)
39 Private Collection (Photo Michael Whiteway)
40 Private Collection (Photo Seiji Okumiya)
41 Haslam & Whiteway (Photo Seiji Okumiya)
42 Private Collection (Photo Seiji Okumiya)
43 Private Collection (Photo Michael Whiteway)
44 Haslam & Whiteway (Photo Michael Whiteway)
45 H. Blairman & Sons Ltd, London
46 Haslam & Whiteway
47 Haslam & Whiteway (Photo Michael Whiteway)
48 Haslam & Whiteway (Photo Michael Whiteway)
49 Haslam & Whiteway (Photo Michael Whiteway)
50 Private Collection (Photo Michael Whiteway)
51 (Photo Michael Whiteway)
52 (Photo Royal Commission on the Historial Monuments of England)
53 (Photo The Bridgeman Art Library, London)
54 Haslam & Whiteway (Photo Michael Whiteway)
55 Parish Church of Ottery St Mary, Devon (Photo Michael Whiteway)
56 Haslam & Whiteway (Photo Michael Whiteway)
57 Haslam & Whiteway (Photo Michael Whiteway)
59 Haslam & Whiteway (Photo Michael Whiteway)
60 Private Collection (Photo Seiji Okumiya)
61 Haslam & Whiteway (Photo Michael Whiteway)
62 Haslam & Whiteway (Photo Michael Whiteway)
63 Haslam & Whiteway (Photo Michael Whiteway)
64 Private Collection (Photo Michael Whiteway)
65 Private Collection (Photo McNeill)
66 By courtesy of the Board of Trustees of the Victoria & Albert Museum

INDEX